Critical Pedagogy in Hong Kong

This book chronicles the author's application of critical pedagogy in Hong Kong secondary schools serving students from working-class families of South Asian heritage, so-called "ethnic minorities" in the local context. Soto used concepts, such as banking pedagogy, generative themes, liberatory dialogue, and transformative resistance, to first understand students' school, online, and community experiences, and then to reshape his teaching of English and humanities subjects to address the students' academic, social, and emotional needs.

This critical ethnography is set against educational reforms in Hong Kong, which re-orientated schools toward developing a knowledge-economy workforce, increased privatization, and competition in the school system, aimed to build national identification with China, and sought to address growing inequality in a territory known for wealth disparity. While these reforms opened opportunities for implementing student-centered pedagogies in schools and increased student access to tertiary education, ethnic minority youth faced ongoing economic and social marginalization on top of academic difficulties. The central narrative captures everyday struggles and contradictions arising from intersections of neoliberal reforms, institutional school histories, students' transnational realities, and collective efforts for equity and social justice. In the course of the book a parallel story unfolds, as the author explores what it means to be a critical teacher and researcher, and is reborn in the process.

The book's "on the ground" story is hopeful, yet tempered, in discussing the limits and possibilities for critical pedagogy. It will be of a great resource for researchers, teacher educators, and pre-service and in-service teachers who are interested in the topic.

Carlos Soto is a Lecturer in the Faculty of Education at the University of Hong Kong. Previously, he spent a decade working in the public and non-profit education sectors in the United States.

Education and Society in China
Series Editor: Gerard A. Postiglione and Zhu Zhiyong

China's economic rise has been breathtaking and unprecedented. Yet educational opportunities remain highly unequal. China has the essential ingredients to build a great system of education, but educational governance needs an overhaul if China is to realize its goal of dramatically boosting its technological output to world-class levels. As more work by established Chinese and overseas scholars becomes accessible in English to the larger global community, myths will be removed and replaced by more accurate and sophisticated analyses of China's fascinatingly complex educational transformation. This series will provide highly analytical examinations of key issues in China's education system.

Books in the series include:

Family Strategies, Guanxi, and School Success in Rural China
Xie Ailei

Student Learning and Development in Chinese Higher Education:
College students' experience in China
Cen Yuhao

Public Education Reform and Network Governance
Lessons from Chinese State-owned Enterprise Schools
Philip Wing Keung Chan

Social Changes and 'Yuwen' Education in Post-Mao China
Control, Conformity and Contradiction
Min Tao

Critical Pedagogy in Hong Kong
Classroom Stories of Struggle and Hope
Carlos Soto

For the full list of books included in the series, visit: https://www.routledge.com/Education-and-Society-in-China/book-series/ESC

Critical Pedagogy in Hong Kong
Classroom Stories of Struggle and Hope

Carlos Soto

LONDON AND NEW YORK

First published 2020
by Routledge
2 Park Square, Milton Park, Abingdon, Oxon OX14 4RN

and by Routledge
52 Vanderbilt Avenue, New York, NY 10017

Routledge is an imprint of the Taylor & Francis Group, an informa business

© 2020 Carlos Soto

The right of Carlos Soto to be identified as author of this work has been asserted by him in accordance with sections 77 and 78 of the Copyright, Designs and Patents Act 1988.

All rights reserved. No part of this book may be reprinted or reproduced or utilised in any form or by any electronic, mechanical, or other means, now known or hereafter invented, including photocopying and recording, or in any information storage or retrieval system, without permission in writing from the publishers.

Trademark notice: Product or corporate names may be trademarks or registered trademarks, and are used only for identification and explanation without intent to infringe.

British Library Cataloguing-in-Publication Data
A catalogue record for this book is available from the British Library

Library of Congress Cataloging-in-Publication Data
A catalog record for this book has been requested

ISBN: 978-1-138-61180-1 (hbk)
ISBN: 978-0-429-46521-5 (ebk)

DOI: 10.4324/9780429465215

Typeset in Galliard
by codeMantra

For my parents, my wife, my son, my fellow educators, and my students, past, present, and future

Contents

Foreword ix
Preface xv
Acknowledgments xvii
List of abbreviations xix
Prologue xxi

1 **The students, the system, and the teacher**   1
   EM students in Hong Kong 3
   Entrenched inequities, market reforms, and new problems 6
   My life trajectory as impetus 10
   Summary and words of caution 12
   Overview of chapters 14

2 **Critical pedagogy: rebirth in theory and in practice**   16
   Theorizing a pedagogy for liberation 18
   Giving life to new practice 21
   Few inroads for critical pedagogy in Hong Kong 25
   Critiques of critical pedagogy 28
   Tempering rebirth: defining limits and possibilities for empowerment 30
   Summary 33

3 **Critical ethnography and dilemmas of a teacher-researcher**   34
   CE as approach 34
   The research process 37
   Reflexive and ethical commitments 49
   Summary 54

4 Alienation, pain, and possibility at NTS 55
Dreams, love, and conflicts in students' worlds 57
Banking education: textbooks, deficits, and other constraints 66
Additional challenges to conforming to existing structures 74
Constrained empowerment through generative themes 80
Summary 84

5 Curriculum at ISS: setting the stage for resistance 85
Life at Industrial Secondary School 87
The curriculum: multimodality, rigor, and community 90
Critiquing school via Bollywood films 96
Self-revelation in interrogating conflicts 102
Academic themes: a study of dehumanization in "1984" 107
Summary 113

6 The complexities of dialogue 114
Bakhtin's epistemological and ontological affordances 118
Identifying a culture of silence: "The Letters Dialogue" 119
Breaking a culture of silence: "The Pyramid of Hate Dialogue" 126
A dialogic relationship: "The Messaging Dialogue" 134
Students moving into transformative resistance 141
Summary 144

7 Toward critical hope 145
Where do we go now? 146
Advancing critical pedagogy as theory and practice 148
Changing the system 152
Conclusion: solidarity and critical hope 159

Appendix: transcription conventions 163
References 165
Index 173

Foreword

The subject of this book, pedagogy, is at the heart of the teaching profession. The "critical" form of pedagogy studied and advocated in this book can be traced to the late 1960s and the work of Brazilian educator and philosopher, Paulo Freire. While Freire's philosophy of education has since been interpreted, practiced, and challenged, in many places around the world, it remains relatively unfamiliar in Hong Kong schools. Though there are signs that for the teaching profession in China's Hong Kong, it is gaining recognition.

Critical pedagogy is difficult to implement because it challenges many of the taken for granted assumptions about schools – that they teach children to think, that they are relevant to daily life experience of all students, and that they provide equal opportunity to all. Critical pedagogy is about using real-life experience as a basis for learning, as a basis for empowering students, and as a basis for thinking about social justice. Partly due to its origins in Marxism, critical pedagogy has been marginalized in Hong Kong, a territory that abides by capitalist values. Yet, it is more prominently advocated and practiced by teachers and teacher educators in the capitalist West because it is based on a liberating philosophy that eschews social and economic inequality.

All educational transformations are in the final analysis a function of the social transformations in terms of which they are to be explained. Transformations driven by reunification with mainland China, economic globalization, the acceleration of technology, and the surveillance society have affected the working life of teachers. As their qualifications have risen, with more now holding master's and doctoral degrees, new forms of accountability, competitive testing, and longer hours spent on administrative minutia have contributed to a growing sense of powerlessness among Hong Kong teachers.

In light of these changes, the fact that Hong Kong has become one of the most unequal societies in the world, with a concern about losing some of its liberties, has indeed increased the attractiveness of critical pedagogy among some in the teaching profession. As society has become more stratified, as political life has become more contentious, and as the "local" has become on the one hand more globally influenced, and on the other hand more asserted as a marker of territorial identity, the pedagogical styles of the teaching profession have become more diverse, dynamic, and differentiated.

Critical pedagogy has made it possible for more students and teachers to intercept, interrogate, and interpret the knowledge that formal schooling requires of them in ways that acknowledge their membership in particular sectors of the community. But critiquing of the formal curriculum with a focus on how to empower students with activist thinking about social and economic inequalities has risked placing teachers in many schools in an adversarial relationship with their school authorities.

All this has happened after education in Hong Kong has traversed the rapid social and economic transformation of the last forty years. Breath taking changes have taken place in the education system, but public discourse has remained the same—schools are too test oriented, learning is too rote oriented, teachers are over worked, and student intellectual styles are too convergent. The current education system can trace its roots back to 1971 when the government legislated compulsory primary education due to international pressure about Hong Kong's cheap exports and some connection with child labor. By the end of the 1970s, compulsory education was extended to junior secondary education. In 1981, the school system was struggling to accommodate a rising number of children from migrant families. In 1981, the Touch Base Policy that allowed anyone from the Chinese mainland to stay in Hong Kong if they could reach Hong Kong land by sea or otherwise was gradually discontinued. By then the school population had increased the number of students per classroom to unhealthy levels.

As the colonial government worked to construct an education system out of the chaos, the demand on teacher training institutions grew. The University of Hong Kong had been preparing a tiny number of school teachers in a small academic unit since 1918. In 1978, it began to admit hundreds of in-service teachers in its newly established School of Education, expanded into a Faculty of Education in 1985. Much energy was directed toward preparing teachers for the rapidly growing English medium Anglo-Chinese school sector. Similarly, the Chinese University of Hong Kong, established in 1964, followed suit but with a greater focus on preparing teachers for the large number of Chinese medium schools. The government-run teacher training institutes major mission was to prepare primary school teachers.

Secondary schools recruited many university graduates in specific fields in the sciences and humanities, but few had any training in pedagogy. Many of those who were hired in their subject area were also asked to be English teachers to meet the growing demand. The Chinese ethic of diligent study and respect for teachers was ubiquitous but in itself insufficient for attaining an international standard of quality teaching. The universities and teacher training institutes began to chip away at changing that. The elite schools, including the government grant schools, began to build a fully professionalized teacher cohort. To raise standards elsewhere, the government introduced a grant-in-aid scheme that opened the door to the subsidizing schools that adhered to a "code of aid," making it possible to cover the salaries of teachers in the schools that followed the prescribed curriculum. To ensure all students attended and stayed in schools, the government also bought places in the so-called caput schools, non-profit-making private secondary schools, not allowed to charge fees in excess of those in the government/aided schools.

Enrolment in part-time teacher certificate programs was incentivized by promotions and incremental salary increases. Although Chinese language was finally given equal status as an official language in 1971, most secondary schools began to label themselves as Anglo-Chinese indicating that their medium of instruction was English, as the separation from the Chinese mainland deepened in the 1980s and 1990s. Nevertheless, most Anglo-Chinese secondary school teachers used a mix of Chinese and English, a practice that was not considered educationally sound. After 1997, there was an effort, opposed by many schools and parents to require most Anglo-Chinese schools that were unable to meet the standard set, to stick to Chinese as a medium of instruction.

As the Cold War wound to a close at the start of the 1990s, a wave of privatization swept through education systems around the world. The education system of Hong Kong decentralized by introducing a Direct Subsidy Scheme that permitted some outstanding schools more latitude and flexibility to select students and charge fees. A School Management Initiative pushed schools to be more inclusive in decision-making by expanding the influence of stakeholders in their communities.

Major educational reforms took place at the retrocession of sovereignty after 1997. Among them was an attempt to address negative effects of streaming practices, including the gap between high- and low-achieving schools, and the stigma of student "labeling" based on academic achievement. Consequently, the system of using assessments to band primary students into five levels of academic ability (band one being the highest and band five the lowest) for secondary school admission was altered. The result was merely to reduce five bands to three, leaving a system in which higher performing students were concentrated in "band one" schools, and the lowest performing students were concentrated in "band three" schools. Despite the transformation of the Hong Kong education system, glaring inequalities persisted. Another dimension remained stubbornly resistant to change. The gap between what the progressive forms of pedagogy promoted by teacher education institutions and the reality of classroom teaching took several decades to narrow.

Economic restructuring called for students who were more oriented to a service economy, rather than students who were trained to behave and think in ways suited to a manufacturing economy. Despite the many reforms that took place, a content analysis of the educational debates in the popular press over forty years reveals the consistent view that schools are too test oriented, even as secondary schools transformed their function from being terminal institutions after which students enter the labor market to preparatory institutions for college and university.

Yet, by the end of the 20th century, Hong Kong gained global notoriety as it ranked at or near the top of the Programme for International Student

Assessment. High ranking in reading, mathematics, and science belied the high degree of inequality among a population of seven million, one million of whom are living below the poverty level.

The values often associated with critical pedagogy are no longer anathema in Hong Kong's educational scene. This has become true if schools are anchored in a heritage of Confucian values, British colonial ideas, Chinese patriotism, neoliberal economics, or religious values. Values that drive critical pedagogies, including social justice, equity, and exploration of social life, have become grafted onto all the curricular documents guiding schools in Hong Kong. For these reasons, Carlos Soto's book about critical pedagogy in Hong Kong makes for an innovative read.

As a graduate of the University of California at Berkeley, Carlos had been deeply committed to critical pedagogy, not just academically but also in practice. He was awarded a four-year studentship for doctoral study at one of the world's top ranked Faculties of Education. However, he chose to give up the coveted studentship in order to directly engage with Hong Kong education as a teacher in a secondary school that served children from working-class households and ethnic minority communities. As a school teacher, he focused on narrative building and the principles and practices of critical pedagogy. When invited to present his doctoral research progress at an annual conference at the University of Hong Kong, he included his secondary school students in his presentation. His teaching attained international media coverage for his willingness to push the envelope, something that at times placed him at odds with the school administration.

Hong Kong schools suffer from an unending ambivalence. For at least forty years the local media has castigated the schools for their rote methods of learning, examination-oriented methods of teaching, and callous method of overloading students with homework. The pressure on the teachers has become unbearable, with the result that many professionals suffer from overwork and depression, and other leave the field entirely. Resistance to change is ubiquitous, partly due to the fear that the stellar global ranking of Hong Kong students will drop. The tragedy is a loss of the essence of what education is for, and its potential to build an equitable and inclusive society. For teachers who enter the profession with central aspirations to promote learning find themselves with a bewildering set of conflicting demands and difficult choices. Should education be about engaging students in learning about how to strengthen their identity, their community, and building a just world, or should it be about keeping them focused on getting high exam grades?

This insightful study is about the day-to-day experience of a teacher who tried to empower students through an engaging curriculum. Using dialogue as an instrument and goal of the curriculum, he created paths by which his students could not just digest facts. Instead they gained the capacity to question knowledge. They gained a sense that their world could change by directly speaking to the realities that they face on a daily basis. In short, critical pedagogy helped students to gain a firmer foothold in their society so they could better negotiate the obstacles faced by their families and communities.

Critical pedagogy reaches beyond teaching methods, curriculum, and school policies. The book illustrates how a teacher can find strategies that permit students to acquire the resources that can transform their families and communities for justice and social equity. This book is a testament to how teaching and learning, even in an exam-orientated culture and marketized system, can remain grounded in the lives of students. Classroom time slots on any particular day can be places to hear deeply the heartbeat of the lives of students, their families. Education can be the basis for communicating with them and to dialogue with them at every moment about the oppressive yet transformative nature of their life situation – as Freire says: "Without dialogue there is no communication and without dialogue there can be no true education."

Gerard Postiglione

Preface

The period between finishing my doctoral study and finishing this book has been one of turning a critical lens back onto myself and back onto the pedagogical work I share in this book. Some of this self-critique has been featured in co-authored publications with Miguel Pérez-Milans, and our efforts will form the basis of a forthcoming book.

As I re-read the doctoral dissertation on which this book is based, I could see my past self as naïve, stubborn, and arrogant. Feeling skeptical, I considered reframing the book to be more in line with my present view of the past.

But I got advice from an unexpected source: the heavy metal band Metallica, my favorite band from my adolescence. Revisiting their music, I realized that as a teen, their songs were my earliest training in critical pedagogy. Their 1988 classic album, *And Justice for All,* features bleak, punishing songs about familial breakdown, war, discrimination, corruption, loss of civil liberty, and environmental destruction. The songs' lyrics and imagery encouraged me as a twelve-year-old to seek literature and history and put more attention to contemporary politics. I wanted to know what their lyrics meant, so I read.

I understand now that listening to these songs in my youth, I connected my personal injustices to larger social struggles. I could hear in their music that the hurt I felt, was felt by others, and my anger regarding my life became an indignation about injustice in society. Metallica was a cultural bridge to criticality.

However, fans have complained over the decades about what they feel is the lackluster sound quality of *And Justice for All* and have begged the band to "fix" the record. The band's lead singer was recently interviewed and asked if the band would ever remix the original audio tracks and re-release a better sounding version. He responded:

"There are things I would like to change on some of the records, but it gives them so much character that you can't change them. I find it a little frustrating when bands re-record classic albums with pretty much the same songs and have it replace the original. It erases that piece of history. These records are a product of a certain time in life; they're snapshots of history and they're part of our story."

Metallica's "flawed" album was responsible for my early critical growth, not despite its imperfections, but perhaps because of them. Now, I am not calling this book a classic. But there is a story I wrote as a doctoral student, and I envisioned *that* story as a book, as the story I wanted to share with the world. And mostly, that is the story I am telling now. I don't want to erase that history. It's also a product of a certain time in life. It's a snapshot of a time when education gave me hope.

Acknowledgments

I would like to express my deepest appreciation to the educators and students who participated in this study. Your brilliance, faith, and laughter inspired much of this book. Thank you for allowing me to share the ups and downs of life with you.

This book would not be possible without colleagues at the University of Hong Kong who supported my work over the last decade. First and foremost, I am deeply grateful to my doctoral supervisors and friends, Gerard Postiglione and Miguel Pérez-Milans. I am also grateful to Ki Wing Wah, Angel Lin, Wang Dan, Margaret Lo, Cheri Chan, and Benjamin Moorhouse for their support and continued efforts to expand critical approaches to education.

I also acknowledge a wider community of scholars, educators, and activists who work each day for equity in education, and who have advised me, given me spaces to share ideas, or encouraged me along the way. They are Jacob Perea, David Hemphill, Ming-Yeh Lee, James Banks, Melissa Fries, Ronnel King, Bejamin Chang, Paul O'Connor, Jan Gube, Gao Fang, Chura Thapa, Puja Kapai, Carmen Leung, Amod Rai, Dor Arie, Dhiraj Gurung, and Magan Savant.

Portions of this book draw on previously published work. My thanks to Springer for permission to use portions of my chapter, Soto, C. (2019) Critical Pedagogy and Ethnic Minority Students in Hong Kong: Possibilities for Empowerment. In J. Gube and F. Gao (eds) *Education, Ethnicity and Equity in the Multilingual Asian Context*. Singapore: Springer, pp. 197–214. These portions appear in Chapters 1, 2, 4, 5, and 7.

Many thanks to Katie Peace and Tan ShengBin at Routledge for helping this book see the light of day.

Lastly, I share this accomplishment with my wife, Yardley, and my son, Carlos Alexis, whose love and support is unyielding.

Abbreviations

CP	Critical pedagogy
CE	Critical ethnography
CMI	Chinese Medium of Instruction
EDB	Education Bureau
EM	Ethnic Minority
EMI	English Medium of Instruction
HKDSE	Hong Kong Diploma of Secondary Education
ISS	Industrial Secondary School
LS	Liberal Studies
MOI	Medium of Instruction
NTS	New Territories School

Prologue

It is December 2012, and I am introducing my form two English class our lesson's activity. All but one of the students in the class is of Nepali heritage. I tell the students that we are going to read a news article and consider how the Hong Kong Nepalese community is being represented. An excerpt of that article is below:

Most of the Nepalis are the children and grandchildren of Gurkha soldiers, fierce fighters who served the British Army from 1814. In 1948, after Indian independence, the British sent the Gurkhas to the New Territories, where they carried out security duties and border patrols. Before 1997, soldiers and their families lived in army barracks in areas such as Happy Valley, Stanley and Shek Kong. After the handover, the Gurkhas were eventually offered Hong Kong residency, and many moved to areas such as Jordan for the affordable rents. But the military men could not find well-paying jobs in the city and unemployment ran high. "I was born in the Shek Kong army camp," said a young Nepali mother whose family of five now lives in a 150 square foot apartment. The family sleeps side by side on bunk beds in one windowless room. Her husband supports her and their three sons by working long hours as a security guard. Official figures put Hong Kong's Nepali population at 13,000, but Professor Maria Tam Siumi of Chinese University said it should be closer to 40,000, many of whom live in Jordan. Many of the Nepalese work as guards, in kitchens or as waiters and bartenders, said Caroline Simick, a community worker from India who has served the population for the past 12 years. "In many families, both parents each work two jobs and are rarely home, leaving the children without adult supervision. They stay outside until late at night. They have nowhere to do their homework," Simick said"...Drug pushers get the ethnic minority teenagers to sell drugs in local schools, because if they're caught, they won't be sent to prison for life. They'll go to juvenile detention," said a local manager at an organization that works with ethnic minorities. "Less than one per cent of ethnic minority students get into tertiary education, so they lose heart and just want to make money." Puja Kapai, a Jordan resident who teaches courses on law and multi-culturalism at the University of Hong Kong, said minority children could not keep up in mainstream schools without support to help them learn Cantonese.

"When they do not have equal access to opportunities in Hong Kong, it's inevitable that an underclass would emerge," she said.

The excerpt above is from an article published in the South China Morning Post newspaper on 7 December 2012 titled "Jordan, home to a battling Nepali community" (Chiu 2012). It tells a story of Nepalese ethnic minorities in Hong Kong. The narrative first acknowledges the past: a historical legacy linked to the British colonial period, migration, and a multigenerational presence in Hong Kong. It then frames the present within ongoing economic and social marginalization, and family and school difficulties that reproduce and entrench marginalization. The imagined future is bleak, as without support for learning the Cantonese language, the text posits, Nepali youth will continue to occupy a position of "underclass." While this story focuses on a specific group in Hong Kong, it is representative of a mainstream narrative used to represent ethnic minorities in general: victims or troublemakers with a long-term presence in Hong Kong but with persistent difficulties in acquiring Chinese language skills, mobility in employment, and full integration into the local society (Erni and Leung 2014). In the face of such narratives, the realities of life these narratives portray, as well as the diverse stories of youth these narratives ignore, educators working with so-called ethnic minority students in Hong Kong face a choice: to continue with the usual practices that contribute to the status quo or to commit to working against oppression and creating possibilities for a different present and future.

This book tells the story of people who chose the latter, of consequences of that choice, and of their struggle for hope.

1 The students, the system, and the teacher

Stories of critical pedagogy (CP) can reaffirm education as empowering, liberating, and capable of driving social transformation. But no single story of CP is enough. Since CP is not a single set of theories or practices, its story needs to be told and retold, written and rewritten to account for new sets of circumstances.

I first encountered CP as an educator in the United States, via the writing of Paulo Freire, bell hooks, Ira Shor, Jeff Duncan-Andrade, and Ernest Morrell. I brought their stories of CP to Hong Kong, where I met positive, but sometimes hurt, and bright but, at times, confused young people. Engagement with their lives now frames this story of CP, in which I strive to resonate with the hope, compassion, love, and renewal that energized me when I first committed myself to exploring new sets of theories and practices.

I moved to Hong Kong in 2009 to answer this study's central question: *What limits and possibilities exist in Hong Kong for empowering Ethnic Minority students through the practice of critical pedagogy?* Since then, I have worked alongside educators, activists, and ethnic minority (EM) youth to understand their needs, shaping and re-shaping a CP. To me, this means taking an approach to teaching and learning in which teachers and students use dialogue to identify and understand oppression, so they can go about transforming the world, for themselves, their families, and their communities. As a teacher, I have used resources such as movies, video games, advertisements, poems, novels, music, and philosophical texts that allow students and me to explore conflicts, identify oppression, and build traditional academic skills.

What might my CP mean to my former students? Tara, a student of Nepali heritage, once described to a local reporter her experiences in our junior secondary class:

> The way he talked to us, it was like human-to-human, not like teacher-to-student. It was never 'take out your textbook and turn to this'. There was humanity in our class: sharing our feelings, sharing our struggles.

Tara's comments return me to what I believe to be the heart of CP: students and teachers seeing each other, as much as possible, as fellow human beings, and exploring together what it means to know, to care, to be, and to act, what it means *to be more fully human* (Freire 2005). This means recognizing each other's struggles and showing compassion. It means resisting labeling each other in categories that limit us, resisting treating each other as things to be used, exchanged, ranked, or consumed, as objects that are already finished and static, so that we may take more "ownership of consciousness, and thus identity," and find avenues for greater collective freedom and liberation (Shudak and Avoseh 2015, p. 465).

However, humanizing educational practices have difficulties gaining footholds in schools operating to address other pressing concerns. Like other parts of the world, Hong Kong has been grappling with the demands of schooling increasingly diverse student populations while seeking to remain competitive in a globalized economy. Research has documented tensions arising as the economic, political, and social agendas of nation-state sponsored education meet the lived realities of students, demonstrating that for students marginalized along dimensions such as race, ethnicity, religion, sexuality, gender or social class, alienation from schooling can be profound (Harris, Lefstein, Leung, and Rampton 2011; Martín Rojo 2010; Meyer 2010; Valenzuela 1999; Yi 2008). This alienation encounters educators often inadequately prepared to make sense of complex and often confusing classroom situations, as they are armed primarily with training meant to assure the stability of existing social orders, therefore limiting potential for schools as sites for transformation toward social justice and equity.

This process is evident around the world, in cities known for being global centers of power (Sofer 2007). Such is the case in Hong Kong, a major transnational city which mediates global flows of capital, goods, information, and people (Sassen 1996). Hong Kong brands itself as "Asia's World City," hoping to create cosmopolitan allure that will assure its competitive position amongst other global centers of power. Yet research paints a society in which "lower-class people…are trapped in a low-income-poverty vicious cycle," with EM residents occupying a distinct economic, social, and political space:

> For Hong Kong ethnic minorities, they were first recruited into the labour market in order to release the middle-class female labour force and to solve labour shortage problems. As post-industrialization proceeds in Hong Kong, they become competitors with the local working classes for low-paid jobs…Socio-culturally, these ethnic minorities suffer from racial discrimination and exclusion from mainstream Chinese society.
> (Lee, Wong, and Law 2007, p. 27)

It is only in the last decade that local research (see, for example, Thapa and Adamson 2018; Gube and Gao 2019) has begun to more visibly explain that many EM students attend schools structured around inequities, therefore necessitating critical approaches that can "inform pedagogic efforts to question and challenge domination, oppression, and inequality and the beliefs and teaching practices that dominate them" (Shum, Gao, and Tsung 2012). Therefore, the current literature on EM education in Hong Kong does not do enough to identify: (1) the relations of power within a school or classroom that are mediated by structural forces, (2) the struggles and pain accompanying oppression that are endured by students in their everyday lives, (3) the ways in which students respond through agency and resistance, and (4) the possibilities for pedagogies that empower students to negotiate forces of oppression, exclusion and marginalization, and transform their society.

Through these gaps, research and discourse misses an opportunity to prepare Hong Kong teachers and educators to act toward more just models of education based on critical, classroom situated, perspectives. This book steps in by telling the story of my experience in employing a critical ethnographic methodology to develop CP teaching in Hong Kong classrooms, with a committed group of educators and EM students, over the course of four academic years, from September 2010 through October 2014.

This remainder of this chapter first describes EM students demographically and explores how their struggles and needs have been framed in research and wider discourse. Next, I provide an overview of the educational system in which this study was conducted. I will show how, despite a rush of reforms after reunification of Hong Kong with mainland China, schools entrenched with inequities and constraints, and dealing with market-based shifts, took on EM students as a survival mechanism, creating new dilemmas. Then I will discuss how my history of social and geographic mobility and personal struggle, coupled with previous professional and academic training in social justice in education, led to me to investigate the field of EM education in Hong Kong. Understanding these two strands of socio-educational context and my life trajectory will help to make sense of the larger story and drama that unfolds in this book. This story depicts how the realities of day-to-day teaching and learning of EM students at the research sites, and the practices I introduced that challenged the status quo, played out against reforms advocating for student-centered approaches to education. In the end, tensions led to a contentious resolution to my research project, as will be discussed in Chapters 3 and 7.

EM students in Hong Kong

Hong Kong's EM residents compose a diverse and quickly growing group that makes up about 8% of the general population (*Census and Statistics Department* 2017), their numbers having increased about 70% from 2006 to 2016 (Bhowmik 2017). While these figures include foreign domestic workers of Indonesian and Filipino origin, and individuals of other national origins, special attention is often paid to what the Hong Kong government has referred to as "disadvantaged group" of about 80,000 EMs as of 2016. This group is made up largely of residents of Pakistani and Nepalese descent, one that the government claims has "much difficulty integrating fully into the community due to differences in culture, language and ethnic background" (*Chief Executive* 2014, para. 74). Students in this category often trace their presence in Hong Kong to soldiers and policemen brought by the former colonial government from Pakistan, and Nepalese soldiers who were members of the colonial Gurkha Brigade of security forces, who gained the right to abode in Hong Kong in the run up to the 1997 return to China. Post-1997, their numbers grew, and today, the parents of these students are often employed in working-class construction and service-industry jobs as security guards, drivers, and restaurant workers (Law and Lee 2013).

In the early 2000s, declining school enrolments in government subsidized schools, stemming from a low fertility rate in Hong Kong, and increased movement of local children into international schools, put schools under pressure from the government's Education Bureau (EDB) to increase enrolments or suffer consequences such as the cutting of classes and teaching positions. This was especially true for schools that were publicly considered poor quality or had previously served as pre-vocational, non-academically tracked institutions (Carmichael 2009; Pérez-Milans and Soto 2014). In this period, most EM students were relegated to a handful of schools that formerly taught in a Chinese medium of instruction (CMI) (Erni and Leung 2014), as their families were priced out of the expanding English-medium-based private international school market (Ku, Chan, and Sandhu 2005), and the dominant medium of instruction (MOI) in schools changed from English to Cantonese at the time of the handover.

Struggling schools took on marketing activities to attract students, some seeing an opportunity in recruiting EMs, who became "an important source of student intake for the less competitive schools in order to avoid being closed down due to inadequate student intake" (Shum, Gao, and Ki 2016). They competed for EM students by offering an English medium of instruction (EMI), Chinese second-language school-based curriculum, and amenities like prayer rooms for Muslims and cricket teams for students (Carmichael 2009; Pérez-Milans and Soto 2014). When I began my study in 2009, the population of EM students in government-subsidized schools was about 20,900 (Bhowmik and Kennedy 2013, p. 35).

But many of these schools had trouble in educating the students they took on for survival. Assimilationist views of education, which see the need to enlighten EM students through the transmission of Chinese culture and Confucian values, have played out in classrooms (Gao 2012) and in the government's general approach to EM students, which ignores fostering "ethnic minority students' appreciation of their own histories and cultures" (Erni and Leung 2014, p. 125). Attempts at assimilation have been facilitated by educators lacking training in multicultural approaches to teaching, and by limited opportunities for EM students and ethnic Chinese students to interact (Loper 2004). Moreover, many EM students have struggled with EMI classes and have shown a lack of proficiency in English writing (Carmichael 2009).

In the Liberal Studies, a secondary school subject that in theory would allow exploration of identity along with local, national, and global issues, students have encountered teaching materials that have rendered minorities invisible, or cast diversity in a negative light (Jackson 2014). Muslims, specifically, are represented monolithically and are often portrayed as "sexist, patriarchal, and backwards" (p. 4). Invisibility of EMs at different levels is persistent in the wider society (Gube and Burkholder 2019).

Finally, research has for decades documented the lack of sufficient and effective instruction for ethnic EM to master spoken Cantonese and written standard Chinese, a problem perceived as contributing to limited job opportunities and a lack of social integration by ethnic minorities (Kapai 2015; Loper 2004). In this context, EM students' "lack of ability to identify themselves as Chinese could be the source for possibly experiencing indirect discrimination over the question of parity of educational achievement," and this conflict over identity can be confounded by the school system's inattention to fostering "EM students' appreciation of their own histories and cultures" (Erni and Leung 2014, p. 125).

Despite this catalogue of concerns, the idea that opportunities for learning Chinese were limited and led to insufficient social integration on the part of EMs became central in publicly circulated discourses used to explain school failure, higher incidence of poverty, and stunted social mobility for EM youth. This centrality persisted even as research advocated for an ideological shift beyond Chinese language as the "core issue" (Connelly, Gube, and Thapa 2013, p. 209). For example, in addressing through a newspaper commentary the low levels of local university admission for EMs, the head of the Hong Kong Equal Opportunities Commission (Chow 2013, para. 2) claimed that:

> In reality, the hardship ethnic minority students face in accessing higher learning and potential employment opportunities stems primarily from their struggle to master Chinese in their school years. Only 120 non-Chinese-speaking students were admitted to degree courses last year, representing fewer than 1 per cent of the offers of study places made via the Joint University Programmes Admissions System.

If the most significant problem was one of limited Chinese language skills, then the solution lay in increased funding for and provision of Chinese as a second language curriculum, or so repeated media outlets, non-governmental organizations, researchers, and government officials. Accordingly, the Hong Kong government allocated 200 million Hong Kong dollars toward developing a Chinese as second language curriculum and providing additional vocational study opportunities for EM students (*Chief Executive* 2014).

Notwithstanding individual stories of achievement that occasionally appear in the local media, EM students as a whole have encountered difficulties in attaining academic success in Hong Kong. While failure has often been attributed to problems with Chinese language education, research highlights a web of interrelated factors (Bhowmik 2019), some of which were present before the post-reunification reforms, and some which arose after, beginning with a school system long known for exam-driven teaching and learning practices. In the post-1997 period, reforms to the Hong Kong education system were introduced which emphasized the need for the territory and students to be oriented toward economic competitiveness, but also contributed to privatization of the system and fierce competition amongst schools and individuals that marginalized values of "community, solidarity, and social justice" (Choi 2005, p. 239), affecting opportunities for all students.

Understanding the past, present, and future addressed by Hong Kong's educational reforms is essential to understanding the developments in this book. These are taken in turn next.

Entrenched inequities, market reforms, and new problems

In the run-up to the British handover of Hong Kong and its reunification with China, Postiglione (1996) pointed to staggering income inequality in Hong Kong which left some living "without running water or legal electricity" (p. 113). According to Postiglione, schools in the colonial period played no role in democratizing Hong Kong. Furthermore, through the 1980s the school curriculum had "virtually ignored raising political consciousness" (p. 107). Instead, Hong Kong schools had historically stressed responsible citizenship, minimizing political involvement for students (p. 108). Rather than educate to fight against inequality, schools in Hong Kong contributed to a pattern of social reproduction, increasingly through a middle class that was gaining more control over the educational system, attempting to ensure inherited middle-class status for their children (p. 113). Class-based inequities were maintained partly through a meritocratic ideology that was based on the "notion that anyone who is capable and works hard in school, regardless of social class factors, can achieve success" (p. 113).

The pre-handover period was one in which such inequities became entrenched in Hong Kong's stratified schooling system. Students were separated by a banding (or streaming) system based on academic achievement, but also along lines of social class and language, with greater privilege provided to students with higher English proficiency. By the early 1990s, Hong Kong had four main types of schools—government, aided, direct subsidy scheme (DSS), and private/independent schools, as Chiu and Walker (2007) explain:

> The first three types are supported by government money and generally follow the banding system. The government fully funds government schools, hires their principals and teachers, and selects their students. In contrast, aided schools are run by non-profit-making sponsoring organisations and hire their own principals and teachers, while being 90 percent supported by government funds. Aided schools can also charge small fees pre-approved by the government, [usually under $HK3,000], for school activities. DSS schools can charge up to [$HK68,000] in annual fees, receive government funding inversely proportional to their tuition, and have greater freedom in selecting students, language of instruction (Cantonese, English, etc.), hiring and remunerating staff, and curriculum. DSS school fees are determined largely by the school's reputation, which is often built on outstanding academic results. Thus, many Band 1 schools have chosen to become DSS schools.
>
> (p. 726)

Such structural conditions, which granted greater freedom to schools charging the greatest fees, shaped the day-to-day experiences of teachers and students within so-called "non-elite" low-banding schools. For example, in a study exploring experiences of students at the lowest banded schools, Yung (1997, p. 160) describes teacher perceptions of students:

> No matter what label one attaches to this group of students or schools, one very common character shared by these students is that they are described by their teachers to be very weak in learning, very hard to teach and very difficult to manage...And they are obviously not able to catch up with the planned curriculum. Some teachers even complain that the students are not able to write out the English alphabet in the proper sequence. This phenomenon attracted much media attention. The public just cannot believe or accept this to be true of our secondary students. Teachers teaching in these schools are at a loss as many of them are not too sure how they should teach or how they can adjust the curriculum for meeting the educational needs of this particular group of students. This feeling is usually reinforced further by the fact that most of the teachers in Hong Kong are still urged by their senior colleagues to keep up with the syllabus that is strongly geared towards public examination requirements. Not only the teachers feel quite helpless, their students also feel rather helpless (Au 1995) due to the prolonged failure experience of the students. Nobody seems to be winning in this battle against the weak foundation of the students.

Yung points to hopelessness felt by teachers who do not see a way to help students with a lack of English language proficiency. Students are portrayed in terms of their deficiencies that create difficulties for others; they cannot be taught and they cannot be "managed." There is a sense that the teachers in this pre-handover period had to follow the curriculum in order to meet the demands of public examinations, and even if they wanted to adjust it to meet the needs of students, they did not know how. This feeling of helplessness was shared with students. Interestingly, the enemy is portrayed as the "weak foundation of the students," rather than any structural forces. We will see similar observed dynamics in my fieldwork in Chapter 4.

In the wake of the 1997 handover, the new Hong Kong Special Administrative Region of the People's Republic of China government set on a mission to overhaul its system of schooling, as political, social, and market forces converged to create new demands, leading to changes in educational policy and practice that, while informed by notions of progressive education and equity, reinforced managerial efficacy and competitiveness (Chan and Mok 2001). These forces included global economic restructuring, a newly implemented "one country, two systems" mode of governance, and locally increasing class distinctions and disparities linked to use of English (Pérez-Milans 2017). Yet schools seemed unprepared to meet the demands generated by forces of change. Schools maintained alienating and constraining conditions, and arduous yet ineffective practices that if not changed, would harm Hong Kong's competitive standing, as the government (Education Commission 2000, p. 4) acknowledged:

> All in all, despite the huge resources put into education and the heavy workload endured by teachers, learning effectiveness of students remains not very promising; learning is still examination-driven and scant attention is paid to "learning to learn." School life is usually monotonous, students are not given comprehensive learning experiences and have little room to think, explore and create. The pathways for lifelong learning are not as smooth as they should be. To make up for these weaknesses, we need to uproot outdated ideology and develop a new education system that is student-focused.

In the following two decades, there was a transformation in terms of structure of schooling and curricular guidelines meant to combat alienating conditions in schools and meet pressing demands. At the level of the school system, reforms were introduced to infuse "diversity in education ideologies, modes of financing and focus of curriculum" (p. 5), leading to the expansion of the DSS system of fee-charging schools. Within schools, reforms aimed to counter monotonous school experiences with inspiring environments "conducive to the creative and exploratory spirit" in which students could develop international outlooks (p. 5).

These aims would be sustained through a focus on students, granting them increased agency in organizing and directing their learning, casting them "the main protagonist in learning," and assuring their needs and interests would be "the foremost consideration" (Education Commission 2000, p. 36), while also expecting them to be vital voices in the reform process. It was envisioned that through a "no-loser" principle, all students would achieve a basic level of education and would benefit from a commitment to "not give up on any single student, but rather let all students have the chance to develop their potentials" (pp. 36–37).

Based on these general aims and principles, specific reforms took shape. A new academic structure was introduced, offering twelve years of free education, leading to the Hong Kong Diploma in Secondary Education Examination (HKDSE), and publicly subsidized undergraduate studies for a quota of qualifying students. This change contributed to an increase in the number and proportion of students able to access university places in Hong Kong. Beginning in the mid-1990s, the government expanded the availability of publicly subsidized first-year, first-degree places to about 17% of the 17–20 age group, a significant increase from 2% in the mid-1980s (see Law 2007 for a historical overview of these changes).

The Education Bureau also revised its official curriculum guides, redefining curriculum as "learning experiences" rather than "documents" (Curriculum Development 2000, p. 19). Supplementing subject knowledge, learning of nine generic skills such as creativity, collaboration, and communication skills, and development of "positive values and attitudes" such as responsibility, commitment, respect for others, perseverance, and national identity were included across eight

Key Learning Areas (p. 11). Additional values such as freedom, human dignity, individuality, justice, love, trust, and solidarity are suggested for inclusion in curriculum (p. 15). The result is touted as an open framework providing flexibility to adapt the curricula to students' needs (p. 19).

This flexible, student-centered approach emphasizing collaborative and enquiry learning penetrated curriculum guides, including those for the two areas in which I taught during my research. For example, schools were granted autonomy to develop school-based English curriculum meeting the abilities, interests, and needs of their students, with panel heads, the teachers that oversee each subject, and school administrations responsible for creating an environment making innovation possible (Education Bureau 2002). Similarly, the Personal, Social, and Humanities Education Curriculum Guide (Education Bureau 2010, p. 5) shifted from a content-focused curriculum to a flexible curriculum based on participatory enquiry learning and "social involvement" that allows students to have experiences "beyond the curriculum" and "contribute to the life of their school and community." It mandates that the "content chosen should be closely linked to daily life and social developments" and "the acquisition of knowledge" should not "be confined to textbooks." To support enquiry learning, there should be use of "a variety of materials" (p. 107) and these resources "are not all necessarily all chosen or developed by the teacher ... students can use their initiative to identify, propose, and select learning resources" (p. 138). In this Key Learning Area, students are expected to ask questions and seek answers, engage in dialogue, enhance learning skills, participate in knowledge construction, and develop positive life values. Chapter 4 will describe how these envisioned curriculum guidelines were enacted at my first research site, and Chapter 5 will clarify how I chose to enact them within my CP.

Yet, a decade after the handover of Hong Kong and a series of reforms, structural inequities and constraints persisted. Reformed schools were described as "hierarchically structured and operated" spaces which "rarely empower teachers," relying on top-down decision-making processes (Chiu and Walker 2007, p. 726). Moreover, changes in MOI that promoted "mother tongue" Cantonese teaching and a biliterate, trilingual policy meant to ensure Hong Kong's citizenry could read and write English and speak English, Cantonese, and Putonghua promoted the status of EMI teaching, rather than demote it (Law 2007). In effect the MOI policy consolidated "the status of English as important socioeconomic and cultural capital" leaving students tracked into schools using CMI "in a disadvantaged position for acquiring higher-value cultural capital and attaining upward social mobility" (p. 116) compared to students at EMI schools.

Even though market-based reforms created opportunities for further education, they further entrenched inequities and had further human costs affecting all Hong Kong students. The increased competition for university places and social mobility has taken a troubling turn. Government research shows that while teachers are generally better trained than ever and are committed to their profession, they experience demanding workloads, frustration with performativity and accountability measures, loss of professional dignity, and problems with stress and anxiety (Legislative Council, 2006). Similarly, a government report describes how between school and after-school activities, Hong Kong's children often bear with an average of fifty-five study hours per week, sleep deprivation, stress, and declining mental health, factors that in the past five years may have contributed to an upsurge of suicides committed by primary and secondary school students (Legislative Council, 2018).

Much work needs to be done to assure the student-centered pedagogical approaches and no-loser principle that underpin the EDB's educational reforms apply to all students, including EM students. Hue and Kennedy (2014, p. 131) recognize the enormity of this task and advocate for collaboration and commitment in order to bring about equity:

> Commitment and advocacy for the welfare of ethnic minority students can only be cultivated successfully through collaboration between policymakers, practitioners and researchers. These participants in this process should share their concerns to work together as allies with schools and communities, to take the concerns of individual ethnic minority students to heart, and to develop strategies that enact educational change at both the policy and practical levels. The strategies they create need to foster social justice, multiculturalism, cultural diversity and anti-discrimination.

Given the state of education in Hong Kong, and the growing body of research accompanying EM education, the next section explains how I became involved, why I advocate for equity through a critical approach to education, and why I continue to do this work despite challenges.

My life trajectory as impetus

As much as this book is about CP, schools, and students, it is also a story about me. My motivation to examine the field of EM education in Hong Kong stems from my work as an educator and graduate student in the United States. But understanding my commitment to my students, and ultimately the impetus for this study, requires reflecting on my life trajectory, which includes using education as a way to transform self, other, and communities, and a lifetime of collecting experiences that I could turn into teaching capital. This section begins a story that will be told through this book, of my evolving criticality in teaching and researching, how I relate with the others in the world. I hope that through this story, you are able to "see your story in mine," and as I "theorize the commitments and contradictions in a radical teaching life through my lived experience," you do the same in yours (Camangian 2014, p. 38).

I began working in education in 1999 as an educational assistant for students with special needs in United States public schools, then in 2001 I began work with an organization called the Bay Area Education Program in San Francisco, California. This long-term support program served low-income students from marginalized communities with the mission of helping them graduate from university and so they could serve communities as agents of change. Working closely with students and families over the course of eight years, I became intimately aware of how my students were disempowered within the education system, and society, through a system of complex power structures and social relations, and this view of the relationship between students, schools, and social reproduction continues to inform my work.

With a desire to better understand and address the experiences of my students, I pursued graduate studies, and as a result, my interest and in the field of CP grew and matured. As I continued to work at the Bay Area Education Program, I became a strong advocate for critical practices, seeking ways to help the program and fellow educators develop their critical awareness so they could in turn develop within students a sense of "transformational resistance" that would allow them to create counter-hegemonic narratives and build the work ethic and hope necessary to engage fully in academic pursuits and social change (Solorzano and Delgado Bernal 2001). Part of helping my students build their narratives was sharing stories from my own life, so that they would open their stories to me and maybe find lessons in mine.

When I came to Hong Kong, I brought with my advocacy for critical theory and practices and value of narrative building. I continued sharing my life experiences with new students and collaborators. It was important to be open, both from an ethical perspective as a researcher (see Chapter 3), and also as a tool for developing a CP (see Chapter 5). In fact, students I taught asked me why I was teaching *them*, as EM students in a band-three school. They wanted to know why I continued to do the work if it brought difficulties to my life, and why I was interested in EM students in the first place.

I would answer them by sharing some of the struggles that led me to identify and feel solidarity with struggles they faced, as I will share here. I was born in Tegucigalpa, the capital of Honduras, a small country in Central America. During my time there, my family, consisting of my father, mother, and three sisters, was what I consider middle class. My father had attended university and become a lawyer and university lecturer. My mother had also attained a much higher level of schooling than her parents. Her father never attended school and was illiterate his whole life, and her mother had dropped out of school in primary three. My mother finished secondary school, and moved to the United States for three years where she took secretarial vocational courses. Having attained social mobility, my parents owned a house, a car, and sent my older sister and me to a private school.

But all was not well at home. In the first few years of my life, I witnessed scarring domestic violence and alcoholism in my home. When I was six years old, my parents divorced, and at seven years old, my mother took my three sisters and me to live in Los Angeles, where our new lives in the United States were drastically different, even as familial conflict and substance abuse persisted. We were now a household headed by a single mother who struggled psychologically, physically, and financially to raise four children on her own. We were no longer middle class, we were a working-class family straining to make ends meet, getting by with the help of free breakfasts and lunches provided by our public schools.

Growing up in the United States, I had two major on-going conflicts that in Hong Kong would help me identify with my students and some of their predicaments. First, I had to figure out a racial identity. I was growing up as a "Latino" or "Hispanic," terms used to designate my non-white, EM status. Second, I was also growing up without a father. From the time I was thirteen to twenty-one, I had no contact with him. I felt internal anguish at the absence of a paternal relationship during a time of adolescence when I was figuring out my masculinity. In senior secondary, I attended a special humanities themed school in which I learned about art, philosophy, critical theory, history, literature, and sociology through interdisciplinary study. This program awakened my intellectual curiosity and challenged me to think and question the world around me, but did not address my internal struggles, which came to a head after my first year of university.

I was escaping my problems with drugs, and my academics suffered, and I was put on probation and threatened with expulsion. Yet, in the midst of my tumultuous university years, I stepped into the world of education, volunteering and working for programs serving students from working-class minority communities. I found that I was working with students with whom I identified, and this realization that I could help others changed my course and took me into the field of education after university. For some students in this study, hearing these stories would build enough trust in me to allow them to commit to the rigorous effort I demanded of them. In my story, they could see theirs.

Years later, in 2007 and 2008 I visited Hong Kong and Guangzhou with a graduate summer course exploring educational practices in transnational spaces. Through participation in this course, I was familiarized with educational systems in these two Chinese cities and gained interest in how San Francisco and Hong Kong, as transnational centers of global capital, were accommodating international business "city users" while restricting the claims that marginalized youth can make on each city (Sassen 1998). Upon returning to San Francisco, I began to wonder how I could fashion a pedagogy through which students struggling for educational opportunities in separate global cities like Hong Kong and San Francisco could come to understand common transnational dimensions of their struggles, in order to resist in solidarity. So I was motivated to come to Hong Kong to understand marginalization in a context of urban education less familiar for me, so that I could consider the possibilities for a CP that works for transnational solidarity amongst marginalized communities. That question brought me to Hong Kong to pursue a doctoral degree, where I am now married and have a son of mixed Chinese heritage. My home is Hong Kong, and I am committed to working here for greater equity in education. The rest of this book will pick up the story here.

Summary and words of caution

Overall, Hong Kong's educational reforms of the past two decades have, on the surface, offered inroads for CP projects. Curricular documents are orientated toward equity through the EDB's no-loser principle. There is attention to students' needs and interests, emphasis on values such as love and solidarity, and calls for teachers to innovate, promote enquiry and dialogue, and bring students into the learning and curriculum development processes, in order to counter the monotony and alienation of previous modes of teaching and learning. These steps point to the removal of constraints and the discovery of new possibilities in pedagogy. However, there is also an insistence on schooling for competitiveness and internationalization, and the reform documents and curriculum guides do not explain how any possible contradictions between education for equity and education for supporting the capitalist market could be negotiated. Ultimately, there are still conditions in schools that constrain teachers and students, and further disempower already disadvantaged students.

Within this environment, EM students and their needs have been marginalized. Moreover, they face an education system that maintains a myriad of obstacles that make reaching tertiary-level education in Hong Kong, especially university, difficult. Situated in Hong Kong secondary schools serving EM students from low-income families, this book outlines possibilities and obstacles to employing CPs as a response to the material conditions students face, while illustrating theoretical concepts with examples of curriculum that were implemented in classrooms.

However, I must offer important words of caution. Shor and Freire (1987, p. 26) warn, "Liberatory learning cannot be standardized. It has to be situated, experimental, creative—action that creates the conditions for transformation by testing the means of transformation that can work" in that place and time (p. 26). Because CPs cannot be standardized, this study offers no quick fixes or step-by-step instructions for educators and policy makers looking for a magic bullet to improve teaching practices. At best, this book offers a framework, practices, and materials that offer possibilities for empowerment and can inspire educators to adapt them to new contexts. This remains true for other teachers in Hong Kong working with EM students. My CP was primarily driven in response to the students, primarily of Nepalese and Pakistani heritage, I encountered at one of the research sites, a local secondary school. Yet other schools serving EM students in Hong Kong may have a much different ethnic and even socioeconomic composition. Moreover, my analysis related to my students often takes them for granted as a group, seeing them as a unified EM group of adolescents, and is limited in its understanding of how dynamics such as differing familial trajectories of migration and movement, class, gender, religious affiliations, and sexuality play out in individual students.

Finally, a key component in educational change is largely absent in this book: parents and care-takers. Though I had some contact with parents and care-takers, and many were aware of my practices and its effects on their children, my contact was limited by our differences in language proficiencies and the time I had available for communication with them, especially since many worked more than one job. Their experiences, perspectives, and collaboration must be included in further research.

Therefore, I encourage readers to be critical about this book.

14　*The students, the system, and the teacher*

Overview of chapters

This book tells the story of the development of a CP over four years of fieldwork. First, it focuses on the data gathered through critical ethnography during the course of an academic year at New Territories Secondary School (NTS), where, as part of my research, I was allowed to assist English teachers and co-teach form one Liberal Studies. Data gathering served to illuminate the context of schooling for the students at the school, and more importantly to uncover generative themes and vehicles for engagement: the former referring to the personal conflicts in students' lives that are parts of larger social patterns, and the latter referring to the texts and other pedagogical tools that allow students and teachers to investigate these themes. Second, the book presents how generative themes and vehicles for engagement became the foundation for a curriculum based on CP at a second site, Industrial Secondary School (ISS), where I extended my research project after I was hired as a part-time teacher. Third, the book reflects on how students at ISS engaged in dialogue related to generative themes in their lives and the world around them, and explores the kinds of individual and collective actions students took to empower themselves and their peers.

Chapter 2 presents CP as the theoretical framework and a literature review. Though the field of CP is diverse, Chapter 2 narrows the theoretical framework to focus on conceptions and applications of pedagogy highly influenced by work of the late Brazilian educator Paolo Freire (1970), including work done in Hong Kong. This chapter introduces important concepts including banking education, critical consciousness, generative themes, and dialogue that shape subsequent chapters. The chapter also defines key concepts in the research question: empowerment and limits and possibilities.

Chapter 3 outlines and justifies the critical ethnographic approach used in this study. I outline key distinctions between traditional and critical ethnography, and position critical ethnography as a method that is explicitly political. Next, I describe the two research sites and how I gained access to them, providing histories of each site, and introducing key collaborators at each site. I take time to consider special ethical considerations attached to critical ethnography, and how adhering to a set of ethics brought about internal and external dilemmas for me as a teacher and researcher.

Chapter 4 analyzes data collected at the first research site, NTS, where I spent a year doing fieldwork. The chapter focuses on the generative themes and vehicles for engagement I uncovered as I became an everyday part of life at the school and began co-teaching form one Liberal Studies classes, and it also sheds light on how inequities for EM students are produced and reproduced through actions of well-meaning educators. The chapter explains what constituted a banking method of education reliant on textbooks, with little room for dialogue and developing of academic literacy, despite attempts by some teachers to care for and understand students. It shows how I used fieldwork to bring myself closer to understanding students, their concerns, and the popular culture they used to make sense of the world, and how I began to test teaching approaches that were alternatives to the norm at the school. I end the chapter with a discussion of how my work contributed to empowering students by giving them opportunities to express identities while showing academic investment, but was unable to effectively move students to empowerment based on transformative resistance. Through stories of students and teachers, this chapter also challenges discourses focusing only Chinese language education to the exclusion of considering students' additional linguistic needs across the curriculum.

Chapter 5 reviews data collected at the second research site, ISS, where I worked for over three years as a part-time teacher. The generative themes and pedagogy present at NTS will be shown to also be valid at ISS. Then I outline a three-year English junior secondary curriculum I developed, focusing on content and products of the curriculum, and tell the story of how I introduced a CP based on generative themes through examination of units and materials that met standards set by the EDB and built students' academic literacy. I highlight some of the difficulties of implementing the curriculum and provide viewpoints of other educators who participated in it, and in the end discuss how students were empowered through the curriculum in terms of the spaces for expression and voice they were provided, and vocabulary and social critique that moved them toward transformative resistance.

Chapter 6 centers on situated accounts of dialogue and student actions at ISS and opens a window for understanding the interactional process of CP in day-to-day practice. I share three episodes illustrative of how various students engaged in dialogue based on the generative themes that informed the curriculum, within the classroom space, on the social media site Facebook, and through written personal letters. Dialogue will be shown in terms of dramatic encounters that take on epistemological and ontological dimensions, addressing the building of knowledge as well as how students are in the world. Student empowerment will be exemplified through actions of transformative resistance, in and out of the school setting, that show students linking up to wider struggles for education and equity, while my own limitations in dialogue are exposed.

Chapter 7 responds to the research question by exploring some of the limits and possibilities for furthering CP in Hong Kong. The chapter advocates for better meeting the needs of students through deconstruction of oppressive social conditions and school practices, and construction of new CP theory and practice. It also calls for attending to teacher and administrator development, opening of new institutional spaces, and moving toward solidarity with other marginalized and disempowered groups in Hong Kong's educational system and beyond.

In the course of these chapters, a parallel story is told. It is a story of how I explored what it means to be "critical," making and remaking how I teach, how I come to knowledge, and how I act in the world. The difficulties I faced along the way, including ethical dilemmas arising from committing to students and research, and tensions and stresses in dealing with administrative concerns at my second site, provide some of the conflict in this story. Ultimately, this is a tale of birth and rebirth across space and time, of acknowledging my limitations in order to tackle them. It's a story about my belief in the power of stories.

2 Critical pedagogy
Rebirth in theory and in practice

> When I began teaching working class students, I wanted to transfer my own knowledge to my students. You see the problem? I naively imposed my own experience on them. I didn't know what it meant to critically reinvent knowledge with them from their place in society.
>
> – Ira Shor

Shor's reflection into his teaching was on my mind in March 2010. I was in Hong Kong, but had not yet commenced fieldwork, and was recollecting my work with students in the United States. In these words, I saw a past version of myself, a naive teacher. To preserve my reflection and to share it with the world, I wrote a post for my blog, inspired by the quote above:

Extract 2.1 "I recognize my own naïveté"

I know that in my early days as an educator, I too thought that the way to help students succeed in schooling was by replicating the knowledge I credited for my own success. Therefore, I did not question the curriculum being taught to my kids. At best, I advocated for more engaging and fun ways to teach that curriculum. At the same time, I thought that a combination of "interesting ways of teaching" and a rock hard will on my part would break down student resistance. Now I recognize my own naïveté; I see that what I accomplished was not education, but imposition.

{Carlos (researcher), blog post, March 24, 2010}

In my nascent days as an educator, I equated education with transferring knowledge to which students would connect. As I matured, I increasingly drew on personal experience, bringing to students theories and popular culture texts dealing with race, gender, and power that were formative in guiding me to positively cope with and surpass my familial and personal difficulties. But during my time as a graduate student, I had a profound rebirth (Freire 2004, p. 61). Through reading critical pedagogy (CP) theory and witnessing its practice, I came to a philosophy of education that situated educational practice directly within the experiences of students, seeing "education as a crucial site for social transformation" (Viola 2009, p. 7), and understanding that resistance was not something to break down, but to build up. As I gained political and ideological clarity (Bartolomé 2004), I continued my educational work at the Bay Area Program and had a space in which to develop a fledgling pedagogy informed by new sets of theory and practice. I had arrived at a CP.

CP forms the framework for this study, which seeks to understand limits and possibilities for developing an empowering pedagogy with ethnic minority (EM) students in Hong Kong. Chapter 1 teased out the research problem, and proposed that CP is a necessary alternative to addressing problems experienced by EM students within constraining schools. But CP can be difficult to pin down because it does not "constitute a homogeneous set of ideas" (McLaren 2007, p. 186). Rather, it is defined by its objective: "to empower the powerless and transform existing social inequalities and injustices" (p. 186). Consequently, there is no clear delineation of a body of literature that in and of itself constitutes CP (Tarlau 2014). Furthermore, there is no single definition of CP, though ideas and terms like student empowerment, social justice, liberation, transformation, equity, democracy, and citizenship are often at the core of the contemporary field (Thomson-Bunn 2014). As we will see, lexical clarity is made more difficult to attain across the field of CP because practitioners of CP develop their own ways to theorize the context of their practice as well as the practice itself.

To educators taking on CP, the term may refer to work rooted in struggle against racism, the development of feminist pedagogies, training youth in social activism, study of language and social structures, or raising of critical consciousness to find new social possibilities; activities that could be placed in the classroom or other arenas (Canaan, Amsler, Cowden, Motta and Singh 2010). Beyond the lack of a uniform definition, CP as a term can be elusive because there is sometimes a perceived split within the field, between those who focus on CP as theory, and those who focus on CP as practice. Attempts have been made to reconcile this split by distinguishing between CP and critical teaching as two necessary aspects of educational work for social justice (Weiner 2007). CP can be thought of as a framework for one's pedagogy within various educational contexts, what Weiner calls "critical teaching," and at the same time CP can be the epistemological model for more general educational projects and social and political critique (p. 66).

I understand this CP study under the umbrella of critical teaching. Therefore, this chapter leans on literature that theorizes and presents examples of CP as such. Yet the literature presented here is not meant to pigeon-hole CP theory and its application. Instead, this chapter and the book as a whole operate assuming that "educators must develop their own versions of critical theory, as well as the curricula and pedagogies that are developed logically from the former" (Brosio 2006, p. 85).

The remainder of this chapter describes my version of CP, and uses my rebirth into CP as an organizational device, mirroring my encounter with CP theory, the exposure to its practice, and my reflections about its limits and possibilities for empowering students. Though CP inextricably links the dual elements of theory and practice, I first describe CP as a theory of pedagogy for liberation, detailing how education can function as a force to unmask and address oppressive conditions, and counter "banking" modes of education, via transformed dialogic relationships that investigate generative themes and prompt action with the participation of revolutionary leaders. Reflecting on this set of theories was a catalyst for my educational rebirth, and it comes into play beginning in Chapter 4, as a way of analyzing what "education" meant at New Territories School, and then as an instrument for evaluating my pedagogy in Chapters 5 and 6.

Second, I provide examples of how CP has given life to new practices. First, I review the work of several critical teachers who guided me in creating my own version of CP. The tools they shared for understanding and engaging with students influenced how I moved from theory to practice in my pedagogy. I also conduct a brief overview of how teaching practices directly informed by CP have been adapted in Hong Kong, showing that while few inroads have been made for CP, small victories should bring optimism for possibilities. Finally, I review a range of critiques of CP that run from questioning of its vague terms, to interrogating its potential to empower and transform. Taking account of CP as theory and practice, along with its critiques, I define the terms "empowerment" and "limits and possibilities". For now, let us examine CP as a tool for liberation.

Before moving on, some words of caution may be necessary: using CP theory and previous accounts of practice does not fully prepare one to take on a redefined critical practice. Teachers must reflect and construct, along with students and collaborators, curricula that addresses their immediate contexts (Hinchey 2004, p. 20):

> Critical educators believe that all such curricula must be based on classroom context...For this reason, and to the chagrin of many traditionally educated teachers, critical theorists and educators have no standard curriculum and pedagogy to offer. Instead of saying, as traditionalists so often do, 'Here's the way to do xyz in the classroom,' critical educators speak instead of praxis: action based upon reflection...

Theorizing a pedagogy for liberation

CP as a field is rooted in the Frankfurt School of Critical Theory which considered the changing nature of capitalism after World War II and "analyzed the mutating forms of domination that accompanied this change" (Kincheloe 2008, p. 46). Contemporary CP though, often traces its genesis to Brazil, and the work of educator Paulo Freire. Using the ideas Freire developed while building literacy amongst poor rural farmers in the 1960s, educators have since countered alienation, such as the alienation mentioned in Chapter 1, through a pedagogy of liberation that rejects transmission-based modes of education and uses praxis and changed relationships between teachers and students to achieve humanization.

In a pedagogy for liberation, the teacher takes reality not as fixed, but always in transformation, necessitating us to seek humanization by supporting pursuits for self-affirmation, rather than support dehumanization through hindering or exploiting others (Freire 2004, p. 55). Those who find themselves in a dehumanizing situation, the oppressed, must work to liberate themselves rather than have liberation done to them or for them (p. 28).

To reach this potential, we must discount the "banking concept" of education, in which teachers merely deposit knowledge into students without providing the means to develop a critical consciousness, an understanding of oneself as both an object and subject of history that moves one towards transformative action (p. 62). The banking method generally treats teachers as the active subject of learning, while students are objects to which is done (p. 73). Teachers become the sole sanctioned actors, speakers, and thinkers in the room, in effect minimizing the students' creative power for transformation while creating conditions under which they internalize a self-defeating consciousness. On the other hand, a critical consciousness allows oppressed students to see that they are not "marginal" and turns their attentions to identifying the social structures that oppress them (p. 74).

A critical consciousness allows students to "read the world" (Freire and Macedo 1987), not as a technical act of manipulating words, but as naming and questioning relations of power in their immediate environments, to develop new understandings of one's world that unlock possibilities for action. This critical literacy situates itself within the students' subjectivities; their histories, languages, cultures; and their ongoing struggles for power (McLaren 1988). Yet, while critical literacy affirms students as "the experts on their own lives," there is recognition that students need skills and forms of communication that allow them to move in the world, through explicitly teaching and deconstructing with them codes of power carried in speaking, reading, and writing (Delpit 1995, p. 47).

Therefore, liberation from oppression must involve an acquisition of a critical awareness of oppression through praxis. Praxis is a cycle of "reflection and action upon the world in order to transform it" (Freire 2004, p. 51) and takes the shape of educational projects carried out with oppressed groups with the purpose of mobilizing them to take action based on their world views and ethics (pp. 54–55). These projects can be done through a "problem-posing" dialogic approach in which problems and their solutions are generated by the oppressed subjects themselves (p. 72), allowing them to move beyond further adaptation to or integration into oppressive structures and into becoming active agents in resisting and reshaping reality (p. 74).

Carrying out problem-posing education projects and reading the world with students requires new dialogic relationships between teachers and students. In a liberatory CP, teachers and students are not conceptualized as separate, contradictory entities. Instead, both teacher and students become active agents in the act of knowing (Shor and Freire 1987, p. 33). Through dialogue, "the teacher-of-the-students and the students-of-the-teacher cease to exist and a new term emerges: teacher-student with student-teachers" (p. 80). This allows teacher-students and student-teachers to practice "co-intentional education" in which both teacher and students are subjects of the education, and not only critically unveil reality but also jointly "recreate" reality. The task of the learner becomes "committed involvement" in the struggle for freedom (Freire 1970, p. 69).

Despite breaking down the contradiction between teacher and student, CP still places the teacher in a position of responsibility. Rather than taking a neutral social function, a teacher should act as a knowledgeable social and moral agent and invite students to see beyond current relations of domination by fashioning "a language of hope that points to new forms of social and material relations" (McLaren 2007, pp. 255–256). These responsibilities call on critical teachers to become "transformative intellectuals" (Giroux 1985), or rigorous, reflective scholars preparing students for active citizenry. Furthermore, teachers should be researchers of their own students to uncover generative themes in the lives of students, and hold a "rigorous body of knowledge" to which "students then react to, reject, reinterpret, analyze, and put into action" (Kincheloe 2008, p. 21). Thus, teachers must develop their ability to manipulate two significant tools in the pursuit of liberation and humanization with students: generative themes and dialogue.

Generally, a problem-posing approach is rooted in generative themes, or "common experiences across participants' lives or relevant to participants' realities" (Souto-Manning 2010, p. 9) that are codified, or represented visually for study (p. 19). Teachers "uncover" generative themes and the materials through which they are studied, based on "emerging knowledge of students and their sociocultural backgrounds" (Kincheloe 2008, p. 20). To initiate dialogue around generative themes, the teacher builds "an unfamiliar critical inquiry around familiar problems while also connecting daily life to larger issues of power in society," thereby embedding "concreteness in the learning process while positioning the local in relation to the global" (Macrine 2009, p. 120). By "establishing grounds whereby these experiences can be questioned and analyzed in both their strengths and weaknesses" (McLaren 2007, p. 249), problematizing should allow subjects to question "the natural, cultural and historical reality in which s/he is immersed" (Freire 2005, p. ix). Following engagement with generative themes, students eventually move from dialogue to communal problem solving and action, only to return to reflection on their actions and begin posing problems again.

Any investigation into students' worlds, should be dialogical (Freire 2004, p. 96). Dialogue in a CP is not understood as a simple communicative function, nor as a series of questions and answers that lead to a final destination. Both its definitions and its practice are messier than that:

> Dialogue is profound, wise, insightful conversation…interactive visiting… Dialogue involves periods of lots of noise as people share and lots of silence as people muse. Dialogue is communication that creates and recreates multiple understanding… [and] rejects telling people what the problems are and what the solutions should be and instead uses participatory activities that allow people to explore their existing knowledges and responses".
>
> (Wink 2000, pp. 47–49)

It should not be thought of as "a simple education technique leading to the attainment of certain results" but instead as an "existential reality" of humans who get to know themselves and the world through others (Durakoglu 2013, p. 104). In dialogic encounters, telling stories to young people, and allowing them to tell stories that contextualize their worlds, creates possibilities to explore influences in their social lives, including their ethnic membership, traditions, or the stories told to them (Greene 1997, p. 6).

These encounters, existential realities, and acts of story-telling move students towards emancipatory action and cultural synthesis, led by "revolutionary leaders" who are committed to students and freedom, and have reflected on the group's domination, though they may not yet be lucid on the state of their own oppression (Freire 2004). Revolutionary leaders use cooperation and unity to further communication that names the world in order to transform it (p. 167). They name oppression in the world, when others cannot, to initiate them into doing the same (pp. 177–178). Moreover, revolutionary leaders build trust, empathy, and humility through cooperation, and unity through actions that build critical awareness in a group, rather than slogans and "mere speech-making" and "ineffective 'blah'" (p. 175). Ultimately, a cultural synthesis is achieved, wherein the views of revolutionary leaders and those of the students are resolved, enriching the perspectives of both (p. 181).

CP can produce a profound transformation in one's *philosophy* of education (Camangian 2014), as it did for me, but giving life to a new *practice* takes additional hard work, struggle, and commitment. After understanding education as a tool for liberation, I looked at the teaching work at the Bay Area Program where I worked differently (see Chapter 1). Though I believed in our mission of helping students go to and graduate from universities, it seemed like much of our work was predicated on helping students conform to oppressive banking education practices. So, I began experimenting with my teaching there with the support of the program. Fortunately, the transition into a new practice for me was eased through studying previous accounts of CP theorizing and teaching, and also learning directly from some of those practitioners.

Giving life to new practice

A review of CP literature reveals its application in wide variety of contexts, early childhood education to tertiary education, from (most often) economically marginalized schools to schools of economic privilege, and in nations around the world. For example, scholars have documented development of CP and critical literacy with senior-secondary school students within the disciplines of mathematics (Yang 2009) and science (Emdin 2011), applying CP via participatory action research with students in an after-school setting (Cammarota and Romero 2009), and using CP for teaching in bilingual settings with children (Cummins 1996, 2000, 2009), or theorizing a compatible place for CP within Muslim education (Hussien 2007). All these stories offer wisdom to aspiring critical educators and researchers, whether as an illustration to visualize CP as a starting point, or for a grander vision of what an articulated and developed practice looks like, along with some tools for getting there.

These researchers and critical educators grapple with race, gender, class, language, media, technology, violence, post-colonialism, and religion, not just as concepts or issues, but as sites for educational inquiry and transformation. What often ties their accounts of CP though, is a similar discourse structure enacted in classrooms (Sarroub and Quadros 2015, p. 254):

> To use critical pedagogy, practitioners attempt to reconstruct their classrooms as a three pronged discourse structure. Structurally, these three aspects include a curriculum that needs to be founded upon students' interests, cultural needs, and community empowerment. In terms of the dynamics of interaction, the teacher/educator in the classroom usually focuses on participation and skills in dialogue in a rational articulation of one's context with others who are differently situated…In this regard, the participatory dynamics and dialogical skills involve the construction of dialogues amongst peers, questioning concepts and common behavior, doubting the ritualized form, explaining one's perception of reality, providing evidence of assertions, advancing arguments from diverse knowledge and/or disciplinary perspectives, drawing upon experience with the curriculum and topics addressed, and listening to a variety of voices in different discourses. In essence, this is the capacity for critique, reflecting the critical agency of participants.

The attention to curriculum based on interests, needs, and community; the attention to dynamics of interaction via participation and dialogue skills; and the attention to capacity for critical agency via critique are three structural factors I sought to bring to my CP. I encountered tools to do this work by engaging in study of, and with, other critical educators. I will now share some of the accounts of CP that greatly influenced me, and these come from critical educators in the United States who engaged in long-term pedagogical projects lasting at least several years (Camangian 2008, 2010; Duncan-Andrade and Morrell 2008; Morrell 2004; Morrell and Duncan-Andrade 2002).

Following my philosophical rebirth, the shape my CP took in practice was in large part to reading accounts written by these educators and their wider network of teacher-researchers. Duncan-Andrade and Morrell (2008) worked as senior-secondary teachers with students of color in a low-income urban American setting, within classrooms, in a summer university access program, and even with a basketball team. In all cases, academic achievement and university attendance rates for their students greatly improved, a feat they attribute in large to the act of reading the world of their students in order to find "countless vehicles for moving forward their critical pedagogical agenda" (p. 70). They describe "vehicles for engagement" as tools or avenues that involve students in academic work while informing teachers about students' needs, concerns, and interests. These vehicles for engagement, which included basketball, hip hop music, American films, and media literacy, "[captured] the hearts and minds" of students, and were placed within a "programmatic vision...students [could] believe in" (p. 71). Moreover, they were a bridge between the generative themes that students and teachers identified and entering into further dialogue and engagement with academic rigor. Later, the teachers used these vehicles for engagement to bridge with canonical academic texts (Morrell and Duncan-Andrade 2002).

In their CP, the practices of research and teaching are part of the same process of creating "communities of practice" recognizing "the existence of a dominant set of institutional norms and practices and intentionally sets itself up to counter those norms and practices" in order to "[respond] directly to structural and material inequalities in the school and the larger community" (Duncan-Andrade and Morrell 2008, p. 11). A community of practice operates via shared critical praxis between students and teachers allowing them to jointly identify and analyze problems, and then develop, implement, and evaluate plans of action. This critical praxis "breaks down the inherent power relations in traditional pedagogy and identifies students as collaborators with adults" (p. 13) while allowing them to build crucial core academic skills.

To make this praxis possible, Duncan-Andrade and Morrell (2008, p. 15) established themselves within a critical research tradition defined by a desire to explicitly use research with marginalized populations for social change and a positing of both teachers and students as researchers. In their model of critical research "instead of just doing research 'on' young people, which makes them the objects of our research gaze", students are repositioned as "the subjects of their own research" (p. 106). For marginalized students, a potential for the formation of powerful identities as intellectuals is created. Students engage in research through a model called "participatory action research" which is facilitated by the teacher to collectively investigate a problem using "indigenous knowledge to examine and understand the problems that are the greatest concern to indigenous researchers" (p. 108).

Camangian (2008, 2010), who I first encountered when he gave a guest lecture in a graduate course I took with Duncan-Andrade, likewise shared a well-articulated theoretical foundation and programmatic vision for his practice, and isolated poetry and auto-ethnography as a vehicles to critically engage economically and racially marginalized secondary students in an American urban setting. He details the school in which he worked as a teacher as one in which, "Administrators directed most of their attention to managing the campus' massive in-school ditching and tardiness, instead of providing training and time for teachers to develop culturally empowering instruction for their students" (p. 38). In a community and school fraught with tension, he used critical poetry writing which analyzed community conditions and individual struggles within oppressive structures "to move from competitive social orientations toward a collective space" by having students "share critical social analysis of power across socially constructed sets of differences" (p. 38). In this way, poetry constituted a dialogue that took place through shared storytelling. A unit of study is shared by Camangian (p. 39) has been formatted for display in Table 2.1.

24 Critical pedagogy

Table 2.1 A curricular poetry-based curricular unit

Unit Module	Activities
A. An ideological critique of Marc Levin's *Slam (1999)*	1 Introduction: Background on the Black Arts Movement (BAM) & *Slam* & Thesis 2 Historical overview of the BAM 3 Theoretical significance of the BAM 4 Film Analysis of *Slam* based on the BAM 5 Conclusion
B. Two Poems	1 Students write two poems
C. A 5–7-minute performance of their poems	1 Students perform poems

Within this curricular unit, Camangian relied on interdisciplinary study of art, history, film, and race, and finished the unit with the production and performance of poetry. This strategy not only allowed him to engage students critically, but meet the demands of curricular standards. Camangian shared samples of student poetry that reflect what he sees as the empowering political and social analysis students conducted. One poem was titled "On the corner":

On the corner

On the corner of nowhere in particular
Crumbling pieces of human beings
Scavenge for crack rocks and exchange their humanity for clouded vision
While traveling from bag pipe back to slavery
From the gateways of X to see the traces of first and second hand weed smoke
Lying on who killed the brain cells and blocked the development of those men
In cellblocks
Who think that prison is their natural habitat
So they form tribes behind bars
Because their whole village is locked up...
Strength is hard to find so smokers smoke for the feeling of false freedom
Until they find themselves in a fetal position
Squeezing their teardrops dry
Wishing they could back track their lives from right now
To the first time they were offered to pick their poison...
And we all become the feature of the transatlantic holocaust
That ends like every bad day in the past
As we hang to get high as just another drug slave

(p. 49)

The poem uses poetic devices such as imagery, extended metaphor, and alliteration to convey the agony of drug addiction linked to systematic oppression.

Beyond these formal elements, it reframes the sights of drug addiction that are familiar to some of Camangian's students with an alternate narrative that links drug addiction to legacies of slavery, contemporary incarceration, and a search for freedom. For Camangian's students, a pedagogy rooted in hip hop culture, a shared cultural referent between him and students, created a vehicle for engagement which allowed students to produce narratives which countered the dominant narratives in their community.

Within these accounts, we see how educators took on constraints within educational contexts, reflected on their practices and relied on various tools to engage students in rigorous academic study, including participatory action research, poetry, and popular culture. These are not the only accounts of CP that influenced my work, and much of what I learned about CP came from peers who were invested in such approaches in various settings, including schools, community-based organizations, and labor organizing. With these accounts of in mind, we move onto Hong Kong, where stories of comprehensively articulated and enacted, long-term, CP are needed.

Few inroads for critical pedagogy in Hong Kong

There are teachers in Hong Kong who work daily against constraints and limits to humanize their students and make learning relevant to their lives. They may not be informed by CP literature, and their stories may not have been captured by scholars, but I have certainly met some of them. It is important to acknowledge their work, while seeking to increase access to CP theory and practice.

The very small number of accounts of CP teaching in Hong Kong schools, mostly focused on English language teaching, is not surprising given that mainstream Hong Kong teaching tends to be "teacher-centered, textbook oriented and test-centered" (Moorhouse 2014, p. 80). Furthermore, subjects such as English tend to be viewed by both teachers and students "as a barrier to overcome for examination and future studies or job purposes, rather than as a tool to explore the world, to communicate, to create and re-create meanings, and to construct and express themselves", and "direct importation and extension of western pedagogical models", such as communicative language teaching, cooperative learning, or integrated language projects, "often proves to be counter-productive and alienating" when they are not integrated with local socio-cultural conditions (Lin 2012, p. 4). Despite these constraints, attempts have been made for inroads. The Hong Kong accounts of CP in this section highlight the potential to engage learners in important topics, the difficulties in staging a CP, the positive effects of using hip hop music as a vehicle for engagement, and the small victories that can come through introducing small changes in day-to-day practice. But because even small pedagogical shifts proved challenging, these accounts also reveal the possible difficulties in enacting a CP with a radical, openly politicized goal of transformative education. As this book unfolds in Chapters 5 and 6, the story of my pedagogy, and its radical orientation, should stand in contrast to the accounts told here.

For example, an English teacher working in Hong Kong through the Native English Teacher Scheme, and now a colleague of mine at the University of Hong Kong, used CP theory in designing lessons to give students voice, relate learning to their experiences, and to raise awareness about social injustice over five, one-hour sessions (Moorhouse 2014). The sessions were carried out with a hand-picked group of ten students from working-class families in a primary school to raise their awareness to social issues identified as important by the researcher, including poverty, Hong Kong identity, and domestic workers. Through dialogue, students were engaged in the sessions and had their stereotypes challenged, however, the five sessions were too short a time to see how students thinking might change over time, there was difficulty in finding materials suitable to the students' English proficiencies, and the study did not impact the practices students encountered in the regular English lessons.

CP was also introduced within a Master's level course that was part of a teacher development program (Lin 2004). In engaging in-service teachers in CP, emphasis was placed on reading critical theory, rather than beginning with the experiences of the class members. The in-service teachers found the critical theory tough to grasp, too time-consuming to read, or difficult to connect to practical work and the difficulties they faced. Teachers complained about conditions in their schools and did not see a way out through critical theory. The lesson was that a critical education must be dialogic and lead to action, a similar lesson learned by Shor in his teaching (Shor and Freire 1987). Reflecting on students' difficulties in the course, Lin (2004) shifted away from excessive theory and moved her students to become publishers in an online journal discussing education. Consequently, teachers saw themselves as intellectuals capable of authoring materials for others to read and use to reflect.

Greater success was experienced in a project through which ethnic Chinese students from working-class families improved their English skills and self-confidence using hip hop music and dance (Lin and Man 2011). Over the course of several weeks, project members introduced elements of hip-hop culture to teach English. Challenging traditional notions in Hong Kong of who constitutes a teacher, a graduate level university tutor, and local rappers, djs, and dancers were brought into a school as after-school instructors and prepared students for a performance. These instructors were steeped in hip hop culture and were able to act as cultural ambassadors who could explain the culture to students and guide them to use it as a vehicle for expression.

This project challenged standing notions of education by using popular culture to humanize students. English became a gateway to increase self-concept and build relationships with fellow students, rather than just a subject required by a government syllabus. However, hip hop was not used in this project to allow students to understand the oppressive power structures in their lives. Instead, it took a more benign form that was able to positively affect students along affective dimensions, while not stirring critical consciousness. Because of funding restrictions of the government-funded project, it had to position itself as serving the primary function of increasing English fluency and not generate controversy.

The last example of CP in Hong Kong offers the tale of a pre-service teacher, who stepping into a school dominated by failure in English, tried re-making learning for students (Lin 2012). Initial attempts to have students learn through "western progressive liberal pedagogies", including cooperative learning and integrated language projects, without making sure they had the resources to do so, led to feelings of depression and loneliness in the pre-service teacher after classroom chaos ensued. As Lin explains it:

> The western progressive liberal pedagogies that the student-teacher had learnt, however, had not prepared her for what to do when students did not respond well to these pedagogies, because these pedagogies, as we understand, have originally arisen from middle class conditions and have not built into their canons ways of adapting them to non-middle class conditions....
> (p. 7)

> Despite initial setbacks, the pre-service teacher maintained commitment to these pedagogies and persisted with collaborative project work, assuring explanations of the importance of tasks, and what might be learned in the process, were provided. Working on her own, this pre-service teacher did not "totally change the examination system and the textbook-exercise-driven curriculum and school culture" however, she did introduce alternatives to the existing practices at the school.
> (p. 7)

These examples of CP in Hong Kong illustrate the mountain critical educators must to climb to introduce pedagogical alternatives to Hong Kong schools. A significant obstacle for potential critical educators, and an issue I take up in Chapter 5, is

> how to carve out a space for doing critical work under a highly packed curriculum, driven by pressures of high-stake examinations, especially in schools where the administrative culture is not supportive of any critical, creative work that departs from drilling students for examinations and tests.
> (Lin 2012, p. 11)

Within these school environments, teachers have high workloads, including the completion of paperwork necessary to assure quality, both internally and by Education Bureau external reviews, as I experienced. This lessens the space available "for teachers to embark on creative, innovative projects that venture out of the safe space afforded by textbook worksheets and drills" (p. 11).

Against the backdrop of some of the critical educators in the previous section, these final accounts based in Hong Kong beg the question of how realistic CP is for most educators, if there is enough literature and materials to support them, and if it can truly lead to freedom. So the next section will take up these questions amongst other critiques of CP.

Critiques of critical pedagogy

When I studied CP in my graduate program in San Francisco, critiques of CP were hardly mentioned. So in my process of philosophical rebirth, I was skeptical, looking for questions to interrogate CP theory and practice. It was not until I was asked in my doctoral program to provide more critiques of CP in my research proposal that I became more aware that even though CP sets out to accomplish lofty goals of empowerment, humanization, and liberation, it is not without its critiques, which mainly originate from within the field. Sarroub and Quadros (2015) point out that researchers have identified shortcomings of CP as a model that include "students' aversion to idealized concepts, teachers' limited understanding of 'critical' in their curricula, lack of support in adopting critical perspectives within the school site, as well as practitioners' skepticism of the 'empowering' outcome in students' lives" (p. 254). This section will focus on three general critiques of CP to which Sarroub and Quadros allude: (1) that it lack explicitness in defining key terms and providing examples of practice; (2) that much of its application is told through narratives of redemption that overemphasize a heroic role for teachers; (3) that CP can fail to meet its political goals of empowerment or social change.

Thomson-Bunn (2014, para. 5) contends that a "major failure" of CP is its lack of "definitional precision and transparency". A lack of explicit definitions makes it difficult to discern what central notions in critical practice, like "student empowerment," actually look like. CP by nature is highly contextual and localized and not subject to simple recipes that can be copied, so these terms can be "imagined and enacted in vastly different ways" (para. 7). Adding to the tension around definitions is the limitation that talk about CP is often limited to academia and does not involve students in defining terms (para. 11). In a sense, if teacher-practitioners of CP keep control over definitions, including defining CP itself, they are enacting power over students, thus undermining the goals of the pedagogy. Backing up this argument, Breuing (2011) shows in her study that self-identified critical pedagogues may vary in how they define CP and its aims and purposes, or may even have no definition for it at all. Consequently, some teachers fail in implementing a CP because they do not even define it.

Accounts provided in this chapter notwithstanding, lack of clarity in CP also comes from a dearth of explicit, tangible tools and sample materials to support teachers in taking on a liberatory pedagogy, making it difficult for potential critical pedagogues to embrace new approaches, especially when working with students with different cultural vantages from their own (Emdin 2011), or when working in an English as second language context (Crookes 2010). An impediment to creating CP-based sample materials, is that there has been no framework for developing specific materials, especially in the context of English second language teaching, where development of language skills and critical consciousness are done simultaneously (Rashidi and Safari 2010).

Or sometimes, CP projects get stuck in critiquing oppressive conditions, rather than expending energy on creating alternative practices (McArthur 2010, p. 493). Over-critiquing forms a contradiction in positioning teachers' agents of empowerment by failing to equip them with contextualized guidance. Expecting teachers to empower students without concrete linguistic, pedagogical, and social tools may be unrealistic (Thomson-Bunn 2014), and akin to "providing them with a boat without a paddle" (Emdin 2011, p. 286). Lin (2012, p. 12) concurs, reflecting that, "Critical work also needs to move away from doing just critique; it should also provide examples of how teaching and learning can be done alternatively; i.e., from doing only critical deconstruction to doing critical construction".

CP has also been critiqued for a reliance on teaching narratives that overemphasize the role of teachers in addressing oppressive school conditions. These "redemptive narratives" paint schools both as a cause and casualty of wider problems with education systems and society, and place a "super conscious critical teacher" as a bearer of hope and as a transformational agent (Fischman and Sales 2010). What could be a false hope is then placed on a "heroic teacher" who can lead schools from an ugly now to a more beautiful later (Fischman and Haas 2009). In contrast to a heroic teacher, teachers who engage in a CP might have as a starting point as kind of "Hello Kitty" hope, a naive belief that by being caring, knowledgeable, and efficient, we can make change that will spread beyond their classes into the wider school system, without causing conflict or creating enemies (p. 566). (That seems to me a sexist, culturally biased term, by the way. Why is Hello Kitty considered naïve?). Alternatively, teachers can be taught to become "committed intellectuals" who avoid narratives of "good versus evil" or inflexible positions (p. 572). These teachers, and the narratives that follow from their experiences, need to acknowledge the daily struggles and conflicts, the repertoire of concepts and practices that teachers develop, and the kinds of everyday dialogue that take place in enacting a CP built on practical collective struggle.

Furthermore, it may be that at its theoretical foundations, CP's potential for empowerment and change is hindered. Burbules and Berks (1999) entertain previous assertions (Ellsworth 1989; Gore 1993) that CP is at its roots rationalistic and through its reliance on dialogue either "masks a closed and paternal conversation" that is exclusionary of "issues and voices that other groups bring to educational encounters" (Burbules and Berks 1999, p. 57), or simply steers students to the teacher's pre-existing conclusions. This critique identifies a danger that CP might reproduce oppression, because dialogue, as part of an epistemology, can be exclusionary in how it is practiced. For example, not enough work has been done to develop teaching and engaging in dialogue with students coming from dominant groups to solidarity with marginalized communities, implying the need for a "pedagogy of the oppressor" (Allen and Rossatto 2009, p. 170). This under-theorizing "inhibits the development of social movements" because it "fails to specifically address, critique, and transform the identity politics of particular powerful groups" (p. 173).

If under-theorizing, over-theorizing, and insufficient critical construction prevent CP from linking with larger social movements or broader coalitions for change, CP's potential for empowerment and change is dampened. Freire's work in the Brazil in adult literacy became connected to larger social movements around popular education, but contemporary CP has not (Tarlau 2014). Because "isolated teachers and students in public school classrooms cannot transform society on their own or by staying in the confines of their classrooms", critical pedagogues must move in the direction of analyzing and acting on "how public schools can articulate with larger community struggles" (p. 390), such as struggles around class inequity, democratic participation, or environmental degradation in Hong Kong. Without this larger goal and vision, CP may maintain its current position outside of public and popular education discourses (Weiner 2007). It risks remaining a "ghettoized paradigm of liberation and freedom," which "can no longer be considered a paradigm of liberation and freedom, only its opposite" (p. 60). This critique is clear: without larger struggle, CP will not bring freedom or change.

Tempering rebirth: defining limits and possibilities for empowerment

Coming into a new philosophy of education, emphasizing a liberatory pedagogy can be an exciting and inspiring time. But there is a danger in rebirth. Reading accounts or hearing talks by well-regarded critical pedagogues, or witnessing directly how students have transformed by gaining critical consciousness and attaining academic achievement, can make it easier to ignore critiques of CP in misled attempts at becoming a heroic teacher. Therefore, we must continuously be clear with ourselves and others about what "empowerment" means for students, to know if it is being achieved, and what its limits and possibilities are within a CP. I reflected on this question in a research note on January 19, 2012, as I finished my first term teaching at ISS:

Extract 2.2 "A mirage?"

> How can I know that I am not just interpreting criticality or empowerment? Camangian has his way of seeing it and requiring it in writing. But I think it is hard to know for real. It is easy to create a powerpoint slide that says "this is how this image of my students or this quote shows critical consciousness". But is this an interpretive mirage?

I was thinking back to a presentation I saw by Dr. Camangian in which a "Five Levels of Analysis" framework used for evaluating writing by senior-secondary students was presented. This framework examined students' writing not just to gauge understanding of central ideas of texts, but also the extent to which they interrogated texts in terms of social justice, connection to their contexts, and applicability for action in their lives (Camangian 2013). In 2012, as I saw my students at ISS engaged in academic work and discussing questions about the generative theme of education (see Chapter 5), I was not sure if they were really becoming empowered, considering if the engagement I was seeing in students was a "mirage" of my misinterpretation. So I returned to my research question and worked on defining the terms, empowerment and limits and possibilities, arriving at the definitions below.

Empowerment in education can be a contentious term to define because "imposing a single definition could be limiting, contradicting in this way the very idea of it, which is about being subjective, flexible and personal" (FRIDE 2006, p. 3). So to open up the notion of empowerment in classroom teaching, I decided to think about it as two-fold. Empowerment is the generating of power amongst actors through a process of interactions that enables students and educators to feel valued, to have a voice for expression, and to engage academically. On the other hand, it is individual and collective acts by students that move themselves and those around them towards transformational forms of resistance. Through this two-fold view, I perceived empowerment as a process that is observed through relations and interactions, as well as a product or outcome that is displayed through behaviors.

In the view of power as relational, empowerment is generated and expands itself through "collaborative relations of power," which have the potential to enable students to achieve academically, as opposed to "coercive relations of power" based on subordination which disempower students (Cummins 2000, p. 44). These empowering relations are understood through "micro-interactions" which "form an interpersonal space within which the acquisition of knowledge and formation of knowledge is negotiated" (p. 44). Therefore, in collaboratively empowering spaces, we should observe students "know(ing) that their voices will be heard and respected" and that the process and space of schooling "amplifies rather than silences their power of self-expression" (p. 44). When collaborative relations of power are established amongst and between educators, students, and institutions, power allows these actors to increasingly achieve, as power generated for an individual or group generates power for others (p. 44).

In the product view of empowerment, critical processes lead to internal, within an individual, or external acts, beyond the individual, of "transformative resistance" (Solorzano and Delgado Bernal 2001) that reflect students' desire to tackle oppression. Transformational resistance refers "to student behavior that illustrates both a critique of oppression and a desire for social justice" (p. 320) and could take the form of a student who pushes themself to achieve academically in order to fight oppression in their community, or a student who organizes or joins activities seeking social change. It is a resistance that is "political, collective, conscious, and motivated by a sense that individual and social change is possible" (p. 320), and stands in contrast to other forms of behavior and resistance defined along axis of critique of oppression and desire for social justice.

For example, reactionary behavior refers to oppositional behavior by students that lacks both critique of their oppression and motivation for social justice. A student displaying this type of resistance may act in "inappropriate" ways in or out of school or may provoke a teacher for entertainment, without understanding the social conditions that contribute to the behavior. Self-defeating resistance refers to students who may have some amount of critique of their oppressive social conditions, but whose actions are not motivated by an investment in social justice. It leads to behavior that is not transformational and reproduces oppression. A student displaying self-defeating resistance may understand inequitable or otherwise oppressive social conditions, and as a result drop out of school, or purposefully fail to submit homework to a teacher deemed as dehumanizing to students. Through conformist resistance, students' actions are informed by a need for social justice, yet have no critique of systematic oppression, often times leading students to "strive for social justice within the existing school systems and social conventions" (p. 318). In other words, students exhibiting conformist resistance may "want life chances to get better for themselves and others but are likely to blame themselves, their families, or their culture for the negative personal and social conditions" (p. 319). A student with this type of resistance might do well in school, and then tell peers, "I worked hard and did it, you can do it too!" without ever seeing the larger institutional and social barriers making their individual accomplishment available to larger groups of students. All things considered, through students' investment in critiques of oppression and social justice, "transformational resistance offers the greatest possibility for social change" (p. 319).

The extent to which students can be empowered to act through transformational resistance depends on the limits and possibilities of a given situation. One could see the ideas of limits and possibilities as diametrically opposed: a limit being what cannot be done, and a possibility being what can be done. In this book, however, limits and possibilities are seen as inextricably linked. Noguera (2003) draws on Freire's (1970) concept of a "limit situation" to define limits and possibilities. A limit situation consists of constraints on "freedom and dignity" that impede humanization, and therefore require engagement through praxis to create change (Noguera 2003, p. 16). They suggest possibilities for change that must be constantly evaluated so that appropriate strategies for countering limits can be devised (p. 16). By avoiding taking reality as fixed and immutable in regard to limit situations, we "consider ways to act on these constraints and gradually expand possibilities for a greater degree of freedom" (p. 17). Therefore, limits are situations and constraints that through reflection and action, allow us imagine what change is possible to existing conditions of oppression. Possibility follows as acts that create more humanizing situations, and consequently pose new limits to be considered. Through identifying limits, we can attempt new possibilities, and by achieving new possibilities, we can theorize new limits, as I will do in Chapter 7.

To achieve empowerment for students, we can challenge existing limits and create possibilities for collaborative relations that open spaces for students' expression, voice, creativity, and academic engagement. Using the expression, voice, creativity, and academic engagement that collaborative relations generate, we can amplify students' empowerment by expanding their understandings of oppressive conditions, and studying with them and modeling what acting for social justice entails.

Summary

This chapter reviewed theories and examples of CP practice that informed my pedagogy and research. I elaborated on a pedagogy for liberation that counters the oppressive banking concept of education through alternative, dialogic, and problem-posing education based in generative themes, vehicles for engagement, the process of action and reflection known as praxis, a dialogical relationship between teacher and students, and literacy as an act of reading one's world. I have also provided examples of educators who have grappled with CP, generating tools at our disposal. Key terms, empowerment and limits and possibilities were defined so as to provide a more explicit manner of evaluating how students may be empowered in relation to a pedagogy, stressing voice, expression, and academic engagement through collaborative relations, and acts of transformative resistance that come about through a collaborative process.

At the same time, my personal story was advanced in this chapter. I shared my initial rebirth into a critical educator, cited influential scholars and texts that facilitated it, and gave an example of reflecting on theory in the midst of my developing practice. The next chapter narrates how I continued to grapple with "criticality," searching for what it means to critically come to know and act in the world. While Chapter 2 told the tale of my becoming a critical teacher, Chapter 3 tells the tale of another rebirth, of how I grew into a radical critical researcher.

3 Critical ethnography and dilemmas of a teacher-researcher

"What does it mean to be *critical?*" It is essential to ask this of a critical research method, the way by which we dive into a reality with the intent to engage in a praxis within it. As we will see in this chapter, critical research demands that *criticality* is regularly questioned and refashioned. In my study, this task became even more important as my roles of teacher and researcher became increasingly intertwined, not just with each other, but also intertwined with the lives of educators and students at my research sites. In this chapter, you will meet some of these people, and learn about some of the dilemmas I encountered in using critical ethnography (CE) as an approach to research, teach, and to conduct my life.

This chapter examines the research approach and methods I devised for moving my pedagogy into greater commitment and action with students and collaborators. Research became inseparable from developing my critical teaching practice, and understanding the teaching practices, curriculum, and classroom experiences that formed the critical pedagogy (CP) I describe in the next three chapters cannot be detached from the research process I provide here. I begin with an introduction to CE, describe its relation to the conventional ethnography, and justify CE as necessary for answering my research question. Next, I provide an overview of the research design that emerged in the course of the study and present the research sites, New Territories School (NTS) and Industrial Secondary School (ISS), explaining how I entered each site, who the students were, who my informants and collaborators became, and how I exited each site, including my account of the problematic exit from the second research site. Data analysis will be presented as process that facilitated my understanding of generative themes relevant to students' lives that would become incorporated into curriculum. Through these accounts, a picture of my evolving criticality will emerge, one that led to a second rebirth as a critical ethnographer.

CE as approach

This study sought to answer the question: *What limits and possibilities exist in Hong Kong for empowering ethnic minority students through the practice of critical pedagogy?* A CE approach was adopted because it provided not just a method for becoming a participating member of the school cultures at my research sites, but also granted room for me to act toward an explicitly political aim of empowerment. CE combines the qualitative research approach of ethnography with critical theory to generate research that is explicitly political in its purpose. It is "critical theory in action," rendering method and theory as "reciprocally linked, yet distinguishable" (Madison 2005, p. 18). Thomas describes it as:

> A type of reflection that examines culture, knowledge and action. It expands our horizons for choice and widens our experiential capacity to see, hear, and feel. It deepens and sharpens ethical commitments by forcing us to develop and act upon value commitments in the context of political agendas. Critical ethnographers describe, analyze, and open to scrutiny otherwise hidden agendas, power centers, and assumptions that inhibit, repress, and constrain.
>
> (1993, p. 2)

While CE is rooted in a qualitative (conventional) ethnographic approach, it distinguishes itself analytically and discursively in order to accomplish its goals. In conventional ethnography the researcher immerses themself via participant observation in the day-to-day lives of people to conduct extended observations and participation in life activities in order to describe and interpret the "shared and learned patterns of values, behaviors, beliefs, and language of a shared culture group" (Creswell 2013, p. 90). Through this immersion, the ethnographer collects detailed data for analysis, to generate a "comprehensive and contextualized description of the social action" within a given context (Pole and Morrison 2003, p. 4), otherwise known as a "thick description" (Geertz 1973). Data collection is done via tools such as those I used in my research: participant observation, interviews, questionnaires, taking photographs and videos, gathering documentary evidence in physical and online spaces, and writing self-reflexive journals to understand my changing roles, assumptions, actions, and positioning within research.

Fifteen semi-structured interviews were arranged (see Table 3.1) and transcribed and provide some of the data presented in the book. Interviews were transcribed (for transcription conventions, see Appendix). In transcribing interviews, I left interviewees speech verbatim, and in presenting extracts for analysis in later chapters, speakers speech is reported as spoken, even if there are grammatical errors that deviate from standard English. I wish for readers to hear my participants as they spoke, and have only used brackets to correct speech when I thought the speakers intention as I heard it was clearly communicated. Likewise, written documentary data are reported as written grammatically and in terms of punctuation, except where I found it necessary to use brackets for clarification. Beyond more formal interviews, communication with participants took place during informal face-to-face interactions, as well as online via social media and messaging platforms.

The process of analyzing the data I gathered was cyclical. Its recursive nature was meant to generate theory about what was happening in the school and why, what the generative themes were for students' lives, how I could engage students in those generative themes, and whether engagement with those themes, and in

36 *Critical ethnography*

Table 3.1 List of semi-structured interviews

	Name	Site	Position	Ethnicity
1	John	NTS	Physical Education Panel Head	Hong Kong-born Chinese
2	Christine	NTS	English Panel Head	Hong Kong-born Chinese
3	Thomas	NTS	LS Panel Head	Hong Kong-born Chinese
4	Paula	NTS	English teacher	Hong Kong-born Chinese
5	Principal Chu	NTS	NTS school principal	Hong Kong-born Chinese
6	Wafa	NTS	Teaching Assistant	Pakistani
7	Lagan	ISS	Deputy Director of International Section	Nepali
8	Jane	ISS	English Panel Head	Hong Kong-born Chinese
9	Pragun	ISS	Science and math teacher	Hong Kong-born Nepali
10	Arjun	ISS	Math teacher	Indian
11	Tara	ISS	Form one student, 13 years old	Hong Kong-born Nepali
12	Maiya	ISS	Form one student, 13 years old	Nepali
13	Omar	ISS	Form two student, 13 years old, previously a student at NTS	Hong Kong-born Pakistani
14	Lateef	ISS	Form 2 student, 15 years old	Pakistani
15	Hamida	ISS	Form 2 student, 17 years old	Pakistani
16	Dr. M	ISS	University of Hong Kong Researcher	Spanish

the research process itself, proved to be empowering and/or disempowering. In other words, part of my data analysis meant becoming involved in a cycle of praxis during data collection. CP theory, as reviewed in Chapter 2, in combination with critical discourse analysis (Blommaert and Bulcaen 2000; Fairclough 2001, 2006), and a sensitivity toward interaction borrowed from linguistic ethnography and critical sociolinguistics (Pérez-Milans 2013; Rampton 2007) were essential tools. Critical discourse analysis provided tools to link language analysis and social analysis by treating any instance of discourse as "simultaneously a piece of text, an instance of discursive practice, and an instance of social practice" (Fairclough 2006, p. 4). Linguistic ethnography offered analytic tools for interactions that could shape accounts that (1) respect "the uniqueness, deficiency and exuberance of the communicative moment," (2) recognize there "is no complete or definitive interpretation either for analysts or participants," and (3) remain "mindful of the scholarly virtues of care, coherence, accuracy, accountability, scepticism and cumulative comparison" (Rampton 2007, p. 4). However, while these methods are indispensable in and of themselves, they are not what ultimately makes an ethnography critical.

What then, does it mean to add "critical" to ethnography? Madison (2012, p. 5) discerns criticality at the starting point of CE, which is marked by "a compelling sense of duty and commitment based on principles of human freedom and well-being and, hence, a compassion for the suffering of living being". This duty and commitment allows the researcher to see that conditions within a context are "not as they *could* be for specific actors" leading the researcher to feel obligated to "make a contribution toward changing those conditions toward greater freedom and equity". This version of criticality, charged with notions of commitment and human liberation, evokes the kind of criticality seen in Freire's view of critical education when he positions the radical actor:

> The radical, committed to human liberation, does not become the prisoner of a 'circle of certainty' within which reality is also imprisoned. On the contrary, the more radical the person is, the more fully he or she enters into reality so that, knowing it better, he or she can better transform it. This individual is not afraid to confront, to listen, to see the world unveiled. This person is not afraid to meet the people or to enter into dialogue with them. This person does not consider himself or herself the proprietor of history or of all people, or the liberator of the oppressed; but he or she does commit himself or herself, within history, to fight at their side.
>
> (1970, p. 39)

In Freire's view, the radical, be it a teacher, researcher, or other actor, is defined by increasing commitment to a chosen position, and consequently greater engagement in creating change. This positioning, engagement, and a sense of solidarity is brought to encounters with others, in the case of this study, to the members of my research sites. This is the beginning of where CE extends itself differentiate from conventional ethnography (Thomas 1993). Conventional ethnography can be thought of as a tradition of describing and analyzing culture in order to understand meaning within a given cultural context, while CE is a process of reflection that leads to the questioning and judgment of actions of both the researcher and other actors within the field of study.

Put simply, "Conventional ethnography describes what is; critical ethnography asks what could be...Critical ethnography is conventional ethnography with a purpose" (Thomas 1993, p. 4). While the traditional ethnographer might see engagement with a community complete when the written ethnography is produced, a critical ethnographer sees the ethnographic project as calling for social and political action (Quantz 1992). Moreover, conventional ethnography is typically research done "on" subjects with the researcher speaking "for" the subjects for the benefit of constructing knowledge that will contribute to a research community. CE researchers, on the other hand, strive to act on "behalf of their subjects as a means of empowering them" and engage their own political positions within their research, attempting to construct knowledge toward social change; CE acts with the purpose of emancipation, "the process of separation from constraining modes of thinking or acting that limit perception of and action toward realizing alternative possibilities" (Thomas 1993, p. 4).

The research process

Putting these theories and methods into practice meant that my notion of "criticality" in research morphed across sites, taking me from more conventional forms of ethnography into a radical CE, a process that was facilitated by the distinct collaborators at each site, individuals who assisted in my research process and worked with me on planning activities for and with students. I will introduce individuals who became my colleagues and collaborators, and in some cases close friends, including Christine, John, and Thomas at NTS, and Lagan, Jane, Tad, and Tara at ISS. They are inseparable from this research process, which took place in five phases across four years, at two sites located in an outer district of Hong Kong about 90 minutes away via public transportation from the central business district.

Research phases: monological to dialogical action based

Table 3.2 provides an overview of my research fieldwork from 2010 to 2014, breaking these years into five phases. During these phases of my research, I cycled through a series of four steps, from describing an existing context and reflecting on what made it come to be as such, to eventually carrying out an agenda for change and evaluating any achievements (Cohen, Manion, and Morrison 2007, p. 187). The first three phases took place at NTS where as a doctoral researcher, I moved from "keeping an eye on nothing in particular", to generating understanding of the site and its members by gathering data related to "physical settings, acts, activities, interaction patterns, meaning, beliefs, and emotions" (Pole and Morrison 2003, p. 28), subsequently generating themes for a CP that I tested by teaching form one students in the subject of Liberal Studies (LS). In the first few months of Phase One, my role as a researcher was "comparatively passive and unobtrusive," as the data gathering remained largely monological in the sense that activities of data collection consisted of observations and note taking in order to create a primary record of the cultural context at NTS (Cohen et al. 2007, p. 206).

Phase Two and Phase Three at NTS became more dialogical, as data were generated collaboratively and discussed with participants in order to find generative themes and vehicles for engagement with them. As I moved to teaching a group of students a unit of academic study in the last six weeks of class, the data collection asked students to "reflect on their own situations, circumstances and lives and begin to theorize about their lives" (Cohen et al. 2007, p. 188). So Phase Three consisted of taking action on generative themes and then trying to reflect on that action and using a larger framework of CP theory, using a systems relation to explain findings.

At ISS, I followed the same stages as NTS. Though in September 2011 I had not yet decided to conduct research at the school, my mind had a research orientation. To understand the students and the school, I began thinking in a monological form to understand of my new context, but quickly moved to dialogical forms of understanding and intervening as I sought to implement a critical curriculum. In Phase Four, I wanted to understand teaching practices and forms of relation at ISS monologically by chatting with students, reading records, and speaking with teachers who had been there the prior year. I also needed to transition students in the main two classes I was teaching to working

Table 3.2 Research overview

Research Phases	Phase 1	Phase 2	Phase 3	Phase 4	Phase 5
Research question	What limits and possibilities exist in Hong Kong for empowering low-income ethnic minority secondary students within a school setting through the practice of critical pedagogy?				
Site	New Territories School (NTS), a "band-three" secondary school in the Tuen Mun district			Industrial Secondary School (ISS), a "band three" school in the Tuen Mun district	
Objectives	a Build relationships and trust with students and colleagues b Build understanding of educational practices and beliefs at site c Build understanding of students' worlds, aspirations, conflicts d Reflect on my experiences in the school and in conducting research	a Analyze and reflect on data gathered to arrive at possible generative themes and vehicles for engagement b Share ideas with students on generative themes and vehicle for engagement	a Test generative themes through curricular engagement with students and by collecting feedback from teachers and colleagues and engaging in self-reflection	a Build relationships and trust with students and colleagues b Validate that generative themes from first site could be used for critical pedagogy at new site c Create a "transition pedagogy" to move students toward critical learning d Reflect on my experiences in school and in conducting research	a Test generative themes through curricular engagement b Collect feedback from students and colleagues c Reflect and generate new themes for engagement d Reflect on my experiences in carrying out a CP
Position	Doctoral Researcher			Teacher, Doctoral Researcher, Research Subject, Advocate	
Main collaborators from the site	a Christine, English Panel Head b John, Physical Education Panel Head c Thomas, LS Panel Head			a Lagan, Deputy Director of International Section b Jane, English Panel Head c Tad, Native English Teacher d Tara, student	
Main period of data collection	September 2010–May 2011			September 2011–October 2014	
Presence at site	Usually five days per week, about five to six hours per day			Three to five days per week, six to ten hours per day	
Data collection methods	Participant observation, including teaching, interviews, gathering video and audio recordings, and documentary evidence (screenshots of online chats and other online activity, institutional documents, web links, images), self-reflection journals				
Orientation of data collection	Monological	Dialogical	Dialogical and action based	Initially monological, then dialogical and action based	Dialogical and action based

in more interactive ways during my lessons, in a sense preparing for Phase Five that would consist of curricular engagement with generative themes and reflection to generate new themes. Ultimately, Phase Five would end with reflecting and analyzing data on the CP that was developed.

A more conventional ethnography at NTS

While similar stages of research were carried out at both sites, my approach at NTS was reminiscent conventional ethnographies that had influenced me (Bourgois 2003; Ferguson 2001; Willis 1977) in that I felt a slight detachment from the site and was more conscious of my role as an outside observer trying to understand a cultural milieu. Several aspects of my experience contributed to this feeling: my sense of "newness" in only having moved to Hong Kong in the previous year, my position as a researcher, how I entered the site, interacted with staff, and how I left, and what I tried to accomplish while I was there. The people, the location, the school system, and being a doctoral student were unfamiliar to me, so I had much to soak in.

Quickly, I learned about the school. NTS is an Aided School that was founded in 1977 to serve as a prevocational school, training students to enter the workforce after form three. It is surrounded by some of the original public housing estates built in the district, as well as several buildings that were previously used for manufacturing and industrial work, but now lay partially unused. After 1997, it became a comprehensive school, offering a full secondary curriculum, and in 2007 began recruiting ethnic minority (EM) students. By 2010, when I entered the research site, it had become a "designated school" for EM students and received additional government funding. This change in student body was a result of a demographic shift in the Hong Kong, described in Chapter 1, that was felt particularly hard in the district.

As the number of students moving into secondary from primary decreased, the school began recruiting EM, or Non-Chinese Speaking, or NCS, students as the school typically referred to them, as a way to cope with declining enrollments. According to descriptions from administrative staff, by 2010, about 40% of the school's 450 students were EM, and about 10% were classified as Newly Arrived Students from mainland China, students commonly referred to as "NAS". The school did not have official figures that categorized its student population into distinct ethnicities, but the EM students were primarily of Nepalese and Pakistani heritage, though there were also students of Filipino, Indian, Thai, Vietnamese, and West-African descent. The students at school, both Chinese ethnicity and EM, were primarily from working-class families, though the EM families tended to have lower incomes, with many receiving government's financial assistance.

Gaining access to NTS site was a tricky task that took mobilizing my small professional network in Hong Kong. After trying in vain to access another school as a research site, a professor in my faculty leading a project providing assistance with Chinese language education at schools in designated schools introduced me to the principal and staff at NTS, and vouched for me. This experience stayed in the back of my mind during my time at NTS. It made me conscious that my actions could reflect on and affect the professor who had used his social network to assist me, and consequently, I wanted the school staff to regard me as positive and helpful, not troublesome.

So I spent April, May, and the first two weeks in June 2010 volunteering at the school. I was asked to teach English lessons to several classes, including three classes of Chinese students. Additionally, I supervised lunch and after-school activities. During this time, I kept in mind the idea of "'deviance credits…taking on some of the harmless tasks of the institution so that you get recognized as a legitimate part of the scenery" (Shor and Freire 1987, p. 66) thinking this would help me once I began my study. In the meantime, I began to construct an "ideological map of the institution" (p. 61), trying to understand the viewpoints of staff, administrators, teachers, and students.

My official fieldwork began in September 2010, and during the academic year, three ethnic Chinese teachers were essential to navigating my research. John, the Physical Education Panel Head and math teacher, and Christine, the English subject Panel Head, became primary informants who shared insights into the school's history, organization, culture, and students. They had the "necessary knowledge, information and experience" of the school and what it was like to be a teacher there, were "capable of reflecting on that knowledge," and were generous in giving "time to be involved" in supervising and guiding me (Cohen et al. p. 180). They encouraged me to participate in school activities during lunch, and John even invited me to performances by students outside the school. Both were veteran educators, and Carol had been at NTS for over fifteen years, so I felt I had much to learn from them. Even though I had a decade of experience in education, I was new to Hong Kong schools, and felt in a weak position to question the school's dominant practices and propose radically different alternatives. The students and the cultural system of the school felt foreign to me for the first few months. But to continue being helpful, and to learn about the school, I ran an after-school activity with several students and edited official school documents in English.

Thomas, the LS subject Panel Head, was also a key informant who became a collaborator. Thomas was only in his third year of teaching and was in his first year of teaching EM students. Like other teachers I observed, he allowed me to teach lessons to his classes. Seeing that students responded positively, he began seeking feedback from me and asked me to co-teach lessons. As we neared the end of the academic year, he proposed increasing my involvement in teaching. As a researcher without a permit to teach from the Education Bureau, I could not teach any classes on my own, but with a teacher present, I could teach under their supervision. By this time, I had taken on increased confidence as a result of positive outcomes of lessons I had led. So Thomas agreed that I could take one of his form one LS classes and teach the final six weeks of the class with him observing me.

As the school year neared its conclusion, I started thinking about staying on at NTS as an employed teacher. My research looked to be nearly done. I had gathered data for an academic year, I had investigated themes that had emerged, and I was ready to move onto data analysis and writing in order to keep my doctoral studies on the necessary timeline to finish on time. But I thought that with my experience there, I could begin to teach in more critical ways with the students I had gotten to know. The staff at the school had been supportive of me, and I was eager to contribute more in the role of teacher, while furthering the boundaries of my criticality through greater commitment to the students and to introducing change. I set up a meeting with the principal, and he informed me that while he would love to have me, he would not be hiring new teachers for the next academic year. He was dismayed because competition in the district for enrollment of EM students had increased, and NTS was facing drastically declined enrollments for the 2011–2012 academic year that could lead to the redundancy of teaching positions. So I decided that I would complete my data collection before the end of the school, and try to return to the school in the fall to volunteer, if I had the time. The limit of my criticality at NTS seemed to have reached a finality, stymied by market forces affecting the school.

But this withdrawal from the physical site did not mean the end of involvement with research participants. Through social media, I have stayed in contact with John and some students from NTS. I have chatted with John periodically and received updates about the school and its students. John has also followed me as I have appeared in local and international media to discuss my work, offering me encouragement during difficult professional and personal times. Five students from NTS moved to ISS and continued studies there, and I was able to speak with them to compare their experiences at both schools. It is now time to turn my attention to ISS, which will be the focus of the next section.

A radical rebirth at ISS

ISS was established in 1984 as an aided pre-vocational school and followed a similar trajectory to NTS. After becoming a comprehensive secondary school post-1997, it too saw declining enrollments and thus began recruiting EM students for the 2010–2011 academic year. During my time there, it also increased its NAS student population and also recruited students with special educational needs (so-called "SEN students") to fill its enrollment. However, ISS was distinct in that it had set up an "International Section" for EM students. This International Section was advertised in promotional materials as offering pathways to International General Certificate of Secondary Education qualification (IGCSE), the General Certificate of Education (GCE) A/AS Levels, as well as the local Hong Kong Diploma of Secondary Education (HKDSE).

My contact with ISS began when I responded to an advertisement from the school seeking teachers for English and LS around July 2011. After devoting an academic year at NTS understanding the school as a cultural site, I was able to take action by teaching students in form one (to be discussed in Chapter 4), so I saw myself as ready to move more into data analysis and writing my dissertation. Finding a part-time teaching position working with EM students while I continued writing appeared to be a suitable way to use my skills and knowledge. So during the course of two interviews for a position at ISS, I made it clear that I wanted to try different teaching methods to engage and empower students, methods that would be different from what other schools were trying with EM students. In August 2011, I was officially hired at ISS as a part-time English and LS teacher permitted by the Educational Bureau.

As I began to work at ISS, I saw that I could use the ethnographic knowledge gained at NTS to further investigate my research question. According to the ISS school marketing brochure used for recruiting the 2011–2012 cohort of students, English at the junior secondary level, which I was teaching, would be offered as "English Language with English Language Arts" which would offer "integration of the teaching and learning of content and process within the curriculum" so that students would "become skilled readers, build abundant vocabulary and write a variety of genres including poetry, letters, journals and short stories". This promotion of a different pedagogical approach, and the attitude of the school's principal and some fellow staff members, and my early teaching experiences led me to believe a critical practice would be possible at the school. Therefore, I decided to extend my research to this second site, to continue to test the limits and possibilities of a CP with EM students, now from the point of view of a teacher researching my practice.

Yet, I felt tentative about doing research at ISS. I was not sure how extending fieldwork would affect completion of my study, and by the time I asked for permission to conduct research in late October 2011, the principal who had hired me had been dismissed, and an interim principal who was previously a vice-principal of the school had been appointed. But in the first few months after my research at ISS began, I felt a strong conviction that my research there should continue, despite my initial trepidation. My position as an employed teacher, which I felt conferred on me "professional" ethic to seek best practices for my students, my expanded knowledge of Hong Kong, students, and the school system, my knowledge of generative themes and vehicles for engagement gathered at NTS, along with the new collaborators I met, led me to a rebirth as a radical teacher and critical ethnographer at ISS, more willing to speak out about injustice, openly committing myself to critical approaches and resolutely seeking change.

At ISS, I also developed a group of primary informants who became close collaborators in this study, and all had commitments to challenging the status quo that colluded in the development of my radical practices. Lagan, an educator born and raised in Nepal, was the Deputy Director of the International Section, and had a history of activism, seeking better educational opportunities for the Nepali community in Hong Kong. During his time at ISS, he continuously advocated for my pedagogy, even speaking out with students about it in the Nepali language media. When I met him, he spoke in favor of "multicultural" education valuing diversity, and had persuaded the school to let him hire a teacher to teach English literature at the junior secondary level.

Jane, an ethnic Chinese teacher, was the Panel Head for the English subject. Though she had over fifteen years of experience, she had not previously taught

EM students when she began at ISS the same year as me. She recalled to me in an interview that she was under pressure to increase public examination results for the English subject (school records showed that only 13% of students from ISS who sat for the previous year's public examination had passed English). That first year, Jane was overseeing my work, but was not a part of the International Section, and we ended up disagreeing strongly about what should be done with the students I was teaching.

By the end of the 2011–2012 academic year though, she had seen that students in my English classes were engaged and offered increased support, which I took. In fact, the engagement shown by the students in Class A and Class B helped to gain the trust of my collaborators and their faith in my research project, leading to extensive efforts by them to collaborate with me. Gaining Jane's professional trust was essential. Over the next two years, Jane brought incredible resources to the school and to my projects, especially as she began to work with EM students and better understood their academic and social needs. More importantly, she gave me a carte blanche to pursue my practices and helped me cope with the administrative demands required of teachers. With a different Panel Head in place looking to limit or sanction my activities, this study would not have been the same. Jane facilitated and colluded with my increasingly radical approach, and by the time I interviewed her in 2014, we were able to laugh about our initial interactions. When I asked her to recall those interactions, she teased, "Tell you about those fights…Have you got tissue paper?" suggesting we would be shedding tears together. Then in the middle of an ongoing conversation, she explained how her thinking changed:

Extract 3.1 "The curriculum didn't actually help"

JANE: I didn't teach [EM] students in the first year, so that's why I didn't, you know, pay too much attention on the curriculum on whether it would actually have catered their needs. I didn't really care because I was just too busy that year. But last year, ah, I started teaching Pakistani girls, and I quickly realized that the curriculum didn't actually help fulfill their needs and stretch their potentials because it was actually way below their level and then they need literature curriculum. Actually not only in English, but for all subjects. For example, for science they need, ah, something like a non-fiction reading program. But sad to say, you know, a band three school has been a band three school for so long for a reason, it's because of the teachers. If the teachers themselves are passionate, you know, uh learners, the of course the students would always be ready to learn.

{Jane, interview, May 20, 2014}

In working with EM students, Jane comprehended that many students needed additional challenge and assistance in English across the curriculum, but in her view, teachers who were not passionate were to blame for the lack of change to meet those needs. While Jane's consent furthered my committed and engaged criticality, Tad expanded scope and reach of it. Tad was a Canadian-born English teacher who had worked in Hong Kong local schools for fifteen years. Lagan recruited him to start working at the school for the 2012–2013 school year. He had some familiarity with the name of Freire and basic concepts of CP. Though he had not developed CP theory-based curriculum, he was eager to try and get away from the constraints he faced in teaching at his previous post. For over two years, he provided much input in improving curriculum and putting his own style on it. Tad's work showed that the curriculum I developed, including its generative themes and vehicles for engagement, could be applied by another teacher, and that collaboration could strengthen it.

My criticality was also shaped by students, who in committing to me, inspired me to commit even more to them. One of these students, Tara, started in my form one class, and in form two became an important informant who transformed to a collaborator. Her evolving criticality will be examined in Chapter 6. I relied on Tara for her insights into my teaching and her classmates and the way she could articulate her inner world and concerns. Over the course my involvement with her, I have asked her to reflect on her experiences in and out of my classes, and these reflections were made into presentations at various university conferences in Hong Kong and beyond. She also presented at a community center and for her school peers. Interacting with her shaped my work at ISS, and continues to shape my ongoing research. She asked questions that forced me to reflect on myself – inquiring as to why I was doing the research, or how I knew that I *really knew* students, or if I even knew them at all.

Besides Lagan, Jane, Tad, and Tara, there were other important collaborators connected with ISS. This community of like-minded educators were trying to enact their own pedagogies to challenge dominant practices, spoke out about teaching, curricular planning, family involvement, and student disciplinary practices at the school they found hurtful to students, and were always willing to learn from me and share their knowledge with me. Pragun, a math and science teacher, was born in Hong Kong of Nepali heritage. Pragun already had a medical degree, and during our time as colleagues, he earned a master's degree in public health and undertook research into the problem of obesity in EM youth. He also launched creative public awareness campaigns online to spread awareness of EM experiences in Hong Kong. Amir was Hong Kong-born of Pakistani heritage and was a teaching assistant. He assisted in one of my English classes during the 2012–2013 academic year and was a window into the experiences of students from Pakistani heritage and Muslim families. Dr. M was a University of Hong Kong researcher conducting an ethnographic study in my classes. He turned me into his research subjects and collaborators, and eventually began to invite my students and me to give presentations to his classes. Since 2011 he has helped me to reflect on my work.

What all my collaborators had in common was that they moved beyond providing data and being researched to a "praxis-based dimension" in which they

46 *Critical ethnography*

wanted to know more about my theory and became increasingly involved in the actions I was taking. This allowed both me, as the researcher, and these collaborators, as the researched, to move "in the direction of self-determination of [our] own consciousness construction" (Kincheloe 2003, p. 223), and to varying extents, they all became agents in the construction the CP I claim as mine in this book. But despite forming close collaborative relationships at ISS, my exit from the school was problematic and controversial, as the promise of liberal teaching approaches at ISS became negated.

My criticality brings opportunities and dilemmas

At the end of each of my academic years at ISS, I was not sure of my return for the following year. My employment at ISS was based on yearly contracts, a situation common to many newer teachers in Hong Kong, and the school would not offer new contracts until it was sure of its enrollments, causing insecurity for all contract-based teachers. Moreover, as a researcher, this caused a sense of instability to my project and its potential to extend through three years of junior secondary, but that was at the mercy of the school continuing my employment, and my choosing to remain working there.

As the end of my third academic year neared, I decided stressful working conditions and lack of support from the administration were overwhelming, and I would not return to the school. Moreover, I needed to find full-time work rather than continue with several part-time jobs in order to support my family. By this time, I had seen ups and downs with students working through a CP and had the benefit of three years working with one cohort through their junior secondary years. I felt my data gathering had reached a point where I could examine three years of continuous teaching, so I was ready to move on, finish analyzing data, and complete my dissertation. I started to orally inform students and parents in May 2014, and in this month, the principal for the past two years (who was the third principal since I had started at ISS) had resigned. Jane, also officially resigned, feeling defeated by working conditions that made her tireless efforts for students more difficult. Lagan had also announced to several colleagues that he would not take on a new contract, and Pragun was of like mind. I verbally informed the outgoing principal that I would not be returning.

In mid-June 2014, an interim principal took over administration of the school and convinced me to sign a new contract to work full-time at the school, teaching and developing curriculum. He gave assurances that he would support the work I had been doing with other teachers, and that together we could make ISS the best school serving EM students in Hong Kong. At this time, the administration also agreed to allow Dr. M and me to carry out a new research project with students at the school in which we would teach research skills to a group of students through an extracurricular activity. There was just one caveat from this interim principal: Lagan, who had also been convinced to sign a new contract, and I needed to help with the recruitment of students for the following year, which we did by hosting a student-led event for primary six students from a successful school serving EM primary students where Lagan had close ties.

When work began in September 2014, I felt cautiously optimistic, but that turned to shock when my contract, along with Lagan's, was terminated without warming by the school near the end of October. The day I was terminated, Dr. M had arrived at the school to begin our extracurricular research program, and the school offered him a contract to carry on the project without me, which he refused. Over the next few days, our terminations became a public matter reported in English and Chinese language newspapers in Hong Kong, as sixty of my former Nepali-heritage students boycotted school for two days and parents organized a press conference to protest the school's actions. The school cited "difficulty in cooperation" between the school and myself in my termination, and students reported to me that they were told by the principal I had not been preparing students for the HKDSE public examinations. Thus, my exit from ISS was one fraught with tension and trauma for myself, my collaborators, and for many of my students, and I assume it was also problematic from the perspective of the school's administrators. For now, I want to make the point that ISS was done for me as a site for critical ethnographic work. My radical commitment at the school was complete, yet, it created a new limit for my criticality, and for the criticality of students. We will return to these events and their implications for a CP in Hong Kong in Chapter 7.

For now, my exits from both sites highlight the intricacies of exiting ethnographic research sites. Withdrawal from a site is not just ending data collection and leaving:

> ...it is at the core of the embedded process of disentangling from the field. We adopt this and view exiting field-work as a process (rather than a single act) of ending relationships developed with research participants over a period of time, be it longer or shorter. It is affected by past, present, and future connections, which may be personal or organizational, formal or informal. Exiting the field may occur only once during the course of the study or take place several times when data are collected periodically. Exiting fieldwork is associated with changes in identities and emotions as enacted and experienced by both the researcher and research participants and their (self) learning and reflexivity.
>
> (Michailova et al. 2014, p. 139)

Changes in identity and emotions after exiting sites seemed especially salient to the experiences of students. After I left NTS, I would sometimes run into and chat with students from the school. Some would ask what I was doing, if I was teaching, and why I was not teaching at NTS, especially since they felt bored in their classes. Since leaving ISS, I have kept in contact with my collaborators and have continued working on projects with Lagan and Jane. Ten of my former ISS students continued with a research project led by Dr. M and myself, and I had opportunities to work with other ISS students in other activities organized by

48 *Critical ethnography*

Lagan. It was the weeks following my termination that felt especially difficult for many students who messaged me, sent videos, spoke with me in person, or even sent me written notes, all with similar themes. They felt distraught, they felt my absence, and they felt a sense of hopelessness as the pedagogical practices that became familiar to them in working with me were replaced with drilling-based instruction in their English lessons. I will return briefly to the issue of my exit from ISS later in the chapter in order to consider some of its ethical implications. But first, I want to provide more background about my role at ISS as an ethnographic researcher and a teacher.

At ISS, my participation was at the level of "active membership" meaning that I took on "some or all of the roles of the roles of core members" (Dewalt and Dewalk 2002, pp. 21–22) of the site being studied. This was due to my status as a part-time teacher at the school. The focus of data collection at ISS was on my own classes, the culture within them, and the curriculum I was developing, and less on understanding the school culture as a whole. Table 3.3 breaks down my teaching duties over the three main academic years of work at ISS, where in the three years of teaching included in this study I worked with four groups of students.

Of the classes that I taught at ISS, the most time was spent with a group of students identified as Class A. The students in this class remained mostly consistent, so they became my main research group. I taught Class D for two years, and I also served as their co-class teacher for a year, overseeing the class and reporting to parents. This group was also significant in helping me improve the practices and materials developed with Class A. From the beginning of the research process, I did not think to include Class B because I saw them twice a week, but for only 35 minutes each time, and sometimes less due to holidays or

Table 3.3 Teaching duties at ISS

Academic Year	Number of Working Days	Total Number of Lessons	Lessons Taught per Week
2011–2012	3	18	**Form one, Class A**: 6 Lessons English, 2 Lessons LS **Form one, Class B**: 2 lessons LS **Form two, Class C**: 6 Lessons English, 2 Lessons LS
2012–2013	4	28	**Form one, Class D**: 7 Lessons English, 7 Lessons Integrated Humanities **Form two, Class A**: 7 Lessons English, 7 Lessons Integrated Humanities
2013–2014	3	18	**Form two, Class D**: 7 Lessons English, 7 Lessons Integrated Humanities **Form three, Class A**: 7 Lessons English, 7 Lessons Integrated Humanities

special schedules, I did not see them at all within a week. However, once I became Dr. M's research subject, he helped me to reflect on and better understand my experiences with Class B, which was in contrast to many of the experiences I will describe with other groups in later chapters.

At NTS, I advocated for students by introducing new pedagogical practices into the classes taught by Thomas. My advocacy while at ISS went much further, and reaching closer to the radical position described earlier in this chapter. Because I was in the role of teacher, I considered it acceptable to advocate for wider curricular change and created written proposals for that change at ISS, and I questioned policies I thought were hurtful to students or not inclusive of their needs. I saw these actions fitting the role of an education professional. My commitment to empowering students also took the form of inviting researchers from the United States, the United Kingdom, Spain, Australia, and Hong Kong, along with students from various disciplines and universities to visit my classrooms, observe my pedagogy, provide feedback, and engage in conversation with myself and students.

My advocacy and activism extended beyond the school as I was featured in local newspaper articles about my views on English language teaching and education for EM students, appeared in Nepali language media, and was a guest on an international media program that aired an episode on the problems of EM education in Hong Kong after reports of ethnic stereotypes in LS textbooks went viral. Students also became part of this media advocacy, appearing in newspaper articles, television reports, radio programs, and in the international media. Advocacy also took the form of conducting presentations at local conferences, university classes at various local universities, public discussion events, and at community centers. Students became part of those presentations in which we spoke out for what we perceived to be the academic, emotional, and social needs of EM students, and these presentations were attended by some of collaborators at ISS. Ultimately, I speculate that the school administration at ISS may have perceived my activist positioning, and increasing radical commitment and engagement, which was not one taken up by so-called "local teachers" as counter to the school and its aims, contributing to its decision to terminate my contract.

Reflexive and ethical commitments

Engaging in self-reflexivity and committing to a sense of ethics are key components to conducting ethnography *critically*, as engaging in acts that question, disturb, or challenge a status quo can cause dilemmas for researchers, participants, and bystanders to research, as my experiences exemplify. In writing this ethnographic book, I attempt to keep visible my own power, privilege, and biases, while also keeping my own story and me visible. Toward this purpose, I have included biographical information in Chapter 1 that reveals the privileged education I had in the United States, as I attended an elite public university, and had the benefit of knowledge of CP and other critical social and postmodern educational theory through my master's program. In my educational and professional experience, I had the opportunity to observe dozens of teachers working in diverse contexts and had spaces in which to experiment with pedagogy. As a graduate student, I was fortunate to observe and assist several times in a secondary class co-taught by two distinguished critical pedagogues, Dr. Jeff Duncan-Andrade and Dr. K. Wayne Yang. Meanwhile, Dr. Duncan-Andrade served as the professor for a graduate course I took in which he invited primary and secondary level teachers to present to us students their critical pedagogies.

These educational and professional experiences put me in a position beyond novice in terms of a critical outlook and practice when I arrived to Hong Kong. My own identity formation within the context of growing up marginalized racially in the United States also biased me toward looking at reality from the point of view of the oppressed. So as I critiqued my research sites, I realized that I was privileged with prior theoretical and practical knowledge and firsthand experience about minorities and education, and the position of researcher that allowed me to create that critique. To come to these conclusions required ongoing reflexivity.

Reflexivity, "a turning back on oneself, a process of self-reference", is an essential component of ethnographic research (Davies 1999, p. 4). To aid in my reflexivity, I wrote journals that made me look at my research, the feelings, tensions, and conflicts I had to negotiate, and how my values shaped data collection and analysis as well as my research sites and participants. I wanted to document my reflections during the course of research in an open manner, and keep a written record of my negotiation and management of internal and external conflicts as they arose. One especially salient example of the type of reflection I did was written in 2012 after a trying lesson with Class C:

Extract 3.2 "I feel a total loss"

> Today I came in to Class C and became very frustrated. Yesterday I yelled at them, and then we were able to get some work done. Today Ali returned after being absent for a few days. I also got the news that Danish left the school, and Rizwan is working at either a laundry or DHL [a shipping company] (Ali told me this). The kids were singing songs across the room, talking, or working quite slowly to write down the two assignments I wanted on the assignment list in their folder. Ali and Rahim kept talking to each other. Eventually I told the kids I quit, I can't do this anymore, I don't see how we can learn anything together if I just come in for 35 minutes and there is talking the whole time. I told them I feel bad because the school is not giving them a good education, but they are also not helping. It's amazing that it is only 9 boys, but it is so hard to get anything done, or to build a classroom culture with them. Akin is absent. How is this school contributing to a pattern of marginalization of Pakistani boys; how does it contribute to a hegemonic process? How do other teachers, including Pakistani teachers contribute, or create counter-hegemonic practices? We need some real ethnographic research on what is happening with these boys. I feel at a total loss. Would this class be any better if I had more time with them like

with Class B? Would the class be better if it was mixed? If it had different age ranges? Would it be different if the English levels were a little bit higher?
(Reflexive journal, February 9, 2012)

Journals like this one became a place where I could "record personal reactions to the field situation, successes, and failures" (Dewalt and Dewalk 2002, p. 152). In this entry, I describe the difficulties I faced with Class C, a class I decided not to follow in the research. This class had started as a form one class with twelve boys of Pakistani heritage, with extremes in English proficiency levels, but because I only saw them two times per week and only for thirty minutes at a time, I was not able to implement the curriculum I used with other classes. As I was starting to experience what I felt was success with other classes, I felt a nagging sense of failure and guilt with Class C. I was seeing male students of Pakistani-heritage drop out of the school (the references to Danish, Rizwan, and Ali) and I felt ineffective my role as teacher. I was asking myself questions needing a critical research approach to answer, but felt my agency constrained not only by a lack of time and engagement, but also because I had not yet developed a relationship with Amir, the Pakistani-heritage teaching assistant who served as the class teacher and family liaison for Class C.

I pursued the topic of Class C and this reflection with Dr. M, who had spent time observing me in this class and had noted the difficulties. He described the ways in which my interactions with Class C were tense and different from more positive interactions with Class A and Class B. Entering into those classes I was often light-hearted and joking, but entering into Class C, I had described to him as if I was entering into a "prison playground", with inmates roaming. Thus, my initial self-reflection prompted more investigation into myself and the bias against Class C in which I was complicit, and spurred me to take action, even if not within the context of conducting research. Following this journal entry, I thought the least I could do was commit to offering the class more engaging activities, and the following year, I was able to work with Amir to be able to better support students of Pakistani heritage in the new form one Class D.

A final point about engaging in reflexivity through journals is that I pointed a critical eye toward the actual method of CE, rather than taking for granted that the method could lead to the empowerment my research question sought to create. With regard to the method, Hytten (2004, p. 96) warns critical ethnographers:

Critical researchers argue that the hegemony of dominant structures creates a false consciousness in people that disables them from collectively challenging the status quo. Yet what we have not considered enough are the ways in which many critical researchers substitute one form of hegemony for another. That is, they do not truly problematize their own understanding of the social world and rather argue for the oppressed to replace their false consciousness with the "critical consciousness" the researcher has. To combat this problem, the first step toward a postcritical ethnography is genuine reflectivity on the part of the critical researcher that allows for dialectic between macro and micro understandings. In simple terms, this means that critical researchers need to give up the implicit assumption that they know how the world works and power operates and the researched don't.

The journaling established a place where I could reflect, a starting point from which I could rigorously examine the goals of my research project, my methods, and their outcomes. I questioned the notion of criticality, asked whether I or not students were being "empowered," and accused myself at times of being an oppressive teacher, thereby opening the research methods, the data and its analysis, and myself to scrutiny. Thus, data collection was a lengthy and sometimes emotionally demanding process in which relationships between researcher, site, and participants were continuously being negotiated. My experience speaks to the nature of ethnographic data collection: it is "socially situated; it is neither a clean antiseptic activity nor always a straightforward negotiation" (Cohen et al. 2007, p. 181).

Ethnographers must also take caution in how they negotiate close personal relationships that are formed with informants. Ethnographers must be careful in the secrets they hold, the friendships that are formed, or if or how they take sides in conflicts since the line between data gathering and social activity can be blurred (LeCompte and Shensul 1999, pp. 194–195). While this did not appear to be a concern at NTS, at ISS, these concerns became palatable during my exit from the field. The school's administration appeared to me and other collaborators as an adversary in the pursuit of educational equity for EM at the school, and my stance in this conflict must have been clear. What made this more problematic is that beyond a researcher or teacher, many students came to see me as a father-figure, or as source of hope, sentiments students expressed to me verbally, in writing, and publicly in the media and in presentations.

Critical ethnographers consciously aspire for their research to generate liberation rather than domination. To do this, they must reflect on additional ethical concerns. Gonzalez (2003) offers "four ethics": *Accountability, Context, Truthfulness,* and *Community*. She breaks the word "accountability" into "account-ability," meaning "the ability to account…to tell a story" (p. 83). Gonzalez says that as ethnographers we must tell the "story of our story," how we came to know what we know, in a sense unmasking ourselves. We must open up all the details of our entire life, as well the whole story of our ethnography, including "every decision, personal, professional, embarrassing or noble, self-serving or altruistic, that helped create the tale as it has come to be told" (p. 84). *Context* is "the ability to describe the environment within which one's tale is told" including the "political, social, environmental, physical, and emotional surroundings of one's story," (p. 84) both the researcher's and the subjects'. *Truthfulness* refers to a "radical openness to *see* not only what is in one's social world and environmental context, to see not only what one has actually done or said, but also to see that which on the surface is not visible" (p. 84).

Truthfulness further described as a "manifestation of true courage, an opening to the heart, a willingness to be absolutely existentially naked about one's purpose and issues in life" (Gonzalez 2003, p. 84). Though it may be difficult or impossible to achieve the absolute nakedness she identifies as crucial for truthfulness, it is an ethic to which we should aspire and commit to pushing in its limits. Finally, *Community*, is meant to transform conventions in research of "audience," "our colleagues, "the field," and "our readers" into "what is created when naked stories are shaped and one opens both in expression and receipt of those stories" (p. 85). *Community* asserts, "Once we step forward with an ethnographic tale, we can no longer feign separation from those with whom we have shared that story" (p. 85). This notion of community puts us into solidarity with those who participate in our research.

This research project immensely tested my sense of critical ethics as described by Gonzalez. During research, I tried being accountable to students, and when possible their parents, by sharing my life story, including tales of embarrassment and tales of pain in my life. I have tried to be accountable in this book about my exit from ISS and how my radical positioning may be in part responsible for what transpired, and may have challenged my ability to affect long-term, sustainable social change within the school and out of it. I attempted during research to be aware of context, for example, by understanding my privilege even as I left a spacious and luxurious home each day and traversed Hong Kong by bus to enter working-class spaces in one of Hong Kong's most outer and impoverished districts. Furthermore, I educated myself about the political context of Hong Kong education by making a study of school reforms central to the introduction of this book. Maintaining truthfulness was more challenging. It required me to turn a mirror on myself, sometimes causing a sense of instability and internal crisis. I often wondered if the problems I encountered at ISS were my fault, or if they were somehow caused by me. I wondered if I was a bad teacher. I wondered if there was any point to the research.

It is perhaps the fourth ethic, community that caused me the most trouble yet has pulled me through inner conflict and the toughest times. At ISS, I developed a deep sense of love for and solidarity with many of my participants, so when I doubted my interventions or faced difficulties in my personal life, they encouraged me. Yet sharing community with others sometimes changed how they positioned me. For example, some students spoke about me as their "second father" or otherwise positioned me as someone having more significance beyond imparting knowledge. One student, a thirteen-year-old female of Nepali heritage named Trisha, posted a poem on social media that included me among other important people in her life:

Extract 3.3 "When I'm with Mr. C I feel there is hope"

When I'm with my family, I feel safe and warm.
When I'm with with my sister, I feel strong
When I'm with my uncle, I feel logical.
When I'm with my auntie, I feel energetic.
When I'm with Mr. C I feel there is hope.

{Trisha, social media post, March 12, 2013}

In presenting this study at a local symposium, I clearly saw the ethical dilemma arising from my investment in community and the investments many students made in me as I read the reference to me (Mr. C) in the final line, "When I'm with Mr. C I feel there is hope". Chapter 5 will present how I engaged students in the generative theme of discontinuity, the idea that students faced stoppages from separations from culture, history, family, places, and community. In taking on this theme, I did not realize that the pedagogy being created with students, and the relationships with me that brought a sense of not only family, but also hope to some students, would also become another form of discontinuity for students to negotiate. I saw it problematic that students saw a sense of hope and family in me, and questioned if I had done enough to help students recognize hope in each other instead. To some extent, it seems I, in operating within available discourses, replicated the notion of the critical teacher as a hero that I critiqued in Chapter 2.

Summary

This chapter discussed CE as the research method for this study and also advanced this book's narratives of the development of a CP, and the evolution of my criticality. CE is an explicitly political research method that works toward emancipation. Its criticality is defined in part by its required ongoing reflection to understand not only the relationship between structure and agency within a cultural context, but also the researcher's positioning, ethics, and commitments within the research project. As a researcher at ISS, and as a contracted teacher and researcher at NTS, I participated in the life of two schools to understand the limits and possibilities for a CP. My criticality at each site was on a spectrum, from closer to conventional ethnography at NTS, to an increasing radically committed and engaged CE at ISS. Analytical frameworks emerged from both CP theory and the data, which refined research goals and questions, ultimately leading to theorizing of generative themes and pedagogical action to address them.

Throughout the course of the study, and within this book, I have attempted to adhere ethics of accountability, context, truth, and community, telling my story, the story of this research, and the place and time in which it is set, in as honest a way as I know, while maintaining solidarity with students. I hope readers of this book judge it as rigorous and honest, and that the same appraisal is made by members of the communities it seeks to serve. Those communities will be the subject of the next three chapters, beginning with Chapter 4, set at NTS.

4 Alienation, pain, and possibility at NTS

> Instruments that record, analyze, summarize, organize, debate and explain information; which are illustrative, non-illustrative, hardbound, paperback, jacketed, non-jacketed, with foreword, introduction, table of contents, index that are intended for the enlightenment, understanding, enrichment, enhancement, and education of the human brain through sensory route of vision… sometimes touch.
> – Rancho, "3 Idiots"

I have to admit when I started my time at New Territories Secondary School (NTS), I felt a bit of culture shock, a sense of disorientation and heightened awareness to difference. This was partly an extension of adapting to Hong Kong and partly due to my unfamiliarity with cultural conditions at the school. Many languages circulated in the air, there were different scents, body postures and expressions of physical affection, and even different comprehensions of personal space from those to which I was accustomed. I used this feeling to my advantage, keeping an open eye to new experiences, and trying to make sense of my home for the next year. I wanted to demystify my feelings of shock to uncover generative themes, the everyday experiences, conditions, and language that create boundaries and limits to one's human potential and become the problems to study with students (Freire 2004), and to discover vehicles for engagement, the cultural forms or activities from students' worlds facilitating investigation into generative themes (Duncan-Andrade and Morrell 2008).

I became curious about students' dreams, hopes, and aspirations, because they are tied up with their actions in the world, and the obstacles presented by their historical periods (Freire 2004, p. 100). For a future critical pedagogy (CP) to have a chance of generating empowerment, it behooved me to delve into the internal worlds of ethnic minority (EM) students to understand their dreams, and obstacles to self-actualization, to find and test generative themes and vehicles for engagement through which to bring students into reflective and academic work. Otherwise, I would risk creating a pedagogy far removed from students' concerns (Freire 2004, p. 96).

To this end, I used "Campus TV," the after-school activity John, the physical education Panel Head, requested I run with a small group of students of diverse backgrounds, to learn from and about the EM students at NTS. Armed with my iPhone, and a school video camera, we video recorded school events and occasionally wandered the school interviewing students. One day in November 2010, I prepared the students to interview classmates on the playground with three questions that might shed light on students' aspirations and the possibilities and constraints they perceived: (1) Do you have a dream? (2) Do you think you can reach the dream in Hong Kong? (3) Why or why not? Before conducting the activity, I helped the group to consider their own answers and practice being recorded. Qasim, a male of Pakistani heritage, was one of the school's star pupils, atop the form three class amongst the EM students in the school's English medium of instruction (EMI) section. He shared his dream in Extract 4.1:

Extract 4.1 "I am a hard working student"

QASIM: My dreams are to be a pilot, to be a responsible person. The most important dream is to be a university graduate.
CARLOS: Will you reach your dreams in Hong Kong. Why or why not?
QASIM: Yes, because I am hard working student, and the Hong Kong government fully support those who wish to study and are intelligent.

{Qasim, video recording, November 12, 2010}

I introduced the frame of "dreams" to Qasim in this extract as a way to learn more about him and help him practice English. Qasim, a devout Muslim, shared his aspiration to be the first in his family to attend a university, and had a conviction that through hard work, he could do it, and that the government would support him. In Extract 4.1, we see a commonality Qasim shared with most students I met, and a difference. Like most students, and teachers at NTS, Qasim subscribed to a narrative of individual hard work determining life trajectory, divorced from discussion of structural constraints. The difference was in Qasim's conviction that he would attain his dream through investment in an identity as a "hard-working student," which most students did not express, as we will see later in this section.

Instead, after a term at NTS, I felt students were surrounded by conflicts not defined in terms of community or solidarity with others, rather as situations for individuals to resolve for themselves. Students faced tensions in that they had dreams, hopes, and aspirations for social mobility, but they lacked access to the tertiary education that would facilitate making their aspirations reality, and had to battle against other constraints including social class, gender, language difficulties, and trajectories of mobility. Meanwhile, teachers felt ineffective because of conflicts around language, students' knowledge, students' discipline, or connecting with students. Though there were teachers students liked, a feeling by students that many teachers were ineffective was common. Based on these observations, education, conflict, love, and social mobility were emerging as generative themes salient in their lives, so I designed activities for English and Liberal Studies (LS) classes, spoke with students on the playgrounds, and interacted with them on Facebook to further learn about their worlds, find vehicles for engaging with these themes, while simultaneously gauging their academic skills.

This chapter examines the limits and possibilities that arose as I searched for and tested generative themes and vehicles for engagement at NTS over the course of fieldwork lasting an academic year, from September 2010 through July 2011. Analysis will draw on a wide array of data sources, including participant observation in the school and online, semi-structured interviews, and self-reflexive journals. We will see how a text-book and exam-based banking concept of education, in which teachers attempt to "deposit" knowledge into students without joint investigation of the world, combined with deficit views of students, and adherence to narratives of individual effort, to place the school's teachers in weak positions to make sense of and use EM students' complex aspirations, identities, conflicts, multimodal practices, and interests, including love of Bollywood films. Teachers struggled to develop students' English academic literacies and to move students to resist collectively, at best pushing students toward conformist resistance, a result I also came to as I tested generative themes through dialogical practices.

Now, let us return to NTS and begin by getting a general feel for life at the school before meeting more of its youth.

Dreams, love, and conflicts in students' worlds

At a school where very few students went onto tertiary education, government curricular reforms that envisioned inspiring environments awakening the creative spirit of students and countering monotonous and alienating school conditions (see Chapter 1), did not seem realized. Instead, the physical conditions of classroom spaces at NTS lent an air of alienation, feelings revealed through interactions with students in the school and online, to which the general teaching and learning interactions also contributed, a point to be explored in the section "Additional challenges to conforming to existing structures".

Outside the classrooms, the school was generally clean, with fish tanks near the main office and flowers planted near the entrance. During the week, students played sports on the playground, practiced playing guitars, chatted with friends, or joined games and activities planned by John and Christine, the English Panel Head, as part of an "NTS" inter-class competition meant to help students feel the school was their "second home." Back in the classrooms, the physical environments were usually plain. A typical junior secondary classroom at NTS had little to no decorations on the walls and display boards at the front and back of the classes. Though some classes had decorated their display boards with themes of unity and harmony (some classes used those words), those would end up torn, stained, or defaced within a couple months of their completion. Each class had lockers in the back for students to use and individual student desks and chairs all facing the front of the class. There was a teacher's desk and table at the front of each classroom, and each room was outfitted with a computer and projector, though these did not always function. While some senior secondary classrooms had clean floors, junior secondary classrooms tended to be more littered, with candy wrappers and papers laying on the floors. Most classes accommodated between twenty and thirty-five students, some senior secondary classes held as many as forty-five, and one form five class, which I was told had the lowest performing ethnic Chinese students, had only twelve students.

A common feature of each junior secondary classroom was a posted sign with classroom rules. In one form one classroom, this poster was titled "Our Classroom Regulations" and told students that there should be no "playing, shouting, chasing, eating, or drinking" in the classroom, and students should mind their belongings, be punctual, be clean, and not say any "dirty words." Instead, the sign instructed students to "Please keep silent inside classroom," an expectation of lesson time behavior I would also find at Industrial Secondary School (ISS). But the opposite was usually true of classrooms I observed. Particularly in the junior secondary classes, all classes composed of EM students, students littered, shouted, ran around the classroom, and a few times even broke into physical fighting. As Wafa, a Pakistani heritage teaching assistant told me in an interview, it was common for students to curse at teachers or each other in Urdu, Nepali, or Hindi. Students who broke these rules would often be sent out of class and sometimes assigned after-school detention.

In senior secondary classrooms, including in classes made up of ethnic Chinese students, one could find students sleeping during lessons. Sometimes, a dozen or more students could be found asleep in some classrooms (including in the form five class with only twelve students). The school's head of discipline, a former police detective, provided some rationale for the sleeping phenomenon during a conversation on the playground: some students were bored, some had stayed up all night either playing videos or working in paid jobs, and some had used alcohol or drugs such as marijuana or ketamine, the latter more popular with ethnic Chinese students.

While official classroom instructions required silence, instances of self-expression, art, or graffiti could also be found in classrooms. For example, some students drew intricate floral patterns inspired by mehndi, a South Asian art form in which hands and feet are decorated with intricate designs, often for weddings and other rituals, on their materials. Other students though, scratched or used correction fluid to emblazon surfaces with names, nicknames, images such as hearts or sexual words and images onto desks and surfaces in the classroom. In one classroom, someone had written "ASShole Porn Fuck" with correction fluid on a windowsill, while a desk had the message "take it quickly, ASSHOLE, FUCK U", also written in correction fluid. In the course of the academic year, the windowsill and desk were neither cleaned, nor removed, and other marked surfaces were likewise left alone by teachers and janitorial staff, leaving these words to become part of the general scenery of classrooms.

As I interacted with students, I wondered about the connection between classroom conditions evident of feelings of alienation, and internal pain felt by students. If NTS was students' "second home," as John and Christine, two panel heads overseeing my work at NTS, intended, why did "home" feel bleak sometimes? So I investigated students' internal feelings in a lesson I conducted with several classes from forms one through four, in which students created "Where I'm From" poems using my sample poems and a template requiring them to describe categories such as sights, feelings, places, foods, sayings that describe their environments from which they come. The sample poems were meant to familiarize students with me, and invited them to share their lives with me.

These poems written revealed much about students. I saw some of their likes (sports, music, video games, fast food), expectations of themselves and expectations from their families, as well as feelings of alienation and conflict, all while seeing great variation in writing skills. Many students shared dreams of a profession such as doctor, dentist, athlete, or teacher, and wrote of their parents' reminders to "study hard" and "do your homework." But also common were lines such as "I'm from sad, lonely, and bored," written by a form one girl of Nepali heritage. She added, "I'm from the sound I hear from my neighbor is always fighting at night...I'm from my parents saying study hard, sleep early, don't play too much games," here coupling a neighborhood fracas with parental concerns over academics and physical well-being. Or students coupled feelings with sounds and conflicts from their neighborhoods, such as a form two Pakistani heritage girl who wrote she was from "sadness," and from "shouting, fighting, buses driving by and babies crying." Strong emotions rang throughout, as did in the poem from, Sangam, a form two boy of Nepali heritage:

Extract 4.2 "I'm from Love & Hate"

I'm from Happiness, Sad, & Anger
I'm from drinking
I'm from son
I'm from "Get lost"
I'm from McDonald's
I'm from Music
I'm from Love & Hate

{Sangam, class assignment, November 30, 2010}

The poem signals some of the themes I would continue to find through my year at NTS and three years at ISS. For example, in the lines, "I'm from Happiness, Sad & Anger," and "I'm from Love & Hate," there are conflicting emotions reminiscent of the mood swings students at ISS frequently reported to me. The line "I'm from 'Get lost'" refers to a line in the poem template asking students to write common sayings from their parents, indicating here perhaps that a parent says these words to his son and a strained paternal relationship exists. But the mechanisms students used for fulfillment or coping are likewise present: "McDonald's" and "Music," and perhaps "drinking" alcohol, a practice common especially with boys of Nepali heritage as young as thirteen I met at both sites, but that also evidenced itself in females and students of other ethnic groups. Alternatively, the line "drinking" could refer to a parent's actions, signaling to possible domestic conflict.

Physical manifestations of pain, despair, and longing were also visible online on Facebook, through hybrid forms of culture and subjectivity, engagement with global popular cultures, and multimodal literacies that revealed complexity in students' lives. Within my participant observation on Facebook, I had greater access to students' secondary discourses, the ways of talking, writing, and thinking beyond the discourses of their primary social group in which they are raised, as well as their "identity kits," the ways they used language, thinking, and acting to present themselves to the world and signal memberships with groups or social networks (Gee 1989). Through online media, students edited and posted photos and videos they took, reposted or wrote and posted quotes, and employed multilingual linguistic code switching; a single post could contain a combination of multiple languages, including English, Chinese, Urdu, Nepali, Hindi, etc. Students were also conversant in online parlance, means abbreviations such as "LOL" (laughing out loud) and "WFT" (What the fuck?), or alternate spelling such as typing "meh" or "yuh" instead of "me" or "you". Multimodal and multilingual interactions in Facebook by students included obsessions with romantic relationships that were exposed through quizzes they took about who their "crush" could be, or who they might marry in the future, and were tied to struggles over class status and cultural traditions.

Along with images of animals and cartoon characters, football and cricket athletes, marijuana leaves, images of American and British heavy metal bands, "boy bands," and Korean pop groups, some Muslim girls posted illustrations of young women which fused elements of Emo aesthetic (Emo is a music and associated cultural styles focusing on themes of loneliness, isolation, and love that has had global reach) with Islamic culture. For example, one student posted an image of an illustrated female figure wearing a black hijab and donning dark red lipstick and black tears streaming from an eye-lined face. Another student reposted what appeared to be an image of a female self-cutting. The image shows the lower half of a body, with the equation cut into its legs: boy + (heart) = (crossed out heart), perhaps a reference to difficultly in romantic relationships. While the image seemed to have been produced by someone outside Hong Kong, from time-to-time students would post images of their own self-harm, typically composed of a bleeding forearm cut multiple times. At NTS, I saw the remnants of self-harm on several students' arms as scabs and scars, and at ISS, I would learn how prevalent the practice was. Once, with my form three class, I conducted an impromptu survey. Students put their heads on their desks, and I asked for them to raise their hands if they had ever done any self-harm such as cutting. In a class of twenty-eight students, half raised their hands. I then asked how many knew someone who had committed self-harm, and all raised their hands.

Further illustrating this concern, Dawar, a form four male of Pakistani heritage, who was well-liked by teachers, was an active cricket player, and loved rock music, posted a poem in Urdu to Facebook which was layered onto a photograph with a colored effect of him standing next to a tall, barbed-wire fence outside a public housing estate. The poem, which Wafa, a teaching assistant of Pakistani heritage, translated for me, displays an existential dilemma, as seen in Extract 4.3:

Extract 4.3 "Love is pain"

love is pain
love is a trap
a kind of injustice
it's better to be alone and drop tears

{Dawar, Facebook post, January 15, 2011}

This post resulted from an investment in taking a photograph, digitally editing and supplementing it with text to convey a message of a contradictory nature of love as "pain," restraint, and "injustice." It ends with a refutation of love, leaving the speaker preferring crying in solitude.

In an interview, Wafa acknowledged students' preoccupations with matters of the heart and their emotional difficulties. She claimed that traditionally, Pakistani heritage students were not allowed to date or have boyfriends or girlfriends, but had more freedom in Hong Kong, leading them to establish romantic relationships. She was also aware of love as a common topic on Facebook. "So its mean, you see in the Facebook," she confirmed, "many students very concerned about love." She elaborated on the issue in our interview:

Extract 4.4 "The girls no need to...get good education here"

CARLOS: Um, I want to know about, um, the girls and some of the teachers talk about how both, um, Nepali and Pakistani, but maybe a little bit more Pakistani, that some of them see that maybe they have no future because their marriage will already be planned for them.
WAFA: Yes. Yes.
WAFA: Actually, you know, in a—I already mentioned because the many of in Hong Kong, you know, is a—majority in, uh, meet more people here in—in Hong Kong. And this kind of people is not well educated. And, uh, also is not, uh, get very good jobs. Many of them security and like, uh, construction worker and same. And, uh, they live in a—I think so is 30 years, over 30 years in Hong Kong here. And they know Chinese very well yeah, but actually the mind is, you know, is not developed here. Same is, you know, the—the old. And so they think, um, the girls no need to, uh, get good education here. Just they, uh, know, um, how to speak and how to write little

bit and is enough and, uh, is no problem. But is a—this kind of majority people, however, you know already selected boys and, uh, and, uh, also you know some of the girls, you know, already engaged when is, uh...
CARLOS: At what age?
WAFA: Uh, uh, engaged is mostly 10 years old. Yeah, mostly 10.
CARLOS: Wow.
WAFA: And after then, you know, is, um, 17—uh, 16 or 17, they get married.
CARLOS: They marry.
WAFA: Marry, yeah.
CARLOS: So even in Hong Kong?
WAFA: Even in Hong Kong.

{Wafa, Interview, July 18, 2011}

Wafa's comments bring the issues of social class, schooling, social mobility, language, and traditional practices into our conversation. She paints a picture in which families with a decades-long presence in Hong Kong, a command of spoken Cantonese, and stationed in working-class jobs offering little mobility, arrange marriages for their children at a young age, and therefore seek limited schooling for daughters who will become wives before their twenties.

Wafa ascribes these practices to families' "old" thinking and as the conversation continued explained these practices might lead Pakistani heritage female students to view commitment to academic studies as fruitless. Wafa also alludes to the lack of guarantee Chinese language acquisition provides in changing traditional practices that constrain particularly female students. Later, at ISS, I got slightly different takes on this issue. While I met Pakistani heritage female students who said they had no choice but to have an arranged marriage, Hamida, a female of Pakistani heritage told me that her parents supported her pursuits in schooling and would allow her to go university if she could reach it. However, if she could not, she would have to be married by nineteen in order to have some security. Amir, a Pakistani heritage teaching assistant at ISS backed Hamida's account in conversation, stressing that many poorer families wanted their daughters to study, but placed a high value on preserving their future security.

Before this interview, Marina, a diligent and pleasant, and by all accounts hard-working, nineteen-year-old form four student of Nepali heritage dropped out of school without warning and got married, just prior to the end of the academic year. She had been involved in organizing the school's dance team and participated in many school activities, so her sudden departure left John, who had taught her for a couple years, shocked. I had heard in interviews with John, Christine, and Principal Chu that females of South Asian heritage sometimes married in their late teens, a practice Wafa backed up. Therefore, insecurity about one's future, concerns about social class, and mobility, and issues of gender and schooling might come to the fore when discussing dreams and aspirations, as might be the case in Extract 4.5, an interaction between Qasim and a form four girl of Pakistani heritage, Mina, who by Wafa's account, was smart, but not motivated to focus on academics.

Extract 4.5 "I don't study hard, Na"

QASIM: What is your dream?
MINA: My dream is in future I want to be business woman because I love to earn money Very much. I want to buy a big house, a car like BMW, Ferrari. Many kind of car I want to buy.
QASIM: Will you reach your goal?
MINA: Of course I will reach it if I study hard. But I don't study hard, na.

{Qasim and Mina, video recording, November 12, 2010}

In Extract 4.5, Mina reports a dream filled with material goods including a big house and expensive cars, powered by a high-earning future as a business woman. Simultaneously, she might be challenging gender and social class norms by even imagining this future. But she readily identifies her own lack of agency in studying as a barrier to her dreams, as opposed to structural factors and family concerns mentioned by Wafa. There is also an underlying narrative Mina advances, that if one does study hard, then a future with material luxuries might be more possible. But place could also be constraint, even in the presence of individual effort, as we will see in the next extract with Suman.

Suman, an affable sixteen-year-old male student of Nepali heritage in form four, was part of the school rock band. He was one of the first students at the school to introduce himself to me and we spoke about the music we liked and life at the school, so I was interested in speaking more with him, hoping to know more about his musical aspirations. In our conversation excerpted in Extract 4.6, he identifies Hong Kong as a difficult place for the fulfillment of his dream.

Extract 4.6 "I hope I can be successful in music"

CARLOS: What is your dream?
SUMAN: I have interest in music, so I hope I can make a future with music. I work every day hard for it and I hope I can be successful in music.
CARLOS: Do you think you can achieve your dream in Hong Kong?
SUMAN: I think I can't do it in Hong Kong because most of the people is all Chinese and what I do is sing English songs and play English songs. It's hard for me to sing in Chinese songs. I think I can't do much better in Hong Kong maybe I need to find other country to do my dream. I think I can't say that music can really make my future but my second option is to study.

{Suman, video recording, November 12, 2010}

64 *Alienation, pain, and possibility*

In this extract, Suman communicates his investment into working hard "every day" to reach aspirations of a successful musical career, and academics are a second, separate option to Suman, not an option that could enhance and be involved in a joint project with his musical dreams. Yet he is tentative about whether this aspiration can be realized in Hong Kong, referencing social constraints, like the possible lack of an audience for English music, or his inability to sing in Chinese, could limit him, but like other students, he mentions that his individual effort are pivotal to his outcomes. He introduces a theme that recurred with other students, that dreams may not be possible in Hong Kong, and that activating mobility might be necessary, often times expressed as a move to the United Kingdom, or a return to one's heritage or "home" country.

Despite the struggles students exhibited, or perhaps because of them, many students also consumed and circulated images and videos of bright, hopeful, Bollywood films and stars, leading me to discover an invaluable vehicle for engagement. Near the end of the academic year, I learned through an online query into the most popular Bollywood film about "3 Idiots" (Hirani 2009), the global hit about three friends who meet in an engineering college. The movie's protagonist, Rancho, aware of a rising tide of student suicides in India, challenges the banking model of education promulgated by the college's domineering director, Dr. Viru. Instead, Rancho advocates for learning that allows students to develop their talents and follow their passions. Other plot lines revolve around Rancho's buddies, who struggle academically at the college, but must contend with parental expectations of academic success. For example, Farhan's parents have sacrificed their own comforts to provide their son with opportunities, and Raju's family struggles with poverty, hoping for him to get a high-paying job to provide succor. Meanwhile Rancho falls in love, but the object of his affection, Pia, is engaged to a materialistic man.

I shared my enjoyment of the movie with a group of Class 1A form one, and they were shocked that I saw it, as the movie had been extremely popular amongst their peers. So I requested movie recommendations, and they insisted I watch two more Indian movies dealing with themes of education and personal conflict: "Udaan" (Motwane 2010) and "Taare Zameen Par" (Khan 2007). The drama begins in "Udaan" when the protagonist, Rohan, is expelled from one school, only to feel alienated in a second when he cannot pursue his passion for literature. Shortly after watching Udaan, I reflected on how Bollywood films could become a vehicle for engagement:

Extract 4.7 "They have complex mental lives"

These two movies had similar threads in them, though one was a drama and the other a comedy with romance thrown in. Udaan tells the story of a seventeen year old boy who returns to live with his abusive father and half brother he did not know he had. His father drinks and beats his younger brother, and stresses about keeping his factory in business during a recession. Rohan wants to be a writer, but the father wants him to be an engineer and run the [small and struggling family] factory. The film can be used to discuss emotional changes during puberty, as well as decision making, as Rohan takes his brother and runs away to Bombay. Also, Rohan's father can be studied as a stereotypical dominant male who does not know how to deal with anyone's emotions. What struck me while watching the film is that it is very serious and emotionally nuanced; not the kind of film I would expect 12/13 year olds to recommend. It shows that they have complex mental lives (duh!). This really counters the idea I have heard from teachers that the kids are simple thinkers. 3 Idiots is the highest grossing Bollywood film ever. It deals with themes of education, family, pressure, suicide, competition, and social mobility. I showed a short clip to a group of students to illustrate social mobility and they enjoyed it."

{Self-reflexive journal, May 22, 2011}

In Extract 4.7, I recall the mood and feel of "Udaan," and reference comments by teachers that EM students were "simple thinkers," as I oppose the assumption by confirming my understanding of EM students' "complex mental lives," emphasizing it with a sarcastic, "duh!". In the extract, I am solidifying my understanding of generative themes including education, family, and social mobility, and also seeing how the film could connect to some of the concepts Thomas had taught from a textbook that year, such as puberty, gender roles, and decision-making. My recognition of the power of stories is also emerging in the extract. "Udaan" is a slow-paced, almost three-hour film, in which the narrative is composed of everyday interactions involving the main character, his friends, and his family, and is only punctuated by brief periods of intense drama. Scenes are packed with emotional nuances, perhaps mirroring students' lives. However, the pace of the story can draw the viewer deep into the world of a conflicted teen to examine its themes.

I reflected on the second movie "Taare Zameen Par" (Khan 2007), which tells the story of an eight year old named Ishaan who, after being expelled from his local school for failing and withdrawing from his studies, is sent away to boarding school by his middle-class parents, eager for him to fit the middle-class model of success embodied by his older brother. At the boarding school, Ishaan meets an unconventional art teacher who discovers Ishaan's undiagnosed dyslexia, and proceeds to teach him using a variety of visual and kinesthetic approaches. Like "3 Idiots" and "Udaan," "Taare Zameen Par" places the conflicts its protagonists face (all male) within the context of family, social class, and banking-oriented schooling dominated by rote learning that constrain the opportunities its characters have to reach self-actualization.

Via these movies, I recognized education as a generative theme I would introduce for investigation with students, and more specifically to ask them what kind of education they wanted, how they learned, and what it meant to be "able" within the context of school, one I would eventually engage recurrently for three years at NTS. If these themes were central to the popular culture EM students consumed, it was worth testing if they were also central concerns in their lives. These movies not only critique schooling but also offer alternative visions of pedagogy and relations between students and teachers. Their importance will resurface later in this chapter when we look at how teachers wanted to make sense of student's emotional worlds. But for now, against these fictional, imagined accounts of schooling consumed by students, the concerns in their worlds, and their multimodal practices, I want to explore the actual schooling EM encountered daily at NTS.

Banking education: textbooks, deficits, and other constraints

Education at NTS in English and LS classes, generally consisted of banking methods mediated by textbooks, a far cry from the most recent reforms advocating dialogue, diverse materials, and learning driven by students' needs and interests (see Chapter 1). While these methods failed in developing students' academic literacies, the speaking, reading, and writing skills and conceptual knowledge and skills needed for mastery in and across disciplines (Gibbons 2009), teachers explained failure through discourse they circulated related to language, knowledge, and social class, and did not imagine viable alternatives to practices beyond those requiring students' conformity to existing banking models. In the next section, I will provide some background into classroom teaching practices, then through interviews and documentary evidence show the ways in which teachers made sense of dilemmas that emerged as pedagogy was misaligned with the needs of students.

Perhaps because of these dynamics, English and LS lessons observed were often spaces full of frustration. Teachers admonished and yelled at students or a whole class for arriving late, not completing homework, or failing to listen during lectures. Sometimes students shouted back. Students were mostly confined to their chairs during lessons, as teachers taught mostly using textbooks, PowerPoint presentations provided by the textbook publishers, and fill-in-the blank worksheets they had made or modified from textbook materials. Adding to the frustration, many students were being taught beyond or below their levels of English in both subjects. While in classes with higher concentrations of students with higher English proficiency, there was more compliance with teachers' work expectations, more often, students appeared bored or frustrated, either because they could not cope with the linguistic demands of the lesson, or because the lessons were too simple.

Instead, some students who felt disengaged with material for lack of challenge took on other tasks, such as pulling out popular young adult novels like "Twilight" to read whenever they had the chance. Consequently, academic achievement at NTS was low, but countering common discourse on EM students' troubles discussed in Chapter 1, teachers placed the blame on subjects other than Chinese language. For example, in our interview, John admitted that based on math results, only a few students could "fight for the [university] places, maybe a higher diploma or associate degree." "But it is just a minority of a minority," he admitted. Besides math, LS difficulties also contributed to placing tertiary admission out of reach for most EM students.

Teaching and learning in the three form one LS classes led by Thomas, the LS Panel Head, was guided by textbooks and was full of frustration for both Thomas and students. Typically, Thomas used materials from textbook publishers and guided students in completing blanks in worksheets of workbooks. One workbook titled "Who Am I?" dealt with topics related to identity, puberty, gender roles, and aspirations. One section studied in the class was titled "My Aspirations" and its objective, according to the teacher's version of the book, was to familiarize students with pathways to further studies in Hong Kong and "cultivate students' problem solving skills." The section contained an image of four youngsters with distinct aspirations running the gamut from specific (teacher, fire fighter), to abstract (a secure job), to undecided. Below the image, students are instructed to respond to questions about the images, with answers are already suggested to the teacher. The teacher answers provided by the publisher in are what students in Thomas' class would copy from a PowerPoint onto their worksheets or workbooks.

In such lessons, the starting point was not designed to be the students' aspirations (though the next page of the workbook did ask students to write their aspirations on a line) nor the constraints they faced, but the starting point designed by the textbook publisher. The book fails to mention any constraints the students might face in reaching those aspirations, and there was no discussion of this in the class. So though on the surface, the workbook deals with themes that could be of interest to students, in effect most students were turned off. The banking concept nature of the textbook was reinforced by the unit and lesson plans provided by the publisher. Table 4.1 reproduces a typical unit plan for the topic "How do we search for identity?" provided to teachers by the publisher of the "Who Am I?" textbook. It stands in contrast to Camangian's lesson plan

Table 4.1 Suggested unit plan for LS textbook

Teaching Objective	Activity and Objective	Teaching Material	Learning Material
After completing this topic, students will be able to: – examine ways to know about themselves – understand sex role and idol worship – understand the importance of sex role and idol worship to self-identity	How can we know more about ourselves? Activity 4: Who am I? – encourage students to learn about themselves from looking at their performance – allow students to conclude what they have learned in Activities 2, 3, and 4 in order to understand themselves further	– Teacher's guide (pp. 18–33) – Workbook (Teacher's edition) – CD-ROM for Teachers – Q-Setter CD-ROM – Publisher's website teaching tools	– Student book (pp. 18–33) – Workbook – Publisher's website for exercises

provided in Chapter 2, which also explored aspects of identity through cultural forms relevant to students through a variety of texts and activities centered on students.

The unit plan defines the objectives, activity, and materials for the lesson. It requires the teacher to deliver already considered questions and answers to students, who then use the learning material (books and website provided by the publisher) to complete the activities (completing the worksheets) in order to reach the objective, understanding more about themselves. Specific lesson plans within the teacher's book go further in describing the role of students and teachers. In a lesson about puberty, for example, the students' role is to "Listen carefully to the teacher's explanation, and finish the activity," and the role of teacher is to "Guide students to finish the activity. Teach the definition of puberty." In a book meant for identity exploration, students do not ask questions and must rely not on their interests or materials from their experiences, but on activities that even the teachers do not need to think about to complete.

Absent from this unit plan is any mention of students' heritages and patterns of migration, local histories, cultures, and communities to which they would claim membership, influence of class status on identity, or their daily experiences in school and Hong Kong as EMs. Likewise, materials from students' lives are absent. The rest of the unit plan focuses on understanding and "accepting" gender roles and the possible negative effects of "idol worship" referring to overemphasis on celebrities. None of these lesson plans mention or instruct the teacher sharing their experiences. When I met Suman and his friends, they mentioned this, complaining that most teachers would not even tell them about their age or families. But the lesson plans do mention that generic skills such as "collaboration" and "time management" should be cultivated, although how that should happen with the given lesson plan is unclear.

Problematic textbook-based banking pedagogies extended into the English subject across forms. As English Panel Head, Christine, felt constrained in the use of materials, feeling pressure not just from the examinations. Her frustration at constraints materialized in a long conversation about use of materials and pedagogy. In Extract 4.8, Christine explains some of these issues after I ask her about difficulties students faced with levels of English being taught.

Extract 4.8 "Most of our materials are from the textbooks"

CARLOS: Okay. Um, I also saw it in, um, in the English classes for the non-Chinese Speaking students also that often times the level of what was being taught was beyond where they were. And I would say I experienced also the same thing in teaching Form 1 studies with 1-B and 1-C where, um, maybe a third of the class didn't know any English at all, um, and that was very difficult and led to, um, a lot of—a lot of bad situations for me. Um, can you also talk what's that situation? What's—what's the pressure there and do you see any ways around it or different ways to handle that situation?

CHRISTINE: You are teaching LS right?
CARLOS: Yeah.
CHRISTINE: Do you have the LS textbook?
CARLOS: The textbook?
CHRISTINE: Uh, textbooks because students have LS textbook.
CARLOS: The textbooks. Yes, I—I actually never used the textbook myself.
CHRISTINE: Yeah. You know, um, um, for English teachers, the pressure is not just, uh, from the proper exam. Of course, it is the main pressure, okay. We still need to prepare them for the proper exam. Uh, also from the school, we still need to help them to, uh, um, um, catch up with the levels they should be in, okay. But we also have the pressure from their parents because for English, we bought, um, uh, English textbooks okay, quite a lot of textbooks. Uh, the parents will—if we don't use the textbook, the parents will, uh, will say "Why you don't use the textbook but you need my kids to buy the textbooks?" So, um, that's why, uh, we still need to make use of the materials that we have.

{Christine, interview, July 25, 2011}

I begin the extract explaining the problem I observed in some classes and also experienced in teaching two form one classes, where a significant number of students were new or recent arrivals from Pakistan, India, or Nepal, and knew very little to no English. These students, who helped to bolster the school's enrollments, were placed into classes usually with no additional support except the occasional presence of an Urdu-speaking assistant. At the same time, some of the students in the class were some of the most proficient in their forms. This problem was most pronounced in two of the form one classes. So as I asked the question to Christine in the extract, I was trying to navigate what could be a tricky situation that could make her defensive, and I tried to position myself as a teacher who shares her dilemma, admitting to her, "… that was very difficult and led to, um, a lot of—a lot of bad situations for me." Christine asks me if I am using a textbook for LS, as she thought that teachers in LS had more flexibility to choose materials, to which I reply that there is a textbook, but I did not use it, placing myself in a position counter to Christine's teaching.

Christine then cites the pressures she feels to use the textbooks. The main pressure, she tells me, is the public examinations, followed by a pressure from the school to help students catch up to an appropriate grade level. She also mentions that she feels a pressure from parents to use textbooks, as students are required to purchase up to eight text and exercise books for the English subject per term. Therefore, parents might feel something amiss if the books they purchased are not put to use. Ultimately, though, she came back to the pressure of public examinations as the main reason for using textbooks as the primary material, as seen in Extract 4.9.

Extract 4.9 "We don't have much choice to decide"

CARLOS: Because of the pressure for the examination?
CHRISTINE: Yeah, because we are focusing on the four skills and, uh, we have the textbook to follow. Uh, but, uh, uh, some of the part we don't have the textbook just like the newspaper clipping exercise then we can choose our own materials. But for the rest for, uh, listening, for, uh, writing we, uh, uh, we need to follow the scheme of work, okay. So, uh, we don't have much choice to decide, uh, whether to use, uh, uh, other materials from outside.

{Christine, interview, July 25, 2011}

In this extract, Christine alludes to the teaching of four skills in English: reading, writing, speaking, and listening, which in practice means students use a different set of books for each skill. Sometimes, as was the case at NTS and later at ISS, the four skills were not all taught by the same teacher. The presence of four skills then becomes a constraint for Christine against using non-textbook materials, and again this is despite the specific reforms in the English subject that suggest integrated teaching skills. Moreover, in Chapter 1, I reviewed that reforms promoted greater use of resources in English, and that students' needs and interests should be taken into account when choosing materials, even to the point of allowing students to contribute materials to curriculum. However, in this extract, Christine reveals constraints on her English subject, stating, "We don't have much choice to decide…whether to use…other materials from outside," leaving students outside of this process, even to the point that even newspaper clippings used for class exercises were chosen by teachers.

Textbooks used by the junior secondary students in their English classes were pegged to the Territory System Assessment, an exam students take in form three in English, math, and Chinese that helps the Education Bureau (EDB) to gauge the "value" that schools "add" in terms of academic skills to students from the beginning of form one through form three. Classroom instruction did not seem guided by students' knowledge, needs, or interests. Within textbook-based assignments, students were generally provided little to no opportunities for voice, neither in speaking nor in writing. The process of learning in the classes I observed most often meant learning by the filling of blanks on worksheets. Though students shared many common languages, discussion and collaboration were rare. Teaching persisted in remaining aligned with what teachers thought would help students face the "proper exam," the Hong Kong Diploma of Secondary Education, even if students could not cope with the level of the textbooks, or as was the case sometimes, were beyond it. As Christine told me in the interview, "We cannot teach them only primary standard level materials…then they cannot catch up with the proper exam. So we still need to teach them…authentic and realistic so that they can know the standard of the proper exam."

Alienation, pain, and possibility 71

Students' lack of English proficiency was also seen as contributing to failure in LS, but it was not the only factor the school mobilized to make sense of difficulties faced by students and teachers. The following two extracts are from a grant application completed by the school requesting money for additional support measures to assist students in LS. Earlier in the document, the school explained dilemmas over medium of instruction (MOI). Though "non-Chinese speaking" (NCS) students are taught in EMI classes, rather than Chinese medium of instruction (CMI), students' results in LS examinations are "polarized." Here the extract picks up:

Extract 4.10 "Some cannot speak, read, or write any English"

Students' performance during Liberal Studies lessons is also quite surprising, with *both* brighter and weaker students missing a high motivation to participate in learning activities, even though teachers already adopt diverse teaching strategies. After rounds of meetings with all Liberal Studies teachers and evaluating students' performance during lessons and exams, we generated a holistic review of our school's needs. First of all, although students at our school are NCS students, their language abilities are still greatly varied. Some of our NCS students are locally born and raised, and received primary education from local primary schools in which the MOI was Cantonese. Therefore, these students are fluent in Cantonese and comparatively weak in English. Other NCS students are new comers to Hong Kong. Their competency in English is at best sufficient for simple conversations, while some cannot speak, read, or write any English. Furthermore, there is a small number of top-tier students who are fluent in both English and Cantonese. As a result, teachers find that it is very difficult to strike a balance. If they teach slower or simplify the teaching content, the brighter students will be under-learn; vice versa, if they teach faster and try to tackle more complex issues or concepts, the weaker students will be lost easily during lessons and hence de-motivated to learn. Therefore, it is vital to develop different sets of teaching and learning materials so as to cater students' varied learning needs and level of English.

{NTS School Document, June 2011}

In Extract 4.10, the school makes note of the language difficulties I observed and brought up with Christine, and explains these challenges through the varying linguistic trajectories of students, which vary along place of birth and MOI used in primary school. These language trajectories result in a wide array of linguistic profiles, from little to no proficiency in both English and Chinese to "top-tier students who are fluent in both English and Cantonese" that cause problems for teachers in how they deliver content, having to negotiate between "simplifying" or teaching "faster and try to tackle more complex issues or concepts." This extract begins to also show three dynamics that ran throughout school practices and documents: (1) that some students are "bright" and some are "weak," (2) that language determines access to "elite" status as a student, in this case English and Cantonese, and (3) that problems with language lead to students' lack of "high motivation" for learning. These dynamics are then referenced as the reason for students' lack of or de-motivation for engaging in the subject's banking pedagogical methods, despite referring to more "diverse teaching strategies" used at the senior secondary level. The next extract picks up where Extract 4.10 left off:

Extract 4.11 "They lack relevant knowledge"

> On the other hand, the Liberal Studies curriculum frequently requires students to have prior knowledge related to Hong Kong and China when considering issues in lessons. Our NCS students face a great difficulty, as they lack relevant knowledge related to Hong Kong and China to attach to lessons. Even though some of them are born in Hong Kong, their social experience here has severely limited exposure to key histories, customs, and institutions of Hong Kong and greater China. Consequently, they lose interest in learning Liberal Studies. Although there are some teaching materials that are written in English, they are still too difficult for most of our NCS students to understand, especially in the modules of "Hong Kong Today" and "Modern China". Those materials are not suitable for students without sufficient knowledge of Hong Kong and China. What makes the situation worse is that while NCS students' engagement during lessons improves with the use audio-visual aids, there is a great shortage of suitable video clips. Clips with suitable content are either in Cantonese, or in English, but at a linguistic level too difficult for understanding and learning. Last but not least, although all Liberal Studies teachers in our school are qualified to use English as MOI and have experience in using English as MOI, English is not the mother tongue of teachers. Additionally, our Liberal Studies teachers are mainly from the science stream, which means that they may need further enhancement in skills of teaching students to write argumentative passages, as the argumentative passage is not the type of response usually used in science subjects. But the argumentative passage's structure is very similar to the structure of answers for Liberal Studies questions. Therefore, further teachers' training is necessary for more effective communication between teachers and students and helping students to write argumentative passages, hence creating sustainable effects on helping students to learn Liberal Studies in English effectively.
>
> {NTS School Document, June 2011}

Alienation, pain, and possibility 73

In Extract 4.11, new problems are introduced. First, students' lack of knowledge and experience to connect to learning about Hong Kong and China is named as a cause for why students "lose interest" in LS. Next, the lack of both Cantonese and English proficiency in students returns to justify a difficulty in finding suitable materials. Here, the discourse focuses on the technical aspects of pedagogy, rather than relational aspects as a way to engage students, arguing that greater availability of audio-visual materials would increase motivation, as opposed to greater interaction and dialogue among students. The extract finishes with a paradoxical situation: Though most teachers are officially qualified to teach EMI classes, English is not their mother tongue. This conflict is not explained, perhaps it means that teacher's proficiencies are also lacking. More specifically, it is admitted that LS teachers actually come from the science teaching subject, and therefore are not familiar with teaching argumentative writing necessary to answering questions on LS exams. To address the challenges specific to LS exams, greater attention to English and in particular to argumentative writing was emphasized so that students could better cope with the subject.

Beyond losing motivation to study LS because of English language difficulties, lack of suitable materials, and deficit of necessary general knowledge around Hong Kong and China, Thomas also saw class status as causing problems for students in the subject. As part of the school's practice, Thomas conducted home visits for some students at the beginning of the year and shared his impressions in our interview:

Extract 4.12 "Their family background is no good"

CARLOS: What's your understanding of the problems or the concerns that students have outside of school, the NCS students?
THOMAS: You know, NCS students—um, the difficulties you're referring to?
CARLOS: Yeah.
THOMAS: Um, from my experience to home visits to some of the NCS students, I will know that—after home visit, I will know that why their performance in school is not very good as those local students is. First of all, most of their family background is no good. Um —
CARLOS: What do you mean by that?
THOMAS: For example, this give me, this give me a very deep impression that I went to a student's home for visits and I discover that in that home, there is no TV, no computer. And inside the house, including the student, there should be about five to six brothers and sisters in total. Obviously, the mother do not know how to speak English or write English and the father is always absent in the house. And all the equipment in the house is very, are very basic one. Or I would say, it's very old, even some of them are not that, that not good. Now because of this background, so that it creates a naturally disadvantage for them because you know that in Liberal Studies, we always need to follow what's going on in the society. They need to trace

very closely with what's happening. But uh, unlike local students here, no matter how poor they are, they still get a computer to surf on to the internet and know what's going on around the world, but they simply do not have this resource.

{Thomas, interview, June 30, 2011}

Thomas caught a glimpse of a students' private lives through home visits and saw that for some students, home environments lack niceties such as televisions or computers, and families can be relatively large. The parent's lack or English language skills and father's need to work also become points of deficit, and the conditions create a "naturally disadvantage for them" because it prevents students from following developments in society. Thomas compares poverty in the case of some EM students with poverty experienced by "local" ethnic Chinese students who remain connected to the world via the internet. Yet these visits are not used as a launching point for study in Thomas' classes. So poverty becomes a negative state students bring to school, that disadvantages them compared to ethnic Chinese "local" students, rather than a position from which to examine experiences in Hong Kong. Lived realities of disadvantaged social class are not considered by Thomas as a way to question Hong Kong's distribution of wealth, inequality, and notions of Hong Kong being highly developed, all topics that exist within the LS official curriculum. Thus social class became linked with knowledge, language, and access to subject literacy. In Thomas' mind, lower class status meant lower English language proficiency, less LS related knowledge of the Chinese context, and barriers preventing accessing information from the world.

By filling students' gaps and deficiencies, the school thought EM students could be engaged in banking pedagogies used for LS. In the next section, we will further see how teachers imagined students could overcome obstacles by conforming to the school's existing social and pedagogical arrangements.

Additional challenges to conforming to existing structures

Despite the obstacles and conflicts that students faced academically and socially, teachers at NTS primarily imagined avenues for students' aspirations and for resolution of problems within existing academic and social structures, offering assistance to students in forms involving conforming to the banking system that alienated many, while reproducing narratives of individual attainment. Even when teachers had a strong desire to help students, they felt constrained by institutional factors or students' or teachers' mindsets. This was the case with Paula, an English teacher who was in her fourth year in teaching, as well as her fourth year at NTS. In Extract 4.13, Paula introduces the frames of social class and of sharing stories related to her success. She identifies as coming from a low-income family, a factor she said helped her to connect with students at the school. During the interview, I wanted to know how this identification with students shaped her teaching.

Extract 4.13 "I want them to achieve more"

CARLOS: What kind of things do you pay attention to?

PAULA: I would say ah, what I bear in mind at that is that I really need to shape their thinking. Because for example—because as you mentioned before, many of our students came from the lower income families; they didn't really have a high expectation of themselves and even their parents as well. So what I want is that, I just want them to achieve more and to learn more in school because I can really imagine that maybe several years later, they can just go out and work. If they don't have any expectation and don't have any dream at all, they would not be able to be ah, successful person and that's why during my past few years, I really encourage my students to think more and to think of what they really want to be, yeah.

CARLOS: How do you do that?

PAULA: Well, as I mentioned before, both local [ethnic Chinese] and NCS students, they like to listen to my stories. And I also came from a lower income families and…

CARLOS: Do the kids know that?

PAULA: Yeah, I—because ah, it's kind of funny. Because I [live] in the Public Housing Estate and some students, they just live close to me. Let's say, if I live in 10th Floor, some of them they just live in 15th or 17th floor. So maybe in the morning or at night or in the afternoon, when I go back or come to school, they usually see me on the way.

{Paula, interview, July 18, 2011}

Paula believed EM students could be successful academically and attain tertiary schooling, not by schools finding ways to meet their emotional and social needs, but through development of language abilities and individual effort. To do that, she needed to "shape their thinking" and get students to "think more" so that they would "achieve more" and have an "expectation" and "dream". She emphasized, "I think the most, most, most important thing should be helping them develop their language skills both English and Chinese". For Janet, language, both English and Chinese, was a skill that was weak and could be developed by teachers, thereby offering a possibility for change for students, ethnic Chinese and EM, coming from "lower income families" such as the family in which she was raised.

She also placed responsibility on the students to change their mindsets in regard to academics and conform to her textbook and examination-based pedagogy, which I observed. She told me as the interview unfolded, "Sometimes in class, they just totally ignore everything, because they think that, oh, I can write. Oh, you need—you tell me to write 200 words and then I just write 200 words, that's all." Students who could attain passing marks in listening and speaking exams "didn't really think of how to improve or how to um, be—how to get higher marks in the writing because they didn't really pay attention to the structure of a paragraph and even a passage." Paula referenced senior secondary EM students who focused on learning what was required from the Hong Kong Diploma of Secondary Education English subject examination, and she also revealed her orientation toward examination-based teaching, seeing students' performance and achievement in relation to how they perform on writing, listening, and speaking exercises. Because writing exams only required relatively short compositions, many students would not write beyond the short limits set by textbooks, exams, or teachers. Though Paula wanted student to conform to the exam and textbook system, and used her story to get students to "think" or dream, in the end, Paula seemed unconvinced that students can employ agency in their own academic interest.

Despite the well-meaning efforts of some teachers and staff at the school, there was a more pervasive belief that reality had already been shaped and naturalized, either structurally or through individual decision-making. Most teachers at the school agreed with John's earlier statement that only "a minority of the minority" of students, such as Qasim, could be successful in the school's existing arrangements, yet radical changes to teaching and learning were not earnestly taken on, even if the need for more humanizing approaches was recognized in pockets throughout the school. For instance, in an interview, the school's Principal, Mr. Chu, revealed to me his skepticism that EM students could be successful under that structures maintained by the school and the EDB. "We need a new paradigm," he explained to me, "teachers need more training and development. They should know the history of where the kids come from as well as how to cater to the different nationalities. Teaching needs more interaction, not just teacher to student, but also student to student."

In these statements, Principal Chu acknowledged the need for reforms to enter the classroom, so that students might learn through interaction, and also acknowledged that teachers might have knowledge gaps related to students' worlds, as opposed to the grant application in Extract 4.11, which emphasized students' knowledge gaps. However, the Principal's statement may marginalize the importance of teachers knowing the history of students in Hong Kong if teachers assume that where "students come from" is not Hong Kong, and instead elects students' "nationalities" as an organizing principle for understanding others.

Enacting the principles identified by Principal Chu was a task that made difficult by institutional and relational constraints tinted with racism. The school was dealing with high-teacher turnover and declining enrollments of EM students. After the 2009–2010 school year, eleven teachers had left the school, and for the 2011–2012 academic year, the school had only confirmed about thirty student enrollments for form one. According to Principal Chu, some teachers did not "want to work at the school because they don't want to work with NCS students," and some had complained to the administration, "Pakistani students sometimes smell and can be lazy. They are especially low skilled in math and can't even do basic calculations sometimes. Nepali can be better working but still hard to motivate and some don't like working with Pakistani." Compounding these racially charged complaints from teachers, "Nepalese community leaders [had] complained that they don't want their students in classes with Pakistani because they fight so much."

Besides institutional constraints, teachers faced problems in how they related to students. Though there were well-liked teachers at the school, some teachers, including Christine, felt limited in their abilities to connect to EM students. She had mentioned that in teaching, getting into students' hearts was important, so I returned to this point in Extract 4.14.

Extract 4.14 "We cannot know about them"

CARLOS: How important is that you think to get into their heart? Is that important as a teacher?

CHRISTINE: I think it's really important for the teachers because, um, if you have a very good relationship with the students, it's easier to motivate them to learn your—your, uh, subject, uh, especially for the local students because, um, um, they don't like English. English is a foreign language to them. Um, most of them are very uh, resistant to English. So, uh, if we can get into their heart, if we can have very good relationship with them, it's easy for us to motivate them to learn the English. But for South Asian, uh, South Asian students because, uh, English is an easy subject for them, I think, okay, uh, they don't, uh, uh, they—most of them, uh, are very active in—in your classroom but they will not tell you, uh, uh, a lot about themselves. So I think, uh, we cannot have very good relationship with them, okay. Not deep relationship. Okay. Only the, uh, uh, um, uh, we can only know, uh, the—um, something, um, how to say? Uh, we cannot know about them, uh, uh, in details.

{Christine, interview, July 25, 2011}

Christine validates the need for teachers to connect with students and build a "very good relationship," but running into problems building relationships with EM students, and this in turn makes banking pedagogical goals harder to achieve. She contrasts the relative ease she has connecting with ethnic Chinese students, who are "resistant" to "English," with the challenge of connecting to EM students, who are "active" in the subject because "it is an easy subject for them." So while EM students are stronger in English, and therefore more active in class, they do not share as many "details" of their lives with teachers, making "deep relationships" a strained task. Whether with ethnic Chinese or EM students, these relationships have practical component, to open up the student to "learn" the teacher's subject. Like other instances in this chapter, relationships,

78 *Alienation, pain, and possibility*

visits to students' homes, or activities on the playground are not taken as an investigation of generative themes that can be introduced as official curriculum in the classroom, instead relationship building is in part a tool for gaining conformation to banking pedagogies.

Obstacles to building relationships with students that could get them to conform were also seen as stemming from the teacher. After working in Thomas' form one classes for a year, Thomas began to see some of the dilemmas he faced coming not just from students' deficits and lack of knowledge about Hong Kong and China, and implicated his own orientations in the pedagogical challenges he faced. In Extract 4.15, I have turned the conversation to his experiences having me in the classroom, and he brings in an idea I find surprising, that Thomas is constrained by his mindset as a "Chinese teacher."

Extract 4.15 "The teacher needs to be very, very strict"

CARLOS: What was it like having me as a researcher in your classroom? Can you tell me about that experience?

THOMAS: Actually, it was one more—I would say one more teacher coming to the classroom. At least the students can learn in a better environment than before because, uh, before, before you came here, I just work on my own. I'm just using my own mindset to teach them and although the teaching assistant is help, was helping me but still because the class size was quite large especially for Class 1B and Class 1C. So the discipline is still a problem because we only have two person in the classroom and if the teacher assistant is on this side dealing with difficult students, but this group of students already in some other chaos already. I have one more observation in classroom. In terms of discipline problems, it can be better controlled so it is one of, I would say the benefit. And the second thing is because, uh, you are also a, maybe a foreigner here in Hong Kong, you can think and you can, you can think, uh, by using their own mindset or mentality. You would better understand what they are thinking. You will, I would say, you already experienced the things that they experienced before maybe, yes. So when you plan the lessons flow, lesson flow or design the teaching materials, you already consider their difficulties already. So you make appropriate adjustment before you go in a classroom and teach. And even during the process, you can switch the approach according to their response and according to their needs at any time. But for me, it's a little bit difficult for me to change in such a short period of time because I'm still using—till now, I'm still quite influenced by my original mindset as teaching in the previous school. Yeah, I'm still with the mentality of a Chinese teacher, local teacher.

CARLOS: Which is?

THOMAS: Um, I would say because in the traditional Chinese culture, we still have a impression that teacher needs to be very, very strict, very, very controlling. Uh, what I got from my experience, as a student or maybe some of the teachers when they told to us. And then also in Chinese traditional culture, teachers need to be very strict just like their, one of their parents. And then in terms of teaching, in terms of teaching, all the teaching materials are designed actually in Hong Kong student's mindset and even the topics are designed for the Hong Kong students. If, if and only if I only—I'm the only person that deal with these teaching materials, then it would not bring any new elements into it – into the—into the lessons flow or even in the teaching style or teaching materials. Yes, if you don't come, then I would probably say that it would not bring any new excitement to the students. It can't arouse their motivation and arouse their interests to learn.

{Thomas, interview, June 30, 2011}

In this extract, Thomas reflects on my presence in his classes, what he observed from me, as well as on himself as a teacher. He expresses gratitude at my presence in the classroom, having seen me as an additional teacher in the classroom, not a researcher, who could help with student discipline and lesson planning. Following these comments, he turns to differentiating my mindset as a "foreigner" from his mindset as a "Chinese teacher," which Thomas surmises allowed me to understand students' thinking and needs. He is alluding to the way I would sit with him and explain what I would anticipate and the linguistic and cognitive demands of an activity, and how I would consider what instructions to be given to students for tasks, as well as the flexibility I exhibited in changing mid-way through activities or a unit. He mentions, "During the process, you can switch the approach according to their response and according to their needs at any time."

However, even though Thomas was exposed to new techniques for planning and teaching, he found the change difficult to come by in himself, because of his previous working experience and because of his "Chinese teacher, local teacher" mindset which filtered new pedagogical tools from entering his classroom spaces. He explains this mindset as insisting on control in the classroom in the same way a traditional parent would, and that this mindset created a space in which teaching materials and topics are all geared with "Hong Kong student's mindset," meaning an ethnic Chinese, probably locally born student. Instead of seeing a deficit, he assumes EM students occupy a space in which they found materials and teaching styles unfamiliar to their experiences. He credits my approaches for "arousing interest" and "motivation" and "interests to learn." While he exhibits reflexivity about his teaching and about the materials used, Thomas still sees teaching as an act of getting students "aroused" in the interests set by the teacher, the textbook, or the syllabus, not the students' lives. Thus, he may need further reflection and theorizing about himself, his identity as a teacher, his classroom practices, and the purpose of education if he is to arrive at a reborn philosophy of education and new corresponding practices.

80 *Alienation, pain, and possibility*

In the final section of this chapter, I examine some of these practices to show that while students did become re-invested academically, my work was ultimately limited in its ability to generate empowerment with students, a situation not perceived by Thomas.

Constrained empowerment through generative themes

In the second term of the academic year, I led activities to supplement the official textbook curriculum taught by Thomas. For example, we surveyed print media to find examples of gender stereotypes and made collages for analysis, we looked at how transport vehicles are decorated in Hong Kong and other locations to express individual, group, or national identity, then colored buses to reflect our own national identities, and we learned about budgeting by reviewing my personal and wedding budgets. These activities began to convince Thomas that students could collaborate, do group and project work, and learn outside the textbooks and worksheets, as his reflections showed in Extract 4.14. The success of activities in engaging students also made me confident that students responded not just to scaffolding and clear instructions for writing and discussion but also to activities that allowed them to explore their identities. So I decided to test if the generative theme of aspirations and social mobility I uncovered would engage students by placing themes within tasks completed within Facebook and tasks that called for expression of identities as vehicles for engagement. While this unit would re-engage students academically and provide spaces for voice and expression, students were not empowered to a social critique or motivation for social justice that would facilitate transformative resistance. Still, from these experiences, I was able to form the foundation of the pedagogy I would create at ISS.

I created a unit titled, "Who I Am," borrowing their textbook's title, and required students to create a poster with images and writing after reviewing concept important terms for the year related to identity, studying the new concept of social mobility, researching tertiary opportunities in Hong Kong online, and learning to write structured responses that would prepare them for their final examination, as previously there had been no writing instruction in the class. In the course of the unit, students completed a team online scavenger hunt related to find tertiary options, completed critical thinking questions on a class Facebook page I created, had a class brainstorming and mind-mapping session on upward and downward social mobility, created concept maps and put together their posters. The unit culminated in the last two classes with chairs arranged without desks as a mini-theater, and students presenting their posters to the audience of classmates and teachers. Students shared their aspirations, desire for social mobility, and interests in cricket, football, manga, Bollywood, and also love of their families and friends.

Figure 4.1 is a sample of a student's poster, which exhibits the kinds of insights about students generated by this unit. We see their popular culture consumption, thoughts on language, their aspirations for social mobility and tertiary education, and challenges to traditional gender roles. The poster was created by a thirteen-year-old female of Nepali heritage, Julie, and features five sections

Alienation, pain, and possibility 81

Figure 4.1 "Who I Am" student poster.

on a bright pink background with bright yellow and gold lettering and accents, a contrast to the dull colors of the class. On the left is a small mind map of her puberty and includes some of her physical and psychological changes with her ways of coping. She cites "becoming emotional" and "thinking about relationships" as two psychological changes, and "crying," "shouting," and "seek help from adults" as ways she copes with puberty. Other students cited similar points, and it was also common to see changes such as "seek independence" or "enjoy thinking," the latter point challenging the earlier assertion by a teacher that EM students had "simple thinking." Below the mind map is a short paragraph about her aspirations, and she discusses her desire to be an "air hostess," wagering the job, "Can give me social mobility," a job she describes as requiring a multilingual repertoire: "First, we have to have better chinese, english, and we can also Mandarin," however NTS did not offer spoken Mandarin to EM students. On the right is a section where traditional gender roles are identified, which Julie challenges with her statement, "I disagree with Traditional Gender roles Because man can be kind and help women take care of Babys. And women can also be tough and work." Below this section she identifies two American female pop singers as her "idols," Taylor Swift and Miley Cyrus, which helps us see the global network of popular culture from which students draw.

Finally, in the middle of the poster is bus and paragraph representing her "nationalities," and this section illustrates students' previous trajectories of migration and the trajectories they imagine, bringing a sense of instability to some about where "home" is. Julie describes her bus as follows:

Extract 4.16 "I want to go back to Nepal"

I have made two flags. One is Nepal's and one is Hong Kong's. I like my Nepal flag soo much. And I want to go back to Nepal. After I finish my study I will work and earn money and go Nepal. I went to Nepal at march And I like Nepal so much Because it is so Peaceful and Beautiful.

{Julie, class assignment, May 31, 2011}

Julie's response was typical in that feelings of nationality tended to be tied up between one's birth of place, one's heritage country, and place where one had lived, which most often included the United Kingdom. She only makes mention of Hong Kong once, then mentions Nepal again six times, calling it "Peaceful and Beautiful," and after pursing further studies, she imagines returning to Nepal. As it turned out for Julie, she did leave Hong Kong, but not for Nepal. Instead, her family moved to the United Kingdom following the end of the school year.

Beyond this opportunity to learn by examining and sharing their identifications with their class, students re-engaged academically and performed their best as a class on the final examination, pointing to a link between identity engagement in the curriculum and increased academic achievement. In the first term examination, the average of Class 1A was 69%, and that average plummeted to 50% in the mid-term test as students became resistant to the class' monotonous pedagogy. In the final examination, which covered material from the whole year, and for which students received writing instruction by me, the average of class rose to 83%, leading Thomas to his positive assessments of the teaching techniques I used.

Yet the limit of empowerment came in an inability to help students develop a social critique and a motivation for social justice that would help them see the social and institutional barriers affecting more than individuals and take collective action. Indeed, there was no development of critical consciousness for this group, as is evident in Table 4.2, which contains several responses to a Facebook post. In the interaction on our class Facebook group, students responded to several questions after going on an online "scavenger hunt" on which they had to find information related to tertiary institutions in Hong Kong and read articles related to education for EM students in Hong Kong. One online article described the low number of EM students attaining tertiary access. After completing the scavenger hunt, students in Table 4.2 responded to the question, "What can we do to change that, so that more non-Chinese students can go to University?"

All students in the class responded, and all responses relied on the same narratives of individual effort present throughout the chapter. Faced with information of difficulties in tertiary attainment, the students of Class A expressed a conformist resistance free of social critique. None of these students expressed

Alienation, pain, and possibility 83

Table 4.2 Student responses to Facebook post

Student	Response
Student 1	i THINK THAT WE CAN ALSO BE LIKE OTHER TALENTED STUDENTS
Student 2	we non-chinese student should need work hard.
Student 3	they should work very hard to learn more chinese, they should watch chinese news, serial, they should read chinese books and listen to chinese music
Student 4	Non-Chinese Student should study more on the subjects that is hard for us such as [[Chinese]], It's the most hardest for most of us. So we should attend extra lessons or tuitions etc. We should pay more attention in class and study hard to get higher marks in the subjects we think it's hard!

an existing "hard-working" student identity, as did Qasim in Extract 4.1, but implored themselves and others to take on this identity. The first response, from a Pakistani heritage male is optimistic in stating, "i THINK THAT WE CAN ALSO BE LIKE OTHER TALENTED STUDENTS," implying the way to tertiary achievement is following an existing model of success of "talented students." The second response, coming from a male of Nepali heritage, reads, "We non-chinese student should need hard work," and that response is followed by another male of Nepali heritage, who writes, "they should work very hard to learn more chinese, they should watch chinese news, serial, they should read chinese books and listen to chinese music". Why the third student chooses the pronoun "they" rather than we is not clear (maybe he does not identify as a "non-Chinese student").

It may be true that hard work is necessary for achieving further educational opportunities, and the third response offers useful suggestions for learning Chinese, yet in light of the dilemmas defined in Chapter 1, students suggestions might lead to further reproduction of the statistics to which they are responding. The last response, from Julie, whose poster we examined, reasserts the dominant message that better supports in Chinese language studies should be the focus of support efforts for EM students, as she advocates for students to increase studying the difficult subject, and have extra lessons and tuition, and further conforming to existing pedagogies, as she tells our Facebook page, "We should pay more attention in class and study hard to get higher marks in the subjects we think it's hard.!". In the end, students reproduce existing discourses and do not implicate the school and its alienating practices.

After having me spend a year in their class, and studying in a unit under my lead, the students of Class 1A completed project work, collaborated, conducted guided research, and shared bits of their identifications. They were given voice in the class, expressed themselves creatively, yet were not empowered toward transformative resistance due to a lack of building up critique and solidarity to engage in change beyond what individual hard work could attain. As we can see in the extract, dialogue is limited, as students respond to the teacher's question, but do not enter into dialogue with each other around an issue affecting their future prospects and aspirations. The limited empowerment showed that greater empowerment could be possible with further commitment to students. But to do so, I would need greater space for a CP and new classroom discourses.

Summary

This chapter was an overview of my year of ethnographic work at NTS, where I uncovered generative themes such as education, love, conflict, identity, and social mobility, and vehicles for engagement including Bollywood movies, music, and Facebook. I had the opportunity to test these themes through the vehicle of Facebook and study of identity with Class A. While I was able to empower students to share their voices, empowerment was constrained by the inability to challenge the narrative of individual achievement circulated by students and teachers. Yet against a backdrop of alienating pedagogies, difficulties with academic English literacies, and teachers who showed concern with students, but stuck to problematic teaching, alternative pedagogies introduced by me re-engaged the class and significantly boosted examination scores.

Besides considering how to further empower students, my time at NTS left me with additional questions about teachers. I wondered, what might prevent teachers like Thomas from generating themes on their own? My process for arriving at generative themes was lengthy, time-consuming, and non-linear. I moved around constantly between online and physical observation, participation, reflecting, reading literature, experimentation, and trial and error in teaching. For me, it took a willingness to see culture beyond just costume, food, or obvious religious practices, but to also include popular culture. It took seeing identity beyond just simple nationality or dichotomous labels of NCS/local. It took seeing beyond the language skills, Chinese and English, students might lack, to seeing the language and literacy practices students do possess, rather than seeing them from labels that promote a deficit view of their knowledge and abilities. Could Christine see deeper into students' hearts if she viewed "Udaan" and saw her students' stories in the protagonist Rohan? And if teachers would commit to reading their students' worlds, could they find or create the space and resources, especially given the pressures of the Hong Kong Diploma in Secondary Education Examination (HKSDE), to reshape their classroom practices and build narratives of community rather than continue with discourse of the individual?

I had no answers to those questions, but by the time I left NTS, I was no longer the same person I described to open this chapter. Better tuned to my Hong Kong environment, and informed by a year of ethnographic fieldwork, I would take what I learned at NTS and apply it at ISS. I did not know it yet, but my CP was just getting started. I was headed to ISS, where my teaching, research, and personal commitment to the struggles of EM youth would evolve on the basis of a new discourse structure. These developments unfold in Chapter 5. And by the way, if you are curious, Qasim continued to work hard. Though his pubic examination scores were too low for university admission in Hong Kong, he was able to enroll in a Higher Diploma program and further his tertiary studies.

5 Curriculum at ISS
Setting the stage for resistance

In December 2012 at Industrial Secondary School (ISS), my form two students in Class A and I were nearing the end of a unit in which we examined emotional and social changes during puberty, cycles of oppression, and domestic abuse, while furthering our understanding of literary elements, poetry, and writing. Along with reading non-fiction articles related to our topics, we watched "Udaan," the Indian movie, students at New Territories School (NTS) recommended about a teen struggling with his aspirations in a family ruled by an abusive patriarch. One day, I read a local newspaper article titled "Jordan, home to a battling Nepali community" (Chiu 2012). The article, which I excerpted in this book's Prologue, was a fitting piece to for integrated Humanities and English class to analyze for connections to our studies, our lives, and to evaluate how media discourse represented a community familiar to us. After reading and discussing the article in class, students wrote responses they posted to our English and Humanities Facebook group and also to the Facebook page of the newspaper. Astha, a fourteen-year-old female of Nepali heritage responded as follows:

Extract 5.1 "Nepali teens should try to break the cycle"

> Well, I'm a Nepali Student too. I both agree and disagree with this article. I agree with this article because some people in our community do bad things. I see some Nepali teens smoke, drink and fight around the public parks. I'm curious, why do they often like to smoke, drink and fight? What will they get by doing that? Maybe, some of the Nepali people are doing those bad things because they might have conflicts between love, family and friends. Some of the Nepali students aren't having a good pedagogy. The reason why some of the Nepali teens want to quit the school is they think the way of teaching is boring. Some of the teens are having transmission pedagogy. They might feel offended and want to quit the school. They think life is boring. Parents should understand their children and also support them, so that the teens will stop avoiding those harmful things. In my guess, mostly teenagers are spoiling themselves by getting into love. They don't think about the future. Anyhow, some Nepali teens should try to break the cycle."
>
> {Astha, Facebook post, December 13, 2012}

86 *Setting the stage for resistance*

Extract 5.1 indexes much about the curriculum I developed within my critical pedagogy (CP) with students at ISS, and especially Class A, with whom I spent three consecutive years as an English teacher. It shows building of critical thinking and English language skills linked to discourses of community, awareness of education-related concepts, engagement with generative and academic themes, and access to online and academic spaces that amplified students' voices and expressions. Astha analyzes the article and takes a position identifying with the community described, agreeing with the acts attributed to Nepali teens in Jordan, such as smoking, drinking, and fighting, but going beyond the article's suggestion that Chinese language education is the key to solving these problems. Rather than rely on a narrative of individual responsibility and hard work, she cites conflicts around love, family, friends, and schooling that could be behind the problematic behaviors described in the article. She specifically implicates "transmission" pedagogies as a contributing factor and calls on Nepali teens to "break the cycle," a recognition that these conditions are not new, and an application of a theme we studied in our unit.

As the Facebook groups I had created for my students began to include teachers in and out of ISS, as well as various university researchers, collaborators in my pedagogy read students' posts and replied, valuing students' expressions while bringing new discourses to the conversation or repeating existing, and exhibiting here how my classroom curriculum linked students into a wider network of educators in and out of the school willing to share resources, discursive and otherwise, with students. Some of their responses are extracted in *Table 5.1*, and we see Lagan, the Deputy Director of the International Section, and Pragun, the science and math teacher, contribute to a discourse of "community," and adding their take on tone of the article, with Lagan seeing a "one-sided negative story" and Pragun highlighting that the article "is only mentioning negative side of the Nepalese community." Pragun also communicates his pedagogical orientation when he values education in which "students are facing the real world and using education to express their feelings." Dr. M, my collaborator and at this point a professor at the University of Hong Kong, praises the online pedagogical space, questions critiques of the story focusing on "true or false" in the narrative, introduces criticality as linked to story-telling, and then invites students to present at his university to teach pre- and in-service teachers "how real issues in society can be collaboratively incorporated in the classroom in a critical (and multimodal) way," thereby positioning students as teachers with valuable knowledge to share with adults.

How curriculum was enacted and embodied is the focus of this chapter. Curriculum is presented here as a negotiated organization of content, materials, activities, experiences, and networks, coupled with the building of safe pedagogical spaces (physical and online) and practices that engaged students in the investigation of generative themes and the building of academic skills. Through investigating curriculum related to generative themes of education, teen conflicts, and dehumanization, we will see how students gained vocabulary to name and critique the world, were invited to personal revelation, and connected to academic

Table 5.1 Adult comments on Facebook post

Writer	Comments
Lagan	I am very happy to read your comments, it is good step see expressing your feelings toward the community and yourself. Some the comments are very good, in some extent you have also agreed the news is true but is has covered only one-sided negative story but not positive.
Pragun	First of all, I am very happy to read comments from the students. I see this as a wonderful beginning where students are facing the real world and using education to express their feelings. Regarding the article from the newspaper, I believe information media is a powerful tool to report what is happening around us, however it also depends on how and what kind of news is conveyed. I agree with the reporter but as most of you have mentioned, all Nepalese in Jordan are not alike and the article is only mentioning the negative side of Nepalese community.
Dr. M	I have read all your comments and I am quite happy about the space that you have created to share emotions and critique on the topic of Nepali teenagers in HK. I believe social life is all about telling stories. When it comes to people and society, it is really difficult to say one thing is true or false; so to me being critical means asking ourselves what stories get told by whom, when, where and with what consequences for whom… I would like to invite you all to come to the university and reflect about this together with Mr. C. This is an invitation to all of you to teach my university students, who are or will be teachers in primary and secondary schools in Hong Kong. I need you to teach them how real issues in society can be collaboratively incorporated in the classroom in a critical (and multimodal) way. Would you like to take this challenge?

and topical themes wider than their immediate concerns. This curriculum, in negotiating both pre-determined academic aims and spaces allowing freedom, challenged dominant beliefs, practices, and forms of relation between and amongst people and knowledge within ISS, in attempts to empower students and bring them closer to transformative resistance. In Chapter 6, we will see more clearly how this curriculum set the stage for transformative resistance to emerge.

Before exploring samples of curriculum and student work, and the associated generative themes, I will explain how the generative themes and vehicles for engagement uncovered at NTS resonated at ISS, and then give a brief overview of my curriculum and the classroom culture that supported it. This will help to understand how the curriculum I introduced was in response to school life at ISS.

Life at Industrial Secondary School

When I started working at ISS in 2011, the ethnic minority (EM) students' population was similar to that of NTS, though smaller. EM students comprised about 15% of a total enrollment of about 400, but by the end of the 2013–2014 academic year, it had become about 40%. Students at ISS displayed dispositions, behaviors, and skills similar to what I saw at NTS. EM students at both schools enjoyed similar popular culture, engaged in multimodal online practices, and also showed evidence of self-harm. For example, nearly all students of Nepali and Pakistani heritage I taught in the first year had already seen the Bollywood movie "3 Idiots," which was also popular with many students at NTS. Likewise, many students at ISS were interested in football and cricket, or engaged in posting on multiple social media sites, including Facebook and YouTube. Online video games, rock music, rap music, emo imagery were also referenced online and offline. There was also a phenomenon at ISS of students posting images or making references to love and romance, need for freedom, and self-harming practices such as cutting. Finally, the range of proficiencies in English was also much like the range present at NTS. Some students read what might be considered age-appropriate English fiction for students whose primary language is English, while some read English at early elementary levels. Most students could interact socially in English with teachers, but lacked well-developed English academic literacy such as complex vocabulary, research skills, and ability to write genres such as essays, research reports, or even a simple cohesive paragraph.

As I learned about my new students at ISS, similarities between NTS and ISS beyond their institutional histories were evident (see Chapter 3). In everyday school life at ISS, I heard labeling talk from teachers referring to students' abilities and motivation. Through casual observation and speaking with students, I noticed that banking approaches I documented at NTS were also prevalent at ISS. Students shared that in most classes, they used a textbook, and the teachers expected them to sit quietly and copy from the board or a PowerPoint presentation. Hamida, a fifteen-year-old female in form two, and a top-ranked student, recalled her experiences studying at ISS in her form one year, before my arrival to the school.

Extract 5.2 "It was easy for us but there was nothing new…"

HAMIDA: I don't like last year class because there was mostly the students, there was newcomer student from Pakistan and there was, their English was really not good. And then we are good in English like our study was good but we need to go with them like their low level, but it was easy for us but there was nothing new to — I mean to catch up or to learn just nothing new. So it was not good, I don't like —

CARLOS: What kinds of things did you learn then in your English class?

HAMIDA: Just like past tense, present tense, future tense. Because the newcomer, even they don't know these kind of things also. So need to — we need to also do with them and so I don't like last year.

CARLOS: What kinds of things did you write in your English class?

HAMIDA: Like pen letters.

CARLOS: Yeah, yeah.

HAMIDA: Pen letter to friend and some writing we write like you know, the sentence are wrong, we need to rewrite it, just that kind of sentence.

{Hamida, interview, June 20, 2012}

In Extract 5.2, Hamida recollects tensions she attributes to the diversity of English proficiencies in her class, from students who are newcomers to Hong Kong and lack basic grammar to students like her who are "good in English," according to her own standard. She expresses a contradiction, "Our study was good," while also expressing dissatisfaction with the level of proficiency at which the class was pitched (a "low level") as well as the type and range of texts produced in the class, and generally feels the year did not help her gain new skills. She surmises she learned "nothing new" and concludes that her study was "not good." When I ask her what she learned, she focuses on specific grammar items, such as tenses. Though the ISS promotional brochure that was circulated to recruit students for the 2011–2012 academic year said that through the English subject students would "become skilled readers, build abundant vocabulary and write a variety of genres including poetry, letters, journals, and short stories," this was not consistent with the experience Hamida shared in the first year of the school's International Section catering to EM students.

In the same promotional brochure, the Liberal Studies (LS) subject was described as based on modules that were "selected for the curriculum focusing on themes of significance to students, our society and the world." In Extract 5.2, Hamida shares her experience in LS Extract 5.3:

Extract 5.3 "It was all about Hong Kong."

CARLOS: What did you guys study in Liberal Studies last year?

HAMIDA: There was just like entrepôt and it was just similar to History, you know. And the teacher like — it was so funny. It was like no one is listening to him and he was like cannot control the class properly. It was just like, I think because of the kid. Just like that. He just also left and it was not so — it was so easy. It's just like entrepôt and then —

CARLOS: Hong Kong as an entrepôt, that kind of thing?

HAMIDA: — also Hong Kong entrepôt country, just this kind of thing. It was all about Hong Kong. So I think it's just as similar as History. Just that.

{Hamida, interview, June 20, 2012}

In Extract 5.3, Hamida begins by talking about the concept of Hong Kong's history as an "entrepôt," a free port for trade. Then she turns to remembering the teacher and laughs. Instead of elaborating on her learning in the subject, she describes interactions and classroom dynamics, recalling, "No one is listening" to the teacher who could not "control the class properly." She alludes to the teacher leaving his position at the school and concludes by reasserting that LS focused on the idea of an "entrepôt," and that ultimately LS was "all about Hong Kong" and similar to what she studied in the history subject.

Hamida felt discouraged by the limited range of the content. For her rather than focusing on themes of significance to students, the content was akin to that covered in her history subject, and was limited in its focus on Hong Kong and its economic development. I would observe the focus on entrepôt again in my first year at the school, as students in form one would cover it not only in their history class but also the business subject. A narrative was presented of Hong Kong being transformed from a fishing village, to entrepôt, to a global financial center, one that did not include in its account the presence or contributions of members of South Asian communities, missing the opportunity to connect the students' own histories to Hong Kong's economic as well as social development.

In Hamida, we see a student interested in learning new knowledge and skills, but confronted with curriculum in two core subjects insufficient to meet her desires. The perceived lack of a challenging and engaging curriculum made Hamida consider a change of schools, but she stayed at ISS, after hearing the 2011–2012 year would bring changes. She recounted, "Actually, I was planning to change my school this year but I did not. I feel like—I think—first, I have to see. They said they will be having a big change and I said, okay, I will see first." In this statement, Hamida evokes a mix of hope that the curriculum would change, along with skepticism that it would actually happen. In the end, while Pragun, Lagan, Tad, Jane, and I introduced practices students found favorable, the dominant practices at the school remain unchanged. In a presentation she delivered at two local universities in 2013 and 2014, Pramiti, a female of Nepali heritage from Class A, summarized the most common practices she encountered over three years at ISS in a slide titled "The Pedagogical Sequence," presented in Extract 5.4.

Extract 5.4 The Pedagogical Sequence

At the beginning of the unit, teacher tells us the name of chapter in the book.
During the unit the teacher starts to read from the book.
We read along with the teacher.
Raise hand when we need definition or example.
We are given fill in the blanks worksheet or exercises in the workbook.
We are given an essay to memorize for exams.
A paper exam.

{Pramiti, presentation slide, March 18, 2014}

Like at NTS, the existing school curriculum at ISS did not appear set up for critical exploration of students' generative themes and conditions of their lives. Consequently, I decided to extend my research project to include my curriculum development at ISS. The next section will briefly summarize that curriculum and the culture that supported it.

The curriculum: multimodality, rigor, and community

In materializing my CP, I wanted to construct a challenging and rigorous multimodal curriculum that engaged students at their levels of English proficiency

Setting the stage for resistance 91

and had a focus on guiding students in understanding and addressing conflicts in their lives and communities, preparing to address conflicts in the present while simulating how they might handle conflicts in the future. Based on my experience at NTS, I knew I needed to build English academic literacy in students and expose them to reading, writing, and speaking a wide variety of text genres. Concomitant to building academic literacy was a curriculum of talk that developed students' abilities to engage in meaning English interaction that facilitated knowledge building and study in generative, academic, and topical themes (Pérez-Milans and Soto 2014).

These goals were made possible by building classroom cultures and communities which valued communication, appreciation, community, and cooperation. To this end, I developed a set of values called "The Four Cs" which were discussed with students and reinforced by collaborators, throughout my years at ISS, inclusive of the class studying my curriculum taught by Tad. The Four Cs were composed of "Communication," "Cooperation," "Conflict," and "Community," and I explained to students that communication and cooperation were necessary to avoid conflict, deal with conflict, and learn from it, and that through communication, cooperation, and solving conflicts, we could build strong communities. The Four Cs were supplemented by involving students in decision-making and planning, and their input was used in developing curriculum and choosing texts. In fact, some of the most powerful texts used in my CP came from students' recommendations.

Table 5.2 provides an overview of a three-year junior secondary curriculum taught to Class A. The curriculum is an English language curriculum with elements of the Personal Social and Humanities Education Key Learning Area integrated into it. The table includes curricular units, main texts, additional literacy activities, and external connections with the curriculum, referring to outsiders who visited my classes or visits we made to the outside. It is by no means inclusive of all the texts used for study, nor activities in and out of school in which students became involved; I mean to merely provide a snap shot of life in the curriculum. For easier reading, the numbers of the items in the "Curricular Units" in the left column correspond to the numbers of the items in the "Texts Read or Viewed" column, so that if you look at the year 2011–2012, the number four unit, "Multiple Intelligences" is connected to the texts "Taare Zameen Par," a Bollywood movie, "Flowers for Algernon," a short story, and "Non-fiction reading on multiple intelligences." The table also has marked texts that were read in abridged forms, as is the case with the book "Diary of Anne Frank," "Of Mice and Men," and "1984." Because the reading proficiencies were greatly varied, abridged versions suited most of the class, while some students read portions or all of the originals.

The table shows great variety in materials used and activities. It includes texts from varied cultural contexts, and a mix of fiction and non-fiction, though there is shift toward canonical English language literature texts in the form three year. The third column, "Additional Literacy Activities" refers to learning activities and tasks outside of the main curriculum in which students engaged throughout

Table 5.2 Class A three-year curriculum

		Curriculum Units		Texts Read or Viewed	Additional Literacy Work	External Connections
2011–2012 Form 1	1	Education	1	"3 Idiots" film	– Brainstorming	– Visiting my PGDE classes at HKU
	2	Teen Conflicts	2a	"True Life: I'm Clashing with my Parents" tv feature	– Asking questions	– Ethnographic work in classroom by Dr. M
	3	Elections	2b	Non-fiction readings related to "puppy love" and family conflicts	– Agreeing/disagreeing	– Visits by university students to observe
	4	Multiple Intelligences	2c	"7th grade" short story	– Vocabulary to describe emotions	– Visit by students & professors from San Francisco State University
			3a	"Please Vote for Me" documentary	– Writing to Pen pals in the United States	
			3b	Non-fiction readings related to China		
			4a	"Taare Zameen Par" movie		
			4b	"Flowers for Algernon" short story		
			4c	Non-fiction reading on multiple intelligences		
2012–2013 Form 2	1	Cultures	1a	"Koran by Heart" documentary	– Thinking stems	– Presentations at two local universities
	2	Food equity	1b	Non-fiction book, "Birth Across Cultures"	– Think alouds	– Visits by UK, Hong Kong, and Australia professors
	3	Social & emotional changes of puberty	1c	"Spellbound" documentary	– Using a dictionary and thesaurus	– Presentations for Dr. M's classes
	4	Coming to cities, capital, & perseverance	2	Non-fiction text related to food issues	– Personal dictionaries	– Visit by children's author
	5	Love and development	3a	"Udaan" movie	– Blogging	
			3b	Non-fiction texts related to puberty	– "Song of the Week" presentations	
			3c	"Diary of Anne Frank" (abridged)	– Learning word roots	
			4a	"English Vinglish" movie	– Reading & discussing local newspaper	
			4b	Examples of film synopsis writing		
			4c	"Coming to the City" documentary		
				Non-fiction texts and webpages related to birthing issues		
2013–2014 Form 3	1	Paragraph writing		"The Diary of Anne Frank" book	– Newspaper reading skills	– Visit by American novelist
	2	Discussing literature	2	"Of Mice and Men" novel by John Steinbeck (abridged)	– "Literature Circles" reading program	– Visit by US Consulate to discuss elections
	3	Making decisions	3	Romeo and Juliet" by William Shakespeare (abridged and original text)	– Word roots	– Visit by Holocaust survivor
	4	Dehumanization & needs	4a	"1984" by George Orwell (abridged and original)	– Illustrated vocabulary cards	– Conflict Resolution Day Camp
			4b	Non-fiction readings related to World War II	– Reading & discussing local newspaper	– Visit by Muslim Mufti
					– Illustrating idioms	– Visit by documentary producer of "Girls Rising"
						– Presentations at Dr. M's university class

the year. Of note here are activities to develop meta-cognitive skills like "Think alouds," special tactile activities that developed students' abilities to speak their trains of thought in English and use of thinking stems to respond to texts online and in class. Additionally, students spent the form two and three years involved working through literacy programs called "The Daily Five" (Boushey and Moser 2006) and "Literature Circles," (Day 2002), respectively. The Daily Five built students' capacities in independent reading and comprehension, while Literature Circles developed their capacities to discuss texts in a small group setting. The last column, "External Connections" indicates the network of educators and other adults that came into contact with my students, often due to the work of Jane, Lagan, Pragun, and Tad. This column includes the university researchers who visited my classes, authors, and dignitaries who came to give talks and interact with students. It also includes some of the trips class members made to universities to give talks and participate in activities. These activities extended English learning by bringing different speakers and providing different venues in which students could speak.

I organized the curriculum around the study of units guided by questions, texts, experiences, productions, and learning. I gave these the prefix "Key" to indicate to myself, and others with whom the curriculum might be shared, that there were more questions, texts, experiences, and productions that could become part of the unit, but that those termed "Key" would serve as the focus of study, as decided by me. This organizational structure would be used for planning units for the three years I taught junior secondary. In Table 5.3, we can see how a unit taught in fall 2011 on the theme of education focused on questions, "What is education? How do we learn? What kind of conflicts do we face" among others. The key text in this unit was the film "3 Idiots," and as part of this unit, students would experience performing a song they wrote. In all units, students produced a wide variety of texts, and this unit descriptive paragraphs, song lyrics, captioned illustrations were included and integrated specific grammar items such as use of present tense.

It is important to note though that my CP had to be made and re-made each year, as I responded to new classroom conditions and generative themes that

Table 5.3 Teaching unit outline

Unit 1: Education (Fall 2011)

Key questions	What is education? How do we learn? What kind of conflicts do we face in education? What kind of education do you want?
Key texts	"3 Idiots" film
Key experiences	Performing a song for the morning assembly
Key productions	Character and conflict description and comparison paragraphs, song lyrics written as class, illustrated movie scene with caption, plot diagram room display
Key learning	Vocabulary to describe characters, vocabulary related to story plot, writing in present tense, descriptive and simple argumentative writing

emerged. Some of these changing conditions, which required maintaining an ethnographic sensitivity, flexibility, and listening to students and how they expressed their needs, will be discussed in Chapter 6. Extract 5.5 comes from a lesson with Class A in 2012. We were studying a unit on elections centered on a documentary, "Please Vote for Me," about an election from class monitor in a primary three class room in China. In the unit, we also studied the Hong Kong Chief Executive election that was happening and held our own election for class monitor. In this extract, I am preparing students to listen to speeches from our three candidates:

Extract 5.5 "I really want you to open up your mind"

When I talk about listening, I really want you to open up your mind and open up your heart... When we're learning about the elections, it's not just about learning about society. You guys need to think about what kind of leaders you want for your communities...What kind of leaders you guys want to be in the community, in Hong Kong, in your family, in your classroom.

{Mr. C (researcher), classroom recording, February 16, 2012}

I positioned listening as a responsibility involving intellectual, affective, and political dimensions. In other words, besides listening as a technique and an examination skill, listening was about openly thinking and feeling in order to come to decisions affecting a community, in this case the decision being whom to elect as leader. In listening to speeches, I wanted to prepare students for the act in the present of electing a class monitor, and future acts of selecting and being leaders in communities, Hong Kong, one's family, and the classroom.

In teaching this unit the following year, I added a "simulation" element that would engage students in practicing organizing to seek change. At this time in Hong Kong, a social movement for universal suffrage was growing, so we kept up with the news on this topic, and also studied when and how women around the world gained the right to vote. We learned about the women's suffrage movement in the United States, viewing protest posters and reading about the arguments used to justify granting the right to vote exclusively to men. The simulation element of this unit involved telling the students in Class D that only males would be allowed to vote, and justifying it with them same claims used in the past to deny women this right. I told the female students they would have to fight for this right if they wanted it, and eventually they organized a demonstration with signs during the International Section's weekly morning assembly, and together read out the poem in Extract 5.6, written by a thirteen year old of Nepali heritage, Lina, who will meet again later in the chapter. The poem alerts the audience the group is ready to "fight" for the right to vote and addresses the students' "community" in challenging stereotypes used to justify the injustice I set up. Simulations like this one, in which students practiced organizing against an injustice manufactured by me, as a spectacle to be played out by students, was a key element of my curriculum.

Extract 5.6 "Protest Poem"

> Girls should have suffrage,
> Girls should have rights,
> You told us that we couldn't vote,
> So now we're gonna fight.
> A leader we choose,
> For our Form 1
> We should also get to vote,
> Cuz we're a community.
> You said girls are emotional,
> And we admit it too,
> We are going through puberty,
> So boys get emotional too.
> You've listed lots of bad things 'bout girls,
> but what about the boys?
> They aren't very serious,
> but instead they're full of joy.
> Boys get angry easily,
> And they usually start the fights,
> Look at girls on the other hand,
> We mostly try to do what's right.

{Lina, April 2013}

This curriculum presented here, as materials, activities, texts, relations, and discourses, became internalized by many students. They could reflect on it, write about it and discuss it, and share it with others. An example of this is letters I had students write in June 2013. I was not yet offered a contract to teach at the school the following year, so I assigned students to write a personal letter to whomever might be my students in the next academic year, whether at ISS or elsewhere. Like other assignments, multiple purposes were served. I could glimpse students' ability to write a personal letter and the tone and vocabulary used, I could see how they viewed my teaching, and they could reflect on their learning and my teaching, giving me valuable insights. The following Extract 5.7 comes from the letter written by Vishal, a twelve-year-old male of Nepali heritage in Class D who was often in trouble with other teachers and reveals his attitudes toward my teaching.

Extract 5.7 "You will enter a world full of unknown words"

I am going to tell you something you need to know about Mr. C. Mr C can be a little manipulative (search it up!)...He can also become very enraged. When we don't clean up our classroom or when we're disrespecting others, you don't even want to know what's gonna happen. Once when I disrespected a student by teasing him, I got severely punished. In Mr. C's you will have to do a lot of writing and reading. You will enter a world full of unknown words and stories in Mr. C's class. You will get to learn from variety of movie and stories. Well in the beginning of the school I felt worried that English would be hard. I thought we would use textbooks and sit and study like most of the schools would do. In the beginning you may also feel like that but don't worry we seniors and teacher will help you.

{Vishal, class assignment, June 21, 2013}

Vishal's letter takes on a playful tone, even telling the reader to search the word, "manipulative," a word I taught the class in our unit on elections, and mocking my behavior by also mentioning that I could become "enraged" in the class using another word we reviewed as a class (though it is also true I did at times express anger to the class). He describes studying in my class as entering a "world of unknown words and stories," which could be a sarcastic remark, or it could be his take on a class that stimulates him though language and story-telling. Vishal is aware that our class challenges the norm, as he, like other students, was used to banking style pedagogies. The extract finishes with a sense he is part of a larger community of students that looks out for each other, telling my future students that seniors and teachers will help them, and giving an overall impression of me as a strict, and maybe sometimes dictatorial, yet caring teacher.

Now from this general overview, we move into looking at specific moments of curriculum that reveal the ways in which students were empowered and moved toward transformative resistance.

Critiquing school via Bollywood films

While conducting fieldwork at NTS, I decided that the Bollywood movie, "3 Idiots," (Hirani 2009) about three friends meeting at an engineering college and helping each other through personal conflicts while challenging the school's banking pedagogy, would be an appropriate vehicle for engaging students in the generative theme of education, and help them understand what philosophies and models of education existed, so they could figure out what education they each wanted for themselves and their communities, and know that alternatives existed. It was also important for them to consider the role education played in reproducing existing conditions in their communities or changing them. In my teaching of form one classes, "3 Idiots" played a prominent role in accomplishing these tasks while also facilitating building of English skills. Along with "3 Idiots," the Bollywood movie "Taare Zameen Par" (Khan 2007) was used in form one to introduce students to a theory of multiple intelligences (Gardner 2006) that could counter discourses of ability and motivation which defined only some students as able and "talented" as we saw students do at NTS. In this section, we will see how students took on a critique of education and applied it in classroom tasks through our study of "3 Idiots."

In our study of education, students were engaged in brainstorming on questions related to education and introduced to three models of teaching and learning: transmission, generative, transformative. Transmission refers to banking models of education in which learning is a one-way transmission of information from textbook, to teacher, to students; a generative model of education consists of methods in which students and teachers co-construct knowledge; and a transformative pedagogy refers to models of education predicated on creating change in a community. A student worksheet pack asked students to identify features of each pedagogical model based on an image. The worksheets also included sections related to descriptive vocabulary for characters, comprehension questions about conflicts in the story of "3 Idiots" (Hirani 2009), and more important for the theme of education, a table in which students sorted statements related to educational views of the protagonist and antagonist, placing statements under "Rancho" or "Virus," otherwise known as Dr. Viru, the director of the college. The statements students sorted are listed in Extract 5.8, and are inspired by, and in some instances paraphrased from Freire's analysis (2004, p. 73) of banking models of education, in some cases para and brought students' awareness to the practices they encountered daily by having them first attach these practices to fictional characters.

Extract 5.8 Worksheet statements on education

Only read/learn from one kind of book
The teacher knows, the students don't know
The teacher should talk, the students should listen
Cooperation is more important
Learning only happens in the classroom
Education is for money and fame
Learning can happen anywhere
The teacher decides what will be learned, not the students
Students learn so they can change the world
Teacher listens to the students about what they want to learn
Competition is more important
Education is food for our hearts
Teachers are students and students are teachers
Learn not only from books, but from anything in the world
Teachers and students should communicate
Students learn to pass an exam

The teacher is in charge
Everyone is a teacher and a student

{Class document, September 21, 2012}

The statements in Extract 5.8 relate to materials used within pedagogies, the locations of learning, control of pedagogical decisions, and the purpose of education. Statements like "Learning can happen anywhere," "Teachers and students should communicate," and "Students learn so they can change the world" were attributed to "Rancho," while converse statements such as "Learning only happens in the classroom," "The teacher should talk, the students should listen," and "Students learn to pass an exam" were attributed to Virus. However, "The teacher is in charge" was attributed to both. Students then applied learning of models of pedagogy to classrooms tasks, and two examples will be provided here that reveal the multimodality of the curriculum, the skills learned by students, and the spaces created for student voice and expression.

Extract 5.9 includes song lyrics created by students in Class D as part of an assignment. In groups, students had to create a verse for a song that described events of different portions of the plot, including the exposition, rising action, climax, falling action, and resolution, and also had to create a chorus for the song. The exercise was meant to reinforce understanding of plot elements, which was new to students, and require students to practice simple tense, as they would need it to write about literature. In the end we put the song, with a student leading on guitar, to the tune of a song featured in the movie, and performed it on three occasions: once for students of the International Section, a second time for EM parents and family members during a school open-day activity, and a third time for the whole school during an assembly in which Class D shared learning in the unit in an English-Cantonese bilingual, fifteen minute presentation.

Extract 5.9 "3 Idiots" song lyrics

Farhan gets a flashback
Raju likes to pray
The teacher teases Rancho
And Virus drops an egg

Raju gets drunk
Farhan and Raju fail
Rancho falls for Pia
Joy's life ends

Don't be so frightened
Say all is well

No spoon-fed education
Let pressure take a rest

{Class D, performance video recording, November 23, 2012}

The first and second verses summarize the plot's exposition and rising action, with the second verse listing conflicts experienced by characters, including a suicide by a minor character, Joy. The third verse is the chorus and references advice from Rancho to other characters to say, "All is well," when faced with a difficulty, while also stating the character's position against "spoon-fed" (transmission) education and overwhelming pressure placed on students. From these classroom assignments, students began to internalize vocabulary related to education and moved onto critiques of their educational experiences. Extract 5.10 features writing from two male form two Class A students of Nepali heritage, thirteen-year-old Prem and fourteen-year-old Sandesh. This text was written for presentation delivered in front of EM students of the International Section at the school. It is representative of the critique and connection to concepts students in junior secondary exhibited, and how they acquired vocabulary that allowed them to name the practices around them, thereby making informed transformative resistance more likely.

Extract 5.10 "In transmission pedagogy many students fail"

Transmission Pedagogy is a way of teaching where the teachers talk and the students listen. The teachers who want to use Transmission Pedagogy want the students to be like parrots. They usually want to use books to teach students because it saves them time and they don't need to think. Teachers just give students questions and later on the answers. The teachers don't want the students to ask questions because they think it will slow the whole class down. Once I had a teacher who used this technique when I was in primary. He always talked and we had to listen and do what he had said. He never wanted us to ask questions because he thought that if only one person asked questions they could slow the whole class down. The teacher only wanted to students to get high numbers in exams. In transmission pedagogy many students fail because they can't ask questions and can't communicate with each other or with their teachers.

{Prem, Class A, video recording, November 30, 2012}

In the presentation, Prem and Sandesh defined and illustrated, through personal examples, the three models of pedagogy we studied for an audience of their peers. Additionally, they showed video examples of each type of pedagogy at work in our classes, describing the purpose of each pedagogy. In Extract 5.9, Prem describes "transmission pedagogy" using terms and ideas circulated during our studies, such as the description, "the teachers talk and students listen." He supplements this description with his own experiences, including a common complaint by students, "The teachers don't want the students to ask questions because they think it will slow the whole class down" and the complaint that some teachers focused their teaching on exam-based activities. He sums up transmission pedagogy as responsible for students' failure, due to its constraints on questioning and communication

100 *Setting the stage for resistance*

between students. Sandesh concurred with Prem to take on transmission pedagogy, and later offered a description of transformative pedagogy, found in Extract 5.11.

Extract 5.11 "We learn to change our selves"

At last, Transformative Pedagogy is very creative pedagogy because it is a lot different from other two pedagogies. In this pedagogy we learn to change our selves and change the community and the society. We learn in a very different way than other pedagogies. In this kind of class, we don't get bored or don't understand. This pedagogy changes our thought for the world. In place of only reading others' ideas or only reading books, it helps to think of our own ideas. After moving to Honk Kong I study in ISS and I learned a way different style because I used to study Transmission Pedagogy and now I study in Generative Pedagogy, and sometimes Transformative. Nowadays I always attend all the classes. It's not boring any more. I know the different pedagogies.

{Sandesh, Class A, video recording November 30, 2012}

While transmission pedagogy was presented as limiting communication, transformative pedagogy was presented in a positive light and a vehicle for personal and social change. While the statement, "In this kind of class we don't get bored or don't understand," could be an overstatement it is important to take Sandesh's statement seriously that he saw a transformative pedagogy as way to change "ourselves and change the community and the society." Sandesh connects the pedagogical models he learned with the transmission pedagogy he faced in Nepal, and admits that whereas before he would skip classes, the presence of generative pedagogy increased his interest in attending classes as he could be in an environment where students were allowed to "think of our own ideas."

Despite Sandesh's claims of avoiding boredom through pedagogy, commitment to my CP required negotiation and re-investment from both teachers and students. As part of the curriculum, I asked questions such as, "What kind of education do you want? What kind of pedagogies will help you learn best? How can we work individually and as a community in pursuit of our education? What prevents you from learning? What do you want to do with your education? What do you expect from your teacher, yourself, and each other?" as a way to give students voice in the direction of my pedagogy. There were times though, when the question, "Do you want to continue with this pedagogy," became of upmost importance, and sometimes I asked myself this question.

For three years, I was only a part-time teacher at ISS, with additional part-time jobs to supplement my income, but I felt like I was working full-time hours for ISS due to the time I spent developing curriculum materials at home. Despite having collaborators at the school, getting support for our educational initiatives was stressful in a school where administrators and other teachers questioned our practices, even as failure in school-based assessments and public exams in the school was the norm, and this affected my sense of commitment to students. I felt frustrated and fretted that too much of my personal time with my family was being taken to do work in the school that was not recognized, but contested, usually with the refrain of not preparing students for public exams.

In moments when I felt defeated that Class A and Class D were not giving their full effort to the academic rigor I required of them, I shared my feelings, and we had to negotiate whether or not to continue with our CP, or if I should switch to a textbook-based pedagogy matching other English classes in the school, thereby saving me stress. On two occasions, once with Class A, and once with Class D, I switched to a transmission textbook pedagogy as an experiment to see if students would speak up for our previous practices, recommit to my pedagogy, and in the process learn to stand up as a class community for their needs. I made photocopies of books used by other teachers and distributed them to students. We worked from these copied textbooks for two weeks, and I moved the desks back to their original configuration of rows facing the front. The demeanor of the class changed during the two weeks. Students sat silently during this time and only spoke when called on. It was difficult for me to carry on in this way. It did not seem like an effective and engaging way to learn, but I wanted to hold on until students stood up for change. Eventually students did, after a female student of Nepali heritage, raised her hand to speak up, and the rest of the class agreed they wanted to recommit to work for a transformative pedagogy, an incident Dr. M and I described in a publication (Pérez-Milans and Soto 2014).

Even as students recommitted to rigorous work, conflicts would arise again, but I tried to re-frame these conflicts into opportunities to understand students' struggles. In November 2013, I asked students in Class A and Class D to address a letter to me explaining why they were not completing all assigned homework for my class. Admittedly, I realize now students had a strenuous work-load for my class, but I justified it to myself at the time as necessary for building their academic skills if they were to have any chance for advancement to tertiary. Nevertheless, in these letters, students talked about feeling lazy, depressed, or distracted by the internet, and they also shared personal conflicts, as seen in Extract 5.11, a letter written by Tripti, a fifteen-year-old Nepali heritage female in class A who was very quiet in class, and had difficulty speaking with me face-to-face, but told me about herself through writing assignments.

Extract 5.12 "I have to clean the house"

> I didn't do my homework because my computer don't work. I could have done it after school in the library but I had to go home and do household [chores] then I had to study for the test then I forgot about the homework...I can't do homework after school because I will be late to go home and I have to clean the house tidy the rooms, I have to ready the food before 8pm then throw the garbage, prepare the rice for next day, then study or homework.
>
> {Tripti, class assignment, November 1, 2013}

In Extract 5.12, Tripti imparts to me her gender-based household duties, an issue I would later discuss with her father. Tripti's father was committed to her education, but for him it was also important for Tripti to contribute to the household, as both parents worked. Therefore, we see Tripti has cooking and cleaning to do before she can get to her academic duties. Additionally, there may be class dimensions present in this extract. It is prevalent in middle-class homes in Hong Kong to employ a domestic worker, thereby freeing family members to other pursuits. But without access to this luxury, Tripti had to negotiate competing academically with other students in Hong Kong while helping to meet her family's domestic needs.

Thus, studying the generative theme of education did not mean students were free of conflict with education in my classes. Perhaps they were burdened with new educational conflicts. However, the curriculum we negotiated, and culture of communication and solving conflicts provided opportunities for students to be honest and share their concerns. By disclosing to students my feelings of conflict around implementing an academically rigorous CP, they mirrored me and shared theirs. This theme of self-revelation in the curriculum, and its connection to the development of academic skills, will be further explored in the next section.

Self-revelation in interrogating conflicts

"3 Idiots" (Hirani 2009) helped us study more than just the generative theme of education, it was also a way to learn to talk about conflicts. Through studying this movie, as well as other films and printed stories, students had to identify conflicts, why they were happening, and how they might be solved. In this section, I will illustrate how students delved into studying conflicts by identifying themselves in characters, using philosophy to rethink their beliefs, and through invitations for self-revelation put forth by me and the curriculum. The emotional and social conflicts I saw students face at NTS were likewise present at ISS, and here I show how I helped students think through them, through analysis of representative pieces of student writing. In this section, films originating from Bollywood and Nepal will play a role, as will my personal revelations and stories that connected to generative themes.

The Bollywood film "Udaan" (Motwane 2010) became central to our study of social and emotional conflicts during puberty. Its main character, Rohan, moves back home after being expelled from boarding school to live with his father who he had not seen in eight years. Upon his return home, he learns he has a seven-year-old half-brother he never knew about, and deals with conflicts as his abusive father worries and drinks, in part due to financial pressures during a recession, and restricts him from pursuing his desire to be a writer. Rohan exhibits social and emotional changes and difficulties, and to cope, he either writes or finds peers with whom to drink, smoke, and fight. His narrative arc in the film afforded an opportunity to introduce new generative themes into our study: cycles of oppression and discontinuity. To deal with his conflicts, Rohan must also understand how his life has been affected by discontinuity, in other words, the sudden stoppage, reversal, or change in relationships, beliefs and other conditions of life. In addition to being affected by discontinuity, we learn there is an intergenerational cycle of abuse in Rohan's family, and in the movie's resolution, he must find a way to break the cycle of oppression he is facing by resorting to discontinuity as a tool for freedom.

I shared with the class the ways in which I faced these themes through intergenerational domestic violence in my family, and through discontinuities in my life. Extract 5.13 is a text I shared with Class A and D as a model for a paragraph on the theme of discontinuity.

Extract 5.13 "I have had several discontinuities"

> In my life, I have had several discontinuities. At age seven, I moved to a new country, from Honduras to the USA. In the USA, I changed schools five times. At age thirteen, my father stopped communicating with our family for eight years. These discontinuities made me feel insecure, depressed, angry, and made it hard from to trust others. I coped in several ways. In an unhealthy way, I became very private and took drugs to escape life. But I also coped by reading and becoming very interested in music. These discontinuities were difficult, but I was resilient.
>
> {Teaching Notebook, October 12, 2012}

In the extract, I relate some of the difficult moments in my life which I revealed to students. I share my family's migration, my change of schools, and the feelings of insecurity, depression, and anger that were partly responsible for me using drugs beginning in secondary school. By forms two and three, many of the students in the classes I taught were dealing with similar conflicts and adopted harmful coping mechanisms, including self-harm, drugs and alcohol, and retreating into online worlds, so it was important to discuss coping mechanisms in order to arrive at more constructive ways of dealing with difficulties. Extract 5.13 is a model of what I thought appropriate sharing in the class could be, and students could modify what they wanted to explore in their own lives, holding back or giving more, relative to my models.

Extract 5.14 shows a form three students' reflection and self-revelation within this unit. Because the protagonist in "Udaan" is a writer, the film features his poems and stories, which we used for academic study of literature and poetic devices. In Class D, we tied our viewing of the movie and reading of non-fiction texts related to emotional and social changes during puberty to producing what I called a "Personal Puberty Parable," a personal narrative, featuring use of figurative language, imagery, and idioms, that told a personal story of a moment of learning during puberty. Students wrote personal accounts, making thorough use of required dictionaries and thesauruses, that ranged from the hilarious, to the earnest, as is the case with the following extracts taken from the personal narrative written by Lina, a fourteen year old of Nepali heritage in Class D, a top student in her form, but also someone whose struggle with self-confidence contributed to her self-harm practices.

Extract 5.14 "Puberty is a nightmare"

> Puberty is a nightmare most teenagers try to keep under their hat. To some people, it's embarrassing to discuss or share with others, even with your family and close friends. It's a time when your thinking changes and you might feel bulletproof. You may feel self-conscious about yourself and there's not much you can about it. You could also get emotional changes when you're in puberty. For example mood swings. Let me tell you about how my mood swings were in form two.
>
> {Lina, class assignment, October 20, 2014}

Extract 5.14 is the opening to Lina's narrative, which invites the reader into her revelations about puberty, and at the same time fulfills the assigned academic tasks by using an idiom, "keeping something under a hat," and incorporating changes in puberty noted in our non-fiction readings, such as feeling bulletproof or feeling self-conscious. She shifts to a personal tone by introducing the personal topic of her mood swings. The narrative continues describing a typical day at school through hyperboles, one of the available forms of figurative language students were expected to use, during which her mood changed "a million times a day" because of "countless disputes with my friends." Extract 5.15 picks up the narrative to describe Lina's feelings during this time.

Extract 5.15 "Those days were awful"

> I remember my friend and I avoiding each other like the plague for months over a foolish issue. Those days were awful. I didn't want to smile because I thought I had no reason to. I was not communicating to the people I was closest with and it made things painful. I didn't tell anyone about it. To hide my feelings I pretended like nothing was wrong, and I wrote about how I felt instead.
>
> {Lina, class assignment, October 20, 2014}

Here, Lina shares some of the pain she did not share with those closet to her, including with me, her teacher. She writes, "I didn't smile because I thought I had no reason to," and shares the pain she felt by cutting off communication with others. Earlier, she hid her feelings, in this portion of the narrative, she reveals them. It is evident in this narrative that a discontinuity in personal relationships became a site of internal struggle for Lina. Before arriving at the conclusion and parable of her narrative, Lina took an interesting turn by telling another story of finding several old poems she wrote and kept secret buried in a drawer. She provides the poem within her text, seen in Extract 5.16.

Extract 5.16 "If I die, Would people miss me?"

If I die,
Would people miss me?
Would they cry,
or would they smile?
Would they think of me,
every single night,
or would they just, say goodbye?
Would they remember
every little thing about me,
or would they
just forget?
Will they live their life,
like nothing happened,
or will they visit me every day
at my grave?
Oh, how I wonder,
What will happen if I Die.

{Lina, class assignment, October 20, 2014}

Extract 5.15 is a poem written by Lina, included and reflected on in her personal narrative, in which she opens up at conflicted feelings about her self-worth and visibility to the world. In the poem, she wonders how people would react to her death, if she would be missed or forgotten, or if those around her would "live their life like nothing happened." In this writing assignment for our English class, Lina opened her secret internal world to the rest of the class. Reading this narrative made me wonder about the feelings students at ISS were carrying that I could not access, and that perhaps those students also needed a constructive outlet like writing to express and think through conflicts. In this case, Lina was granted a pedagogical space safe enough to share her feelings openly and not feel siloed from her peers. The parable ends by reassuring readers that she patched up relationships and signals a transformed sense of self as she realized by reflecting, "Once you hit puberty, you realize how naive and weird your thoughts were compared to now." Lina's personal narrative is an example of the self-exploration and revelation students conducted in my CP. These acts allowed conflicts experienced during adolescence to be named by students so they did not remain invisible and hidden.

Another example of students' self-exploration and learning to name conflicts comes from a unit dealing with the generative theme of love and centered on the Nepalese film, "Pooja" (Rauniyar 2010), which I learned about after a form two student in Class A posted a link to the movie on Facebook in the spring of 2013. "Pooja" tells the story of a teen girl by the same name living in a remote rural village, who dies in childbirth while her boyfriend is in Hong Kong seeking economic opportunities. The film deals with themes of motherhood, patriarchy, sexism, love, economic development, and making decisions by examining the events leading to Pooja's death, to determine responsibility for the tragedy. Pooja, her boyfriend Rumi, their families, and structural social problems are all parties and factors bearing some blame. Along with the movie, we read articles and examined data related to maternal and infant mortality rates in Nepal, Hong Kong, and other parts of the world. To frame our study of the movie, and begin investigating the generative theme of love, I asked students to write and then share their personal definitions of love. Most definitions were similar to the one written by Jagan, a fifteen-year-old male of Nepali heritage who was considered a trouble maker and a weak student in primary school and by some teachers at ISS when he began in form one. In Extract 5.17 Jagan connects love to a feeling.

Extract 5.17 "Love is a feeling"

Well love is feeling that can make happy and sad. True love is love that is you feel like long and lasting. You just keep on loving the same person. Every day your love increase more and more. You feel like your love is worthless without her. Its like a bright sun to you. When you feel like lonely and sad, you want them to appear in front of you because it makes your dark world to bright.

{Jagan, class assignment, April 16, 2013}

In the course of the unit, students evaluated their definitions of love and determined if the protagonist in "Pooja" had love, based on our reading and analysis of various definitions of love coming from distinct perspectives, including the black-feminist American scholar, bell hooks, who described love as knowing how to be solitary, and a Muslim perspective on love, which defined love in relation to community, marriage, self-care, and Allah. For our English writing examination, students answered the question, "Did Pooja and Rumi have true love?" Below is Jagan's response:

Extract 5.18 "Love is action not a feeling"

According to bell hooks, an African-American feminist writer, true love mean "knowing to be solitary" and "love is action not a feeling". We should know how to alone, take care of ourself and help each other. Pooja and Rumi's does not know how to be alone. For example, when Pooja leaves her home she called Rumi and he takes Pooja with him instead of helping her to take her back to her home. Rumi helps Pooja because he cannot live without Pooja. He don't know how to be alone. After Pooja becomes pregnant,

Rumi went to Hong Kong to work there so that he could make money... When Rumi arrive back to his village, Pooja dies in childbirth. Pooja and Rumi accept each other rather than helping each other. They don't work together and don't take care of each other.

{Jagan, English exam, June 11, 2013}

Despite his grammatical errors, Jagan is able to reproduce the essay genre of writing, introducing a reference to bell hooks, citing evidence from the film to make an argument, using transitions, and coming to a conclusion in this paragraph. The essay examination also forced him and his classmates to look at love from various perspectives so that they could reconsider their definitions, and in this case, Jagan uses the definition provided by hooks to examine love as action rather than his earlier definition of feeling. Some students walked away with new definitions of love, and new ways to name the relationships in which they and their classmates sometimes invested much mental and emotional energy. In presenting this unit to students at a local university in April 2014, Krishna, a Nepali heritage Class A student reflected that she not only improved her essay writing, vocabulary, and discussion skills, but also learned to value her own "mother and taking care of our bodies." She admitted to having fallen in love before, and theories of love we learned, "Were helpful to know about couples around me." Based on our studies, she explained she saw relationships around her, including her own romantic relationships, as based on "immature love" that creates dependence, not freedom.

Through studying film, literature, and philosophy, students were able to take self-revelations and see them in new lights. Eventually, students would use vocabulary of critique they learned and connect their problems of adolescence to larger conditions of cultural discontinuity and historical struggle. To do that, we had to study a theme larger than us and our everyday struggles that connected us to the rest of humanity, as we will see in the next section.

Academic themes: a study of dehumanization in "1984"

In the spring of 2014, my mind was set on leaving ISS. I loved my students, but working conditions were becoming overwhelming in a school culture often at odds with the student-centered practices and curricular changes for which my collaborators and I advocated. I had to spend more time creating, invigilating, and marking examinations than sitting together with colleagues to discuss how to meet the needs of students. Both Jane, my supportive English Panel Head, and Lagan were also talking of leaving the school. I decided I wanted to finish what would probably be my last couple months at the school in the strongest possible way with students, and designed a unit around the themes of dehumanization, human needs, and dignity, centered on the abridged version of the novel, "1984," by George Orwell (2003), though some students read portions of an unabridged version.

I saw these themes as vital to an understanding of life, and that amongst these, "needs" might be the most immediate to students, as their social, emotional, and physical needs were sometimes unfulfilled, both in and out of school. Dehumanization and dignity would be more academic themes for study that I thought they could connect to, and added to these we took additional academic and topical themes, including World War II, the Holocaust, and forms of government. I decided to teach the same unit to both my form three Class A and my form two Class D, though class A covered additional materials and topics. Tad also taught the unit to his form two EM students, and Jane decided to use another Orwell novel "Animal Farm" with her class of form three Pakistani heritage females. Through this unit, students connected to themes outside their immediate experiences, integrated diverse bodies of knowledge, and eventually used academic themes to engage in acts of transformative resistance in Chapter 7.

Along with the novel, my students and Tad's students learned about Maslow's Hierarchy of Needs, as a way to frame how the dystopian society of 1984 stripped away the ability for its citizen to not only meet basic needs but to reach self-actualization. To learn to study history, write historical narratives, and look a historical examples of dehumanization, we studied World War II and Holocaust, read about forms of government, viewed the film "Schindler's List," which shows the pain endured in Nazi concentration camps, read about the "Hitler Youth" Nazi training program for young people, and watched clips of the movie "Swing Kids," which depicts the experiences of young people who wanted to dance to swing music but became part of the "Hitler Youth" during World War II.

Coinciding with our studies, Amir, the Pakistani heritage teaching assistant, and Tad planned talks from visitors. Amir invited a Mufti, a Muslim scholar, to talk to the EM students at our school after a suicide by young girl of Pakistani heritage became big news in Hong Kong. I requested reading material from the Mufti to address human needs and issues of self-harm, and he provided an essay on his Muslim perspective on needs. Perhaps the most powerful moment during the unit was the visit by an artist and Holocaust survivor to our school which Tad arranged. She showed us archival footage of the concentration camp where she stayed and revealed the experiences of dehumanization endured by her family. This visit, and the personal statements of pain and suffering from the Holocaust survivor, allowed students to make the academic themes they were studying more personal.

Figure 5.1 shows our study of topics including imagery, symbolism, setting, and author's purpose in an assignment from a Class D student. Students were assigned to find examples of imagery, language that helps us imagine using our senses, in the novel "1984" (Orwell 2003) and illustrate them, and later they viewed each other's illustrations and with sticky notes, commented on what the author's purpose might have been in using this imagery, or added their inferences. We can see the author's use of imagery which the student has identified, "In the Parsons' flat, everything was broken. There were sport clothes and sports equipment all over the floor…" with the page number (8) added showing where the quote was found. Classmates have added comments, citing the author's purpose to describe the flat, the lack of cleaning from the family, and recognizing the family has a bigger flat than Winston's. There is another quote describing

Figure 5.1 Student illustration for "1984."

the presence of a "telescreen" through which the government in the novel monitors citizens, and a classmate identifies that, "Orwell uses the symbol of the tele screen to show that the people are under control."

From this example, in which students are displaying grasp of basic literary analysis techniques, we move to Extract 5.19 a segment of an English writing examination written by Pramiti, the same student who critiqued dominant textbook practices in her school, including her LS class. This extract is from the introduction of an exam essay in which students were asked to use the texts studied in class, and their experiences, to explain how and why humans struggle to meet their needs.

Extract 5.19 Student English writing exam on needs

> To achieve great goals in our life, we might think we need good grades, getting into well known universities and getting a high-status job. But that's not all that we need. According to Maslow's "Hierachy of Needs" we need five different kind of needs to fulfill, which will help us achieve great goals. They are physiological, love or belonging, safety, esteem and self-actualization needs…But according to Mufti [Shah], a Muslim scholar, the holy Quran says that we need secure community, healthy body and food and water to achieve great goals. Community is more important than individuals and human life is sacred. The person who fulfills his brother needs, Allah will fulfill his need. But unfortunately, these needs are hard fulfill in life. In a novel called "1984" by George Orwell, a documentary called "Girl Rising" and a movie named "Schindler's List," we can see how the characters needs are not met, how they are affected by it, and what they do to meet their needs.
>
> {Pramiti, examination paper, June 12, 2014}

Pramiti meets academic goals of writing in the essay genre while integrating diverse knowledge. She opens with a "hook" to engage the reader, defines needs through psycho-social and religious perspectives, and maps the essay by introducing the texts she will use to engage with the topic of needs and providing a thesis. She includes the British novel "1984," a documentary, "Girl Rising" which told stories of girls around the world standing up to oppression via education (we viewed stories from Peru and Nepal), and the Holocaust drama, "Schindler's List." This developing command of academic conventions was shared with other classmates who studied in the class for at least two years. Even the less proficient students in the class who had been studying continuously with me could put together an academic text like this one, and some of the students who had been amongst the weakest in form one were writing at a proficiency similar to Pramiti's in form three. This general knowledge about argumentation, and instances of dehumanization will be important background for episodes of dialogue around dehumanization and education in Chapter 6, as students involved in those dialogues will be speaking from informed points of view.

Besides responding to our study through formal academic assignments, students also responded in less formal assignments and also took on our themes from this unit outside the school. Extract 5.20 is from a post by Sandesh to our English Facebook group, which included students taught by Tad, Jane, and me, after the visit by the Holocaust survivor, in which we can see the affective dimension of the unit, and also the culture of communication and appreciation at work.

Extract 5.20 "We learned how people painfully suffered"

> I appreciate Mr Tad for arranging the visit [by the Holocaust survivor] to our school and give a sharing about World War 2 and I also like to appreciate Class E students [who hosted the event]. I could feel that strong energy delivered by her sharing, which made me think more about the Holocaust and the WW2. We learned how the Jewish, Homosexual, Gypsies were dehumanized during the Holocaust and World War 2. We learned how people painfully suffered during the Holocaust. Thank for holding this event. It made me think of '1984' in which the people had been dehumanized by destroying the past history and rewriting it.
>
> {Sandesh, Facebook post, May 9, 2014}

It became a normal practice for collaborators and me to ask students to reflect on activities and experiences and share their "appreciations" orally during class meetings or in writing. In Extract 5.20, a now fifteen-year-old Sandesh, who had spoken about pedagogies to his peers, talks about connecting the talk by our visitor to our learning of World War II and the Holocaust, and displays his

Setting the stage for resistance 111

awareness of other groups who suffered, and also empathy he shared in feeling the "strong energy delivered by her sharing." He connects the visit explicitly to the novel "1984" recognizing how characters were dehumanized by having their histories destroyed and re-written.

The theme of history was another taken on by some students with me. Lagan helped me to organize a workshop in a local community center for which I researched and presented Nepali Gurkha soldier history, explaining how this group of soldiers was formed, how they came to Hong Kong, and what their struggles have been. Along with my presentation, Lagan invited a retired Gurkha soldier to tell stories of his experiences serving in Hong Kong. About forty of my students attended this workshop on a Saturday, and Jane also came with a group of her students as they were working on a video documentary about the history of Gurkhas for her English class. Though it was not part of our official English curriculum, this and other activities, reinforced in students the importance of personal history, particularly since many Nepali heritage students knew very little about theirs.

Outside of official school activities, students took on our themes in a variety of online and physical settings. One example brings us again to Sandesh and another fifteen-year-old male Nepali heritage, Bismal. With Lagan's help, we secured sponsorship for Sandesh and Bismal to join a three-day "rock camp" in which they would learn to play and perform cover songs as also original pieces. A song co-written by the pair, "Live Without It," featured the lyrics in Extract 5.21.

Extract 5.21 Song lyrics

I am tired of this domination
I am tired of this world
It's finally time to step up
Nobody's inferior
You can't not enslave anyone
In the eyes of God
The riches kill the poor
but they can never take our freedom
All you have is gold and silver
We can all just live without it

{Sandesh and Bismal, song lyrics, May 3, 2014}

The pair takes the concept of "domination," and sends a message of resistance to it, offering a critique of the world. Instead of retreating from it, the song implores, "It's finally time to step up." They specifically reference economic domination, claiming "The riches kill the poor," but take a position against the need for wealth, preferring freedom and living without "gold and silver." After their performance, I asked the students if they were inspired by any specific experience in their life, and they told me they were just thinking about general "domination" and "dehumanization" in life, with these taking on different forms for different people. In the end, like Pramiti, they took an academic study of themes and topics seemingly far from them, and connected them to their experiences and generated new texts and productions.

In the fall of 2014, Class A was separated when students went into form four. Bismal, who helped to pen the song lyrics dealing with domination, wrote a letter to me requesting to change him to my class, displaying his investment in the themes we studied in our class. In our form one year, Bismal, who attended a Chinese medium of instruction primary school, had the weakest English proficiency in our class, and struggled with the English reading and writing assignments, but persisted with the help of his peers. His letter displayed a vast improvement in his English written expression and also showed a deep appreciation for his learning.

Extract 5.22 "I really want to know more about the world"

> The reason I want to learn with you from you is not because of you have taught me for three years, it's because I really want to know more about the world and humanities, and I really want to step up on music for my community, and you are the only one who can push me up on this.
>
> {Bismal, personal letter, September 12, 2014}

Besides acting as a testament to my CP, this extract shows a burgeoning transformative resistance. For Bismal, study of the world and humanities, including literature, history, and geography that was infused in our class, became a way for him to address his "community" directly. The sense of affection and duty to community was shared with other students in Class A during their three years of study, as seen in Extract 5.22, an anonymous response from a survey conducted at the end of Class A's form one year.

Extract 5.23 "I think our classes are very good"

> I think our classes are very good. Having teachers to teach you many things not only from the book but from outside also. Teaching you to write paragraph, solving problems, teaching you to behave properly, teaching you to feel about community that might be in danger in future have really touch my heart. And I will try hard to change my feeling for community around us.
>
> {Anonymous response, student survey, June 13, 2012}

Summary

Extract 5.23 is useful in summarizing this chapter. The student recounts my CP in its first year as involving learning "not only from the book but from outside also." It is a curriculum that helped students connect study of generative themes to the wider world, and to academic and topical themes. Students built academic skills including writing a paragraph, solving problems, and also citizenship, or what the student calls, "Teaching you to behave properly." There is evidence that this student and others were emotionally invested in the curriculum, sharing, "Teaching you to feel about community that might be in danger in future have really touch my heart."

Students in this chapter were shown to become empowered through curriculum. By Jane's own account which she shared in an interview, and by results of uniform examinations taken amongst English medium of instruction classes, the students being taught through my CP performed the highest overall. In fact, when students going into form four were reorganized according to results, the vast majority of the students in the new "elite" class came from Class A. In addition to opportunities to develop academically, students had spaces in which to share their feelings, concerns, and worries. They used academic study to create songs, or to write in academic genres which would have only been available through memorization of pre-written essays. Through my revelations of my personal struggles, some students came to share on theirs. Extract 5.21, along with other data in the chapter, also exhibits a student on the road to transformative resistance. Rather than reproducing only narratives of individual achievement found at NTS, students in this chapter, including the student in the last extract, took on discourses of community that framed learning and action within wider social struggles. Study of themes of education, dehumanization, human needs, and reflecting on their personal struggles would lead students to arrive at social action through dialogue. Extract 5.23 finishes with a resolution by a student in form one, "I will try hard to change my feeling for the community around us." Chapter 6 will explain how through dialogue around conflict, some students took those words and materialized them into acts of transformative resistance.

6 The complexities of dialogue

> Honesty and openness is always the foundation of insightful dialogue.
> – bell hooks

If you had walked into the classes I taught at Industrial Secondary School (ISS), particularly Class A and Class D, you might have seen all kinds of communicative activities: students and the teacher discussing academic and non-academic content, students reading, writing and presenting, working on art (for both class assignments and sometimes out of boredom), or making posts to their personal blogs or an online class Facebook group. If you had joined some of our learning excursions and activities outside the school, you might have witnessed a wide array of actions by students: lecturing in academia, speaking out in media, raising their voices in political spaces, facilitating workshops with younger peers, or banging drums and strumming guitars, singing lyrics they penned on topics ranging from online love to societal oppression.

You might have responded similarly to other classroom visitors (students, teachers, professors, and journalists), who remarked that the activities they observed countered their preconceptions of what classroom life was like in so-called low-prestige "band three" schools or schools serving ethnic minority (EM) students. Maybe you would have concurred with Joki, a student in a teacher certification program course I taught, who wrote after visiting two of my classes in December 2012, "Unlike the accepted stereotype, these students were certainly not lazy, nor unmotivated nor of a low-ability...I had expected their work ethic to be substandard, but these students wanted to learn." Or you might have been affected in the same way as Venus, a doctoral student in a class taught by Dr. M, who saw several of my Class A students make presentations in March 2013 at a graduate course in education. Following the visit by my students to her university, she gushed in an email about the course, the power of critical pedagogy (CP) presented by students, and a desire to learn by observing a CP at work:

Extract 6.1: "I was sooo touched"

The course...helped transform me. Yesterday, seeing and talking with the secondary school students from Mr. C's class, I was sooo touched. It made me believe that this education towards equality, realizing everyone's potential, can happen, as long as we work hard to do it...If I had the chance, I would like to learn from Mr. C, observe his class and learn how he is trying to use various resources (I particularly like the idea of experiencing and reading life in class) to empower students.

{Venus, email message, March 29, 2013}

Or perhaps, like me, experiencing the day-to-day dilemmas of classroom life, you would have been more tentative and skeptical, wondering if these feel-good moments truly indicated the liberating, empowering, and humanizing effects of a CP built on a praxis of reflection, dialogue, and action.

Despite classrooms that were often lively with activity and discussion, there was a palpable silence that could go undetected, a feeling that there were words that needed to be said that remained unsaid, as if classroom discussion talked around the most pressing concerns held by students, maybe because they were unaware that something needed to change. In his teaching work, Freire discovered a "culture of silence" in his adult students, an "ignorance and lethargy" that were a "direct product of the whole situation of economic, social, and political domination—and the paternalism—of which they were victims" (Freire 2004, p. 30). This culture of silence ensured that "Rather than being encouraged and equipped to know and respond to the concrete realities of their world, they were kept submerged in a situation in which such critical awareness and response were practically impossible" (p. 30). Part of what keeps the oppressed submerged in a culture of silence is that "The dominated consciousness is dual, ambiguous, full of fear and mistrust" (p. 166).

Without trust, dialogue becomes impossible, as was sometimes the case with my students. I was aware that students communicating in or out of school did not necessarily mean dialogue was happening, or that students taking action in or out of school on what *I* considered significant issues did not mean their actions had come out of their reflections. Moreover, I constantly questioned, if any observable dialogue or action against oppressive or hegemonic conditions was empowering to any or all students involved. Freire (2004, p. 79) warns of the dangers of verbalism, words that are spoken without action, and activism, actions that take place without prior reflection and critical thinking. Neither is transformative. Only a praxis, in his view, composed of ongoing reflection to name and act upon the world can lead to "dialogical action," and thus, humanization, the essence of liberation. So was this liberating dialogic action taking place with my students?

Following the 2011–2012 academic year, I pondered this question and shared a dialogue with Dr. M on two sets of data collected in my classes at ISS. The first data set, centered on a classroom interaction with Class B in 2012, at first might portray me, as the classroom teacher, as having difficulty focusing the class on my lesson, in which I wanted them to learn vocabulary that would appear on a paper examination. An audio recording of the lesson featured students making jokes, and I was trying to get them to cooperate with an exam I thought was not fair to them. But through his sociolinguistic analysis, Dr. M helped me understand how a classroom interaction centered on an examination preparation activity, loaded with disruptions and tensions, was also a specific time and place in which students and I negotiated social positioning and institutional demands through employment of communicative resources (Pérez-Milans and Soto 2014). In retrospect, I saw this instance, in which I felt frustrated by the school's demands for standardized assessment, as a missed opportunity for dialogue with students, who also felt that the activity was not in line with our previous modes of learning. I let my frustrations dominate the classrooms and created a monologic environment, rather than listen for the collusion some students may have been asking me to join.

I analyzed the second data set taken from an online pedagogical episode, the "Levitation Dialogue," in which a group of Class A students, Pragun, and I discussed the ethereal photographic self-portraits of a Japanese artist showing her "levitating." Discussion moved around several pages on Facebook, and eventually a group of students produced their own "levitation" photographs. In this episode, students met pedagogical goals as they "used new vocabulary, synthesized art with science learning, and invested in identities as producers of visual texts" (Pérez-Milans and Soto 2014, p. 229). Moreover, I understood that students who felt constrained by a lack of creative association with the world, engaged with the generative theme of freedom, pushing the limiting boundaries of their everyday lives by playing artistically with their bodies, the urban landscape, and a digital camera.

I concluded that in the Levitation Dialogue, moving students from the realm of words toward remaking their worlds meant "thinking and acting in a multi-textual, cross-disciplinary way, and generating temporal, geographic, and participatory displacement as the dialogue shifted across time and online and physical locations, while participants and authors entered and left the dialogue at various points" (Pérez-Milans and Soto 2014, p. 229). In other words, pedagogical intervention and dialogue required the use of a variety of tools in a variety of spaces, in which students and other participants could come and go at any time, as they pleased. While this analysis allowed me to make sense of the complexities of dialogue, I held on to some skepticism regarding its liberatory power in this instance, wondering if "more sophisticated social critique and social action" would follow, and surmised that the "greater value in this kind of dialogue" would come if continuity was maintained between the involved actors while also creating space for "a broad set of voices and resources" (pp. 230–231). I thought greater transformative resistance could emerge from dialogue if the conditions for dialogue, and the participants who contributed to it, remained in place for longer.

In this chapter, I advance my dialogue *about* dialogue through analysis of three additional sets of data from Class A, stemming from the two years following the Levitation Dialogue, that illuminate students' dialogical encounters with their worlds and actions they took following reflection, within the framework of the curriculum described in Chapter 5. Because these encounters, as well as the Levitation Dialogue, are tied to the same class, a sense of continuity will be established that will help us see how a praxis of dialogue and action to change the world developed over time and in interaction with my CP curriculum. In Chapter 5, curriculum was understood as the negotiated organization of content, materials, activities, experiences, and building of cultural spaces and practices that engaged students in the investigation of generative themes and the building of academic skills. Curriculum was crafted to develop students' vocabulary, critical thinking, and communication skills so that they could engage in reflection and talk.

Equally essential were attempts to build pedagogical spaces (e.g. physical spaces in classrooms, community centers, student publications, and non-physical online spaces and emotional and intellectual spaces) in which students felt safe to express themselves and their concerns, spaces in which revelations and critical analysis of my own personal struggles invited students to do the same. Consequently, a culture of change was necessary that challenged dominant beliefs, practices, and forms of relation within ISS. This curriculum, which negotiated both pre-determined academic aims and spaces allowing freedom, will figure prominently in this chapter as a force that provoked, allowed, mediated, and at times limited dialogue, while generating empowerment amongst students. Heeding the recommendation that dialogue be contextualized and its complexities not be taken for granted (Burbules 2000), I will draw on the review of CP in Chapter 2 and introduce a theoretical approach to understanding dialogue in education (Matusov and Miyazaki 2014) that was essential to deepening my analysis of data.

A description of this theoretical approach will be followed by three accounts of dialogic action that describe where, when, and how dialogue took place, what the content of it was, who was involved and in what ways, why the dialogue took place, and what relations, objects, texts, and practices mediated dialogue. I further situate and contextualize these encounters within the institutional processes of the school, classroom experiences, and lived realities of the students to understand what aspects of reality students were attempting to name. We will see how continuity with me, my collaborators, and their resources contributed to ongoing dialogic relationships and to students' willingness to enter into dialogue infused with elements of everyday drama, including risk, and heightened psychological states. By the end of the chapter, we will understand that continuity, drama (events that provoke emotional reactions), discomfort, and listening were all active in the dialogues presented and contributed to empowering students.

118 *The complexities of dialogue*

Bakhtin's epistemological and ontological affordances

In analyzing data for this chapter, I found my theoretical framework insufficient. What troubled me most was the presence of multiple instances of self-reflection to name the world, and these instances felt like dialogue, yet how could dialogue take place between only one person? My investigation into this question led me to more recent developments in dialogical pedagogy, based on Bakhtin theory of language that exposed new complexities (Matusov and Miyazaki 2014). Through this set of theories, I understood my pedagogical role as listening to discover latent possibilities and questions within students (p. 33) and found an answer as to how dialogue could happen as a solitary or even imaginary act. Furthermore, the drama in my pedagogy, and the pain it sometimes involved, was given a theoretical basis. I was already aware of how I pulled students into learning through staged spectacles, lessons, and simulations I set up to provoke students into reacting intellectually and emotionally, preparing students to understand the present, while also preparing them for future actions (see Chapter 5). A Bakhtinian approach clarified how students took to the stage to test ideas and become "heroes" of the narratives I authored (p. 31). Moreover, I saw the converse as true, that I, and other students, sometimes became the heroes of student-authored dialogic encounters. In this role as author, the students' "utterances [were] unexpected for both the teacher and themselves," revealing in students independence, freedom, and a sense that they are unfinished beings (p. 34).

A Bakhtinian approach to dialogue supported that as teachers, we might build a monologic pedagogical relations with students mediated by finalized authoritative discourse, or we might build increasingly dialogic pedagogical relations on "unfinalizability," meaning actors continuously generate new awareness and actions for themselves and others (Matusov and Miyazaki 2014, p. 20). Within this spectrum of pedagogy and relation, instrumental, epistemological, and ontological aspects of dialogue take shape. Instrumentality refers to the aspects of pedagogy and relations that are built around the teacher's goals or preset curricular endpoints. Any pedagogical approach built upon privileging instrumentality will result in a monologic relation, meaning dialogue is severely limited.

Epistemological aspects of dialogical relations refer to investigations into knowledge issues. These investigations rarely become interested in the everyday or mundane (Matusov and Miyazaki 2014, p. 8), rather they are removed from space and time and reduced to a single theme, concept, or corresponding logic, with questions and answers typically already known by the teacher. Thus, epistemological dialogue and pedagogy may ignore the most salient aspects of topics important to marginalized students, including sex, substance abuse, pop-culture, violence, inter-personal conflicts and dramas, students' personal hopes, interests and needs, and daily and historical injustices, including everyday acts of name-calling, prejudice, and discrimination (p. 29). Think of a class in which the concept of "puberty" is read about, mind-mapped, and discussed, but students never talk about their personal anxieties or shames, or the historical dimensions shaping how personal problems are experienced. This purified, mono-topic dialogue is perilous in that it:

> ...can lead to pedagogical violence as a way of 'disciplining the students' minds' so they remain on the theme and only engage in the intellectual framework defined by the teacher, which is always the best. It brackets the complexity, ontological massiveness, and interconnection of the diverse themes and makes certain 'irrelevant' agendas, interests, strengths, desires, and ontological groundings as inappropriate and illegitimate (which in its own turn requires policing the discourse and issuing punitive actions for the violators of the epistemological regime).
>
> (Matusov and Miyazaki 2014, p. 8)

Then there are times when pedagogy and relations between and amongst teachers and students take an ontological turn, sidelining instrumentality and opening dialogue to learning surprises for teachers and students. In ontological dialogue, learning is located in the immediacy and here-and-now of students' lives, yet is not limited in space and time. It takes on challenge, wonder, and transformation as the class delves into the nature of being and humanity, free of the teacher's instrumental concerns that split students' lives from their educations. Consequently, when ontological dialogue emerges, it defines its own endpoints in students that come from the dialogue itself.

With these ideas in mind, I now turn to our first encounter with dialogue.

Identifying a culture of silence: "The Letters Dialogue"

I mark the beginning of this episode, with me as I set up an activity that was instrumentally and epistemologically oriented. In Chapter 5, I explained how bringing students into university and community spaces to present using an academic voice became a component of curriculum that sought to build capital and extend the networks and social fields through which students traversed. To this end, I prepared five students to present at a post-graduate student conference in my university faculty in May 2013, after what had started out as a difficult year evolved into one of significant academic and social growth for many students. I wanted the student speakers to apply the academic skills we developed in class, including writing and presenting and effectively with awareness of audience, purpose, and tone, consider the themes we had studied and the relevance to their lives, and inhabit the academic space of a university, thereby meeting endpoints set by me. Taking on my pedagogical task, Tara, a fifteen-year-old female of Nepali heritage, engaged in dialogue in two letters written a year apart and addressed to her grandmother. This episode is a self-reflexive, partly imaginary dialogue, initiated by my provocation (with knowledge of her previous online activities), in which Tara sought to name and understand the behavior she observed in herself and her classmates, eventually naming a culture of silence. As the episode furthered, it became more ontologically oriented as Tara employed the daily dramas of her life and her class as the valid content of dialogue and questioned her grandmother about basic issues of humanity, love, and trust, receiving answers that led her to more questions. In the course of her two letters, Tara additionally created a sense of drama that pulled me further into dialogue. Before introducing the letters, I will provide some context.

For Trisha and Tara, two form two students from Class A, the year had gotten off to a rocky start. After a successful first year, I expected form two to begin with academic themes students would find relevant and critical to the needs of their communities. But in the first couple months of school, most Class A students were unfocused and detached from our unit on food equity, which posed questions generated by me such as "What kind of nutritional habits do we have?", "Why do we have them?", and "Why doesn't everyone have access to healthy food?" Beyond the detachment in my class, frustrations at school, family problems, conflicts with friends, difficulties with dating and relationships, coping through self-harm, and experimentation with drugs and alcohol started to weigh on the well-being of students. Increasingly their interpersonal relationships became more tense, while their academic engagement suffered. To re-engage students, I dispensed of my planning and re-engaged the class with the generative themes in front of me, leading to our studies of texts like "Udaan" and "Pooja" and themes of adolescence, cycles of oppression, discontinuity, love, and motherhood mentioned in Chapter 5.

So as we neared the end of the academic year and were preparing for our university presentations, Trisha and Tara drew on these concepts to contemplate the struggles they and their classmates had faced. Trisha, who was thirteen years old at the time, spoke about dialogue in her short presentation, disclosing to the audience, "Trust is what I think is the main problem in my class. For me trust means having respect for each other's ideas and being open enough to share them" (see Extract 6.2). After citing classmates hurting each other's feelings as the cause of breakdown of trust in her class in the beginning of the form two year, she echoed Freire's sentiment on the necessity of love, respect, and trust in education as she connected the problem of trust to the class' inability to achieve the "transformative pedagogy" we had discussed in our studies:

Extract 6.2 "Without trust, there's no dialogue"

> One problem that I see is that without trust there's no dialogue, and without dialogue there's monologue and only transmission education. What that means is that when there's no trust, we won't get to interact with each other and we won't really know who we are, and we don't share our problems, and the cycle begins again and then there starts the transmission education with the cycle begins again.
>
> {Trisha, university presentation video recording, May 18, 2013}

Trisha's reflection on dialogue offered an astute analysis of conditions in her class, and of the limits of our pedagogy, seeing a connection between trust, dialogue, pedagogy, and relationships. With a breakdown of trust, dialogue disappeared, leading to a cycle of monologue and lack of trust. But without offering possible ways to move into relationships of greater trust, her account was subject to the trap of verbalism, or reflection without action. She had not yet reflected with her class about how to break the cycle of mistrust, monologue, and return to banking education.

Tara picked up on Trisha's ideas, and the afternoon before the presentation, she was set on connecting the theme of love to the difficulties faced by herself and her classmates, but was undecided about how to convey a message to the audience. As I had noticed she had posted photographs and memories of her grandmother to her Facebook page, I suggested she incorporate her grandmother in her presentation somehow. The next morning, Tara informed me that she had stayed up late into the night working on a letter to her grandmother. She let me revise the letter to make minor corrections to grammar, then she continued to work on it. When it was her turn to present, a photograph of her grandmother was projected onto the screen in the room, and Tara read the letter she had written, presented in Extract 6.3.

Extract 6.3: Slowly, we are dying inside

1 Dear grandmother,
2 I've got many things to share with you! When I saw the picture of you, my initial reaction
3 was how beautiful you were. I remember how closed we were. You were my only true
4 mother and there's no one like you but then you left me alone and I had to live my life
5 without you. I was so much filled by your love but now that you're gone I can't be loved like
6 you love me. I'm scared to live my own life. I always wonder what might happen next. It's
7 like a pages that I'm reading everyday.
8 Everyday when I walk into my classroom, I feel nothing but it's kind of suffocating.
9 Everyday I have to survive, not knowing what might happen next. I feel so empty with your
10 love and it's even harder to live when I don't have father's love. It hurts when I see, how
11 harder my mother tries to live day by day and there I see the same problem that she too needs
12 love. My chest really hurts but try to cope my pain by having fun with my friends. I'm not

13 sure if they really are my friends because they don't share their pains and I think I'm really
14 not their friend because I share nothing painful with them. I'm scared to share because I don't
15 know what they might think.
16 This year, we were going through puberty and a lot things were happening in our class. There
17 was a problem in our class and we couldn't figure it out. We are so smart and everyone in my
18 class were talented but this year something shattered us into pieces. Everyday I could see my
19 friends laughing, joking and having fun but we were slowly harming ourselves. We weren't
20 brave enough to make a move and couldn't figure it out what our problem was. We learned so
21 many things in Mr. C's class by watching movies, documentaries and by experiencing going
22 to university. We also learn teen's conflicts but we weren't looking at ourselves. We weren't
23 studying ourselves. We would be so afraid to the truth, meanwhile we would be so loud
24 when we're having fun. How I wish to share this with you, face to face and I could even
25 imagine how you'd comfort me by your words but it's so bitter when it's not real.
26 Grandmother, how would people feel if they were so loved by their loved ones? They would
27 be the happiest people ever. So, why we couldn't build love in our class? The school took
28 away our beloved teachers and we couldn't learn because there wasn't love in what we were
29 learning. I can see my friends that they need love but they don't know yet. Some people just
30 give up themselves. Life would be great if we could draw our own life and that would come
31 true.
32 Slowly, we are dying inside. We aren't able to build social and cultural capital. We have no
33 interest what we're learning anymore like before. If we could just love each other, and just be
34 honest then we could help with each other. We could stop our cycle that we are suffering
35 from ages. If there could just be Love and Trust within us.

{Trisha, letter for presentation May 18, 2013}

Tara opens the letter in Extract 6.3 by greeting her grandmother and recalling the years she and her sister were raised by their grandmother in Nepal, while her single mother resided in Hong Kong. Her grandmother passed away relatively young, in her fifties, leaving Tara feeling "alone," pointing to our theme of discontinuity in her life. In this paragraph, Tara also presents herself without a sense of agency, describing that life is "like a pages that I'm reading everyday" (line 7). She makes a similar statement toward the end of the letter, "Life would be great if we could draw our own life and that would come true" (lines 29–31). In other words, she felt a lack of authorial power, as her life was written for her, as an object of history, not a human subject who authors her own life.

The second paragraph connects personal conflicts of love to more public classroom experiences (lines 8–15). Tara introduces a paradox, stating that walking into her class, "I feel nothing but it's kind of suffocating." How could she be suffocated by nothing? She cites the lack of love from her deceased grandmother and her absent father, and the pain she also feels by seeing her mother live with a lack of love. She understands she brings this pain and emptiness with her into the classroom, and her classmates also have suffering they withhold (line 13). Because of a lack of trust and dialogue, and love, Tara admits that she coped by "having fun with my friends" (line 12) and repeats the lack of courage to speak up because of how she might be judged (line 15). This brings into focus that a lack of dialogue caused her to feel suffocation, a threat to her life, alluding to dialogue as a source of life or humanity.

The third paragraph references her daily classroom life, one in which despite studying themes related to puberty and conflicts, students were not always studying in a critical way that would re-examine reality. She brings her classmates into the frame with the claim, "We weren't studying ourselves. We would be so afraid to face the truth…" (lines 22–23). Here, she might be recalling a classroom talk in which I accused students of the same. At the time, I told students that it was not enough for me if they learned to write an essay about a character's conflicts if they did not use this knowledge to look at themselves, and that we were all, in a sense, lying about our learning. The paragraph ends with a wish for her grandmother's comfort and a realization that the dialogue she is carrying on is imaginary, as any comfort gained from her grandmother would be "bitter sweet when it's not real."

The concluding paragraphs trace an analytical line across the conceptual terrain of love, considering why love was absent in her class, what the consequences of its absence were, and what its presence would mean. Tara questions her grandmother directly, speculating how people would feel with love, and imagines an answer, "They would be the happiest people ever" (lines 26–27). Then she follows with a second question, one maybe posed to herself, her grandmother, her classmates, or the conference audience, "So why we couldn't build love in our class?" (line 27). She provides two answers: the break in continuity with teachers created by administrative planning and the lack of knowledge on the part of students about their need for love. The most dire consequence of love's absence is a metaphorical or perhaps spiritual death, which Tara identifies as "dying inside" (line 32). More literally, the absence of love within her class community meant that students could not jointly "build social and cultural capital" and lost interest in learning (lines 33). Alternatively, the presence of love, coupled with honesty and trust would lead to action, and therefore be life affirming. It would allow students to "stop our cycle that we are suffering from ages," a reference to intergenerational oppression, another concept we studied.

Tara's understanding that there was a culture of silence in her class, which reproduced reactionary and self-defeating forms of resistance by preventing relationships based on love and trust from forming, is exhibited in the first letter. This culture of silence possibly contributed to her feelings of suffocation, one that in her second letter she saw as partially maintained through patriarchal culture that was part of the class landscape. So while she and others were "loud," they actually were silent on the nature of their oppressive reality, unable "to make a move." Through this culture of silence, students engaged in behaviors that pulled them from academic commitment. For some, this behavior was reactionary because they still lacked a social critique, but for some, including Tara, it was self-defeating, because they did have a critique of oppression, yet were still focused on activities that alleviated pain, instead of figuring out the nature of their pain to take action on it. So it was not just actions and decisions on the part of the school and its agents that maintained oppressive conditions, students also became complicit through their acts of reactionary and self-defeating resistance. Tara made it clear: "Everyday, I could see my friends laughing, joking, and having fun but we were slowly harming ourselves" (lines 18–19).

A year later, in June 2014, I asked Tara, along with three classmates to join me in conducting presentations for the staff of a community center that served EM youth, to share our perspectives on the needs of the youth they served. Because we had no time to prepare, I suggested Tara to read and talk about the letter she had created a year earlier. She indeed read a letter to her grandmother, but it was a significantly revised letter. Not only was she using more advanced descriptive vocabulary, conceptually, her thinking was more clear in synthesizing the concepts we had studied in our class and making personal connections to them. For example, her second letter exhibits a critical consciousness that connects her previous apathy at school more explicitly to issues of domestic abuse, patriarchy, and pedagogy, seen in Extract 6.4.

Extract 6.4 "We have a lack of transformative and generative pedagogy"

In school, I felt apathetic. I couldn't push myself to get ahead and work because…I was worn out by the problems that I had been facing inside my home. In class, some of the girls couldn't concentrate on the lessons because the boys distracted the class, but no one realised that, not even me. In our society, men usually erode women and we don't realise that because…maybe we have lack of knowledge about these things…a lack of transformative and generative pedagogy.

{Tara, letter for presentation, April 25, 2014}

Here, Tara again recounts her feeling of disengagement from school and her conflicts in her home, but now she connects classroom events involving gender to patriarchy, citing "men usually erode women," and the lack of knowledge to the lack of pedagogies that would be more enlightening. She was also more aware of actions she could take to build knowledge and other forms of capital, citing the opportunities outside the school provided by Lagan, Pragun, and myself. This allowed her to use her "agonizing problems" to make herself "stronger to build my academic skills and fight against the distractions that I've been through." Furthermore, she saw a connection between history and intergenerational poverty in her life, stating, "I've learned that it is important to know our own history and by knowing my own history has empowered me not to repeat the cycle of the intergenerational poverty." Still committed to the idea that she and her peers needed to rely on trust and love, she added, "making young people leaders," was key.

Her closing statements might point to greater confidence in seeing herself as an author of her life, rather than experiencing life as pages that appear before her in the first letter. Still, it seems that Tara needs a teacher to set dialogical stages for her, as she saw herself and her classmates "gradually developing these skills like reading this letter in front of everyone to let them think about how young people can change," while needing someone to be a guide. In contrast to her first letter that ended morbidly, with a community "dying inside," her second letter is more affirming by positioning her a subject of history, rather than an object of it. She tells her grandmother, "I hope you are proud of me. Leaving me behind was the only path [through which] I was able to learn these things and giving me the strength to not give up."

This ontological dialogue extended as I was drawn to additional questions about love, trust, dialogue, and my own teaching. By not disclosing the content of her first letter until the day of the presentation, by continuing to edit it until she presented, and a year later, by surprising me with a revised letter, Tara created a sense of drama that pulled me further into dialogue, and was evidence that Tara had taken on the unfinalizability of ontological dialogue. The drama and ongoing nature of the ontological dialogue was also heightened by putting me into relation with her grandmother, who felt both imaginary and real to me, and whose life became interesting to me, leading me again to further wonder. I was compelled to know not just who this woman was, but also understand the experiences of the forbearers of my students. More specifically, I sought to learn how Tara's grandmother influenced Tara in being who she was, and what the grandmother's life in Nepal meant for defining a "Nepali" culture in Hong Kong for Tara.

Through this dialogue over the course of two letters, Tara reflected critically on reality, and despite the sometimes dreary tone of her first letter, maintained a sense of hope that change was possible for herself and her peers. Though in her first letter authorial agency did not suffice to create the transformation she longed to see, Tara took the action of naming love as a generative theme requiring additional dialogue and also pointed the importance of students to understand their own needs. Tara unknowingly positioned herself as a "revolutionary leader," a radical committed to her classmates who had considered the reasons for mistrust in her class and was beginning "to seek out true avenues of communion with them, ways of helping the people to help themselves critically perceive the reality that oppresses them" (Freire 2004, p. 166). Because she had critically reflected and entered into dialogue with herself, her heritage, the generative themes and content of our curriculum, she could "see [her] friends that they need love but they don't know yet" and she was aware of their self-defeating resistance that leads classmates to "give up themselves" (lines 28–29).

However, Tara told me that she felt she was delivering these letters to the wrong audience. She saw the value in challenging discourses about EM youth through her letters and engaging with an academic audience, but was critical of presentations that felt like "monologue" with little feedback or questions from the audience besides compliments. Her letters had been read at the presentations with peers in the audience, still, she felt discomfort at the idea of reading them in front of her class, and thought not enough action had come from the letters. Though this dialogue in itself, simply by being uttered, may constitute action on reality to transform it, later, Tara would take additional action, within the context of dialogue, against the culture of silence in her classroom. This story unfolds as a component of Episode Two, "The Pyramid of Hate Dialogue."

Breaking a culture of silence: "The Pyramid of Hate Dialogue"

In this encounter, Tara broke the culture of silence in her class. It began as a staged drama: a lesson in which students would have to confront and respond statements meant to elicit strong reactions was coupled with the goals of students practicing academic classroom talk and generating epistemological dialogue about forms of hate in life and about the specific nature of hate against Jews in the Holocaust. As the encounter developed, dialogical tensions emerged, opening spaces in which the culture of silence in the class could be partially dismantled through transformative resistance. My initial instructions set the pedagogical goals for the activity and provided students officially sanctioned ways in which they could participate while still allowing confrontation to happen. Throughout the dialogue I negotiated tensions that included my own anxieties about whether all students in class would be able to participate, and whether the activity would be pedagogically successful, and my desire to have a space in which risk, shock, personal revelations, personal histories, and pain could circulate openly as a part of the formal curriculum. The context of this dialogue comes next.

On a Friday afternoon on 9 May 2014, the Class A seats were arranged in a square with all twenty-five students facing toward the inside. I was seated at the corner of the square, and included in our arrangement, was a familiar visitor, Dr. M, the university researcher who was in his third year of ethnographic data collection with Class A. At the front of the room, the projection screen was down, and students were told that a series of statements would be projected, to which they could respond either in suggested ways or any manner they thought appropriate. Students had in front of them copies of "The Pyramid of Hate," a taxonomy of escalating acts of dehumanization in the following order: prejudiced attitudes, acts of prejudice, discrimination, violence, and genocide.

After reviewing the terms in the Pyramid of Hate handout, I set my expectations for how students should act and communicate during the ninety-minute activity, keeping in mind the need to balance authoritarianism with permissiveness. Freire (2005, p. 104) speaks of this mediation:

> Thus, however, just as learners' freedom in the class needs limits so that it does not lose itself in indiscipline, so the voice of the educator and of the learners needs ethical limits so that it doesn't slip toward the absurd. It is just as immoral to have our voices silenced, our "body interrupted," as to use the voice to falsify the truth, to lie, deceive, deform.

To establish a disciplined, ethical interaction, I first reminded participants of the "Step up, step back" rule I often invoked, stipulating that students who spoke up regularly should make room for other students to share, while students who preferred to listen or keep their thoughts outside of the group should make an effort to contribute orally. Second, I gave instructions as an attempt to focus the conversation, prevent runaway discussions, give students English language sentence stems with which to build comments and ask probing questions, and allow as many students as possible to feel comfortable sharing. Though I peppered my explanations and instructions with jokes and examples from our class, I was still using an authoritative discourse that only granted me permission to set rules and boundaries for dialogue. I did not allow students the right to set what they thought might be appropriate boundaries for a discussion that might raise sensitive issues, neither did I provide them the option to leave the activity, two steps I would take if I conducted this activity again. I could have and should have engaged with students in more dialogue about dialogue.

As we commenced, I was a bit apprehensive. This would be my maiden attempt at this activity, and advised the students that the experiment "might go well, it might not go well." Moreover, there were seven male of Pakistani heritage who had joined Class A that year, including five I knew from Class C two years before, and the other two had transferred from other schools. These students were generally academically weaker and had lower English proficiency as a whole than the rest of the class, and with only three days per week at the school, I felt like I did not show them the same commitment I had shown other students in previous years. All seven lacked exposure to the curriculum the rest of Class A had experienced in the first two years, and five did not have the English proficiency to engage in some of the texts from our study of dehumanization centering on the novel "1984," which was discussed in Chapter 5.

In spite of my worries, one by one, we discussed the following statements in Extract 6.5, which referenced our studies, current discourses in the mass media, statements I had heard students make, statements I had seen on social media in which

128 *The complexities of dialogue*

students participated, or the actual lived experiences of students who has suffered from prejudice discrimination, or acts of violence perpetrated against them.

Extract 6.5 Statements from the "Pyramid of Hate

1. Jews cannot be trusted
2. Jewish people are like rats, they cause problems in our country
3. Jews should not be allowed to be citizens of our country
4. Let's make them wear a star of David badge so we know who they are
5. Jews are dangerous, so we should burn down their synagogues
6. Jews deserve to die, it's the only way to get rid of them
7. Girls only care about their looks
8. That girl is a slut, she just cares about getting attention from boys
9. Girls should not be allowed to go to school
10. I did not rape her. Look at her, she was dressing in a sexy way. She was asking for it.
11. During many wars, women are raped, abused, and killed in very large numbers
12. Justin Bieber is gay
13. He is a disgusting faggot
14. Gays should not be allowed to work as teachers
15. Sometimes, gay people deserve to be beaten
16. We should kill all gay people

{Mr. C (researcher), Class document, May 9, 2014}

Statements one through six focused on academic content from our studies of the Holocaust and World War II, as I thought personal detachment from the statements would ease students into the activity. As we moved through the first six statements on the list, students were complying with the intended curricular goals, though they were not yet personally connecting to the statements. Some students began to take apart the concept of humanity or clarify what type of a hate a particular statement actually represented. However the personal detachment started to change once we reached the statements related to sexism. We were discussing the statement "That girl is a slut, she just cares about getting attention from boys," teasing out the meaning of the word "slut." Dr. M was asking epistemological questions in attempts to lead students to recognizing contradictions about who might be considered a "slut," and eventually I asked the students if they had similar words in Nepali, Hindi, or Urdu. At this point, the following exchange in Extract 6.6, the focus of this episode's analysis, occurred:

Extract 6.6 "I heard Danbir was called gay"

1. **Tara:** I don't want to say, but I used to get that a lot from my mother and that made me feel, um,
2. dehumanized.

3   **Mr. C:** You say your mom called you that?
4   **Tara:** Yeah, because she had many problems so she used to shout at me. And, uh, I also want to
5   connect this to another class because yesterday, in bio class, I heard Danbir was called gay,
6   which made me mad. So I think we should not do that. Especially, I really wanted, to be
7   honest, Damini and other girls and boys who called Danbir gay, that made me really mad
8   because he's not gay.
9   **Naija:** Sometimes, wait (addressing male student trying to enter the conversation). Sometimes,
10 Tara, I feel that you stand up. Instead of you, I think Danbir, he should the one to stand up for
11 himself. If someone's calling him gay, he should answer them back that I'm not a gay and
12 talk to them nicely. If he is not taking a stand, others don't say to him.
13 (Jagan, a male student, tries to enter the conversation, but Tara quiets him)
14 **Tara:** Wait a minute. I think he's smiling outside, but maybe inside he's really like, he thinks others
15 as his friends because he doesn't want to admit that he's not gay, but if somebody's not
16 standing for him, I think he won't get that confidence to stand for himself.
17 **Naija:** I totally agree with that (there is audible chatter of other students attempting to speak) and
18 somehow Danbir should get the sense of standing of himself, not matter who is in front of
19 him. If something is wrong, he should stand for that. You get that? If someone is taking a
20 stand ("Yes, yes" is audible from a male voice) for you appreciate them and take a stand
21 for...
22 **Jagan:** No, you can't who is saying him gay they will be like acknowledging the stand for himself.
23 **Naija:** What? (Chatter breaks up with a number of students asking "What?" and giggling and
24 attempting to comment.)
25 **Mr. C:** I want you guys to step back for a second, ok? Let other people. Let's breathe for second, see
26 if other people want to step up. (Silence for about ten seconds)
27 **Tara:** I just, you know, I'm sorry if I took out your name, but that made me really mad yesterday.
28 **Naija:** It's ok. You haven't said anything wrong. You don't have to apologize for that.
29 **Mr. C:** Damini, do you think, do you agree that there are acts of prejudice in your Class A? Do you

30 ever take part in those acts of prejudice?
31 **Damini:** Ah, yes, because Danbir, we tease each other, they also tease me. Ah, they are singing, and
32 they are, only sometimes we all tease each other.
33 **Mr. C:** What kinds of acts of prejudice, you don't have to say names, what kinds of prejudice do you
34 think have come against you?
35 **Damini:** By calling nick names.
36 **Mr. C:** About what, because usually the names are about groups. Like oh, they're this, they're that,
37 Jews can't be trusted. Oh, Jews are like rats. Is that just a joke? Remember, [Holocaust
38 survivor] says that flame grows. If you let that flame keep growing, it keeps growing.
39 (There is some chatter, then after some students notice that Sunanda has nodded along with
40 Damini, Naija enters again.)
41 **Naija:** Sunanda, I want to hear from you.
42 **Pramiti:** Yes, yes, me too.
43 **Naija:** Come on, don't waste our time.
44 **Sunanda:** (Lets out a deep breath.)
45 **Jagan:** You say you agree, why. (There is a little bit of chatter and a few seconds of silence and the conversation shifts onto the topic of schooling for girls.)

{Class A, audio recording, May 19, 2014}

Extract 6.6 begins with a personal revelation of familial strife from Tara that in the past her mother had called her "slut" in Nepalese (line 1). But a shift in topic comes quickly when Tara states she wants to connect her own experience with being dehumanized through name-calling to an incident the day before in Class A's biology lesson. In an act unexpected by me, she does not request permission from the group to make a second revelation, that she heard one of her classmates, Danbir, a Nepali heritage male student, was called "gay" by other students (line 5), and she specifically names Damini, a female born in Nepal, as a culprit. She discloses her feeling of anger because "he's not gay." At this point, it is unclear what the source of Tara's anger is. Is she upset that Danbir had to endure name-calling, that Danbir is being accused of being something (homosexual) he is not or that is itself repulsive or inherently negative, or is she upset that her classmates are promoting homophobia?

Without answering that question, the next few exchanges see students jockeying for a speaking position. Naija, a female of Indian heritage, is the first to respond (lines 9–13) and addresses Tara's standing up for others rather than the issue of homophobia in the class, stating that maybe what Danbir needs to do is to "stand up for himself" (lines 10–11). Tara does not step back when Jagan, a male of Nepali heritage, tries to enter the discussion (line 13) and explains that perhaps Danbir lacks the confidence to stand up for himself, even if externally he puts on a smile, to which Naija expresses her agreement. Several students try to step in, but Naija does not step back, insisting that Danbir still needs to gain the ability to stand for himself against name-calling, to which a male is heard agreeing, perhaps Jagan. Jagan finally enters the conversation (line 22), but his meaning is unintelligible, prompting laughter and attempts by several voices to comment.

At this point, I step in to reshape the dialogue. First, I reinforce the step-up, step-back rule I set at the beginning (lines 25–26), but after about a ten-second break in the exchanges, Tara is the first to step back in with a statement rather than a question to another individual or the group, as she apologizes to Danbir for using his name in the activity and restates her anger. Naija replies directly through an authoritative discourse, reassuring Tara, "You haven't said anything wrong," not stating what Danbir's point of view might be, or what other classmates might think. So I redirect the center of speech away from to Tara and Naija to Damini, and to what I had set as the academic, epistemological focus of the activity, understanding forms of hate and connecting them to our own experiences, both as perpetrators and victims (lines 29–30). I reference the talk we had by a Holocaust survivor, which I also reviewed with students before introducing the Pyramid of Hate activity, reminding the class that unchecked hatred escalates and grows like a "flame" (lines 37–38). The concluding section of the extract reveals some tension. Students respond to my reference to the Holocaust survivor with chatter and gestures of agreement, including Sunanda and Damini who nod (lines 39–40). Naija, Pramiti, and Jagan beseech Sunanda (who has previously been active) to comment, but she only responds with a deep breath (lines 42–45), perhaps signaling something important on her mind that she is not ready to share.

Following the interaction in Extract 6.6, the activity shifted topic, tone, and voices, as the drama of the activity took a narrative structure. The conversation moved from the incident with Danbir onto the statement "Girls should not be allowed to school," bringing in a wider polyphony of voices, and more seeking clarification and questioning assumptions about what the future is likely to be for a girl, and what gender roles are and should be. The conversation became especially boisterous when discussing the statement "I did not rape her. Look at her, she was dressing in a sexy way. She was asking for it." In response to this statement, Aamir, another student of Pakistani heritage who was in his first year at ISS, questioned why a man wouldn't just go to a prostitute instead of committing rape, to which another Pakistani heritage male, Reza, quipped, "Rape is free of charge." In a lengthy exchange lasting several minutes, students sought to understand why he made this statement, what was meant by it, and debated, with most girls in the class agreeing with my assertion that the joke that was made could be seen as an act of violence, or supporting acts of violence against women.

As we neared the end of the lesson, I connected back to our Holocaust survivor visitor and her belief that a genocide has its inception in a small flame, as we finished the discussion with statements related to homophobia. Thus, we arrived to the resolution of the activity, which previously followed a narrative arc, starting from a slow exposition in which a setting was provided by the author (me), to an inciting action by Tara when she broke the silence preventing students from openly connecting to the activity, to a polyphonic climax in which a multitude of voices entered the drama of the stage I had set, and then a resolution in which I reinforced the epistemological pedagogical goals of connecting to texts and developing greater understanding of my preset concepts.

If there was an epilogue to the narrative of the activity that was visible to me, it happened online on our class Facebook group, where I received feedback on the activity and where epistemological dialogue continued. Common responses from students included shock or surprise at the sexist or homophobic statements that were being made in class, a feeling that some classmates still felt like strangers, and also statements of appreciation for the activity. The students with weaker English said that while it was challenging to understand some of the spoken English, they could follow most of the conversation, easing my previous concerns.

Some students furthered epistemological dialogue on the concept of hate. For example, as part of one exchange involving several students and myself, Jayita, a female of Nepali heritage addressed Raj, a male student of Nepali heritage who had seen the statements in the activity as "very familiar to our lives" came to know through the activity that hate existed in his class. She wrote, "Raj, I think 'hate exists almost every place [because] there are things we hate, people we hate and all kind of hates." Raj responded to this invitation for epistemological exchange on the nature of hate, first by agreeing, then by qualifying that "where 'hate' [exists] there is 'love' too, it's like [two] opposite sides of a coin. Let me tell you tell something now, we can see there is a 'hate' in our class room and everyone has forgotten love. We have been studying [the] hate pyramid and we also learned to solve conflicts in our community." Yet he saw that the Pyramid of Hate was "useless" if students did not reflect on it critically and create change by applying it to their classroom community. Jayita also agreed with him and added her own qualification, pointing out that "hate and love both exist in one place" and that not all students had "forgotten about love" in their classroom.

Besides further epistemological dialogue, students who had remained less orally active in the conversation stepped up with written comments. Danbir, who remained silent in regard to being called "gay" posted that it was difficult grappling with the idea that "even something so common like joking, name calling, or thinking untrue statements would be called hate" and was most surprised when Tara "used [him] as an example of [an] act of prejudice," and that the name-calling between him and his peers "would make her furious." He publicly acknowledged Tara's pain and absolved her of any wrong-doing by stating there was "no problem" with Tara using his name. Anjali, a girl of Nepali heritage, who typically stayed quiet in class discussions, revealed that she had some difficulty making decisions about the statements I provided, but on the other hand, "sitting in a square form and facing each other" made understanding other participants "easy." She found it compelling that her classmates "shared a part of their history and what they think about the quotes in a very interesting way," and found that she herself had shared parts of herself, and therefore all students had come out of the activity "more mature."

During the hour and a half activity, my instrumental goals were met as students engaged in instrumental, epistemological dialogue. All students contributed in sanctioned ways by asking questions, making comments, or responding to questions from either me or classmates. There was use of some of the academic speech conventions on which students were instructed. But this dialogue was de-ontologized and intellectually detached from the space and time occupied by students and the class.

It took Tara's intervention, by bringing up her own suffering in being called "slut" and the teasing of Danbir, to move the dialogue into ontological territory, into the here and now of their lives. We can identify that on one hand, she became the hero of the pedagogical activity I authored when she spoke up about the teasing of Danbir as gay, as I did indeed wish for students to move into confrontation of their own being in the world as perpetrators and victims of hate. On the other hand, we might see her as the author of her own unfinalized dialogue, previously visible in the Letters Dialogue. In the Pyramid of Hate Dialogue, Tara put her reputation amongst her classmates, and her personal relationship with Danbir in peril. While in the Letters Dialogue, she referred to her lack of courage to speak, in the Pyramid of Hate Dialogue, she seized an opportunity to break a cultural silence in order to move the class from an epistemological relation with reality, to an ontological one. In writing this chapter and reviewing this episode with Tara, she informed me she did not want for Danbir to be "oppressed" by her classmates, and that also she "didn't want [her] classmates to be homophobic" or for Danbir to perpetuate the homophobia by remaining silent. Therefore, Tara was acting informed by a critique of social oppression and spoke in order to create social change. Her transformative resistance chipped away at the culture of silence, creating a hole through which students could further engage in ontological dialogue as the activity continued.

If Tara was an author, then several students chose to become the heroes of her dialogue, and of the drama she created for the class to witness. Naija became active in legitimizing Tara's revision of the metaphorical script I had created, telling her that she did nothing wrong and had no reason to apologize (line 28), even if she was not aware that others might want to enter the ontological space that was opened up by Tara. There are moments of chatter when a clamor of voices is heard wanting to enter the conversation (lines 13, 23, 39, 45), as well as moments an individual voice seeks space to enter (9, 13, 20), however, the space for them to enter the ontological dialogue, orally, is not widened. Yet, even if the dialogue was limited at that point in its polyphony, the comments posted to our Facebook group made it clear that students participated in the ontological space as the audience to the heroes of the drama Tara initiated, and also participated in the epistemological dialogue I set up, all despite the wide range in English proficiencies that caused me anxiety. Anjali, in commenting that the square seating allowed her to easily understand her classmates, also alluded to the experience of having a front-row seat, as the rest of the class did, to the drama that played out in front of them. Though some students took on the heroic role of "stepping up," students who "stepped back" were still engrossed in dialogue, feeling shock, surprise, or hurt, and shared an experience of being in dialogic relations while they also built knowledge.

As the activity continued, the space for epistemological and ontological dialogue and breaking of the culture of silence expanded, both in the class and online, and brought in more voices, challenging me to listen and tease out my role. What drove the drama, propelling students to ongoing questioning, and therefore engagement in dialogue, were the ways in which students improvised on the stage that was set for them by me. Improvisations were enacted by students, and by me, as was the case when Tara brought up Danbir and when Reza made a "rape joke." These were utterances that were unexpected to both the students and me, and I licensed the revelation and the slur as content for dialogue.

From the Pyramid of Hate Dialogue, we now move onto the third and final episode, which is more intimate in nature. In this episode, there will be no university audience, no class full of students, just two people, a teacher and a student who become teacher-student and student-teacher (Freire 2004) through the act of dialogue. To get to this final episode, we flash forward five weeks from the Pyramid of Hate Dialogue.

A dialogic relationship: "The Messaging Dialogue"

The "Messaging Dialogue" is indicative of an ongoing dialogical relationship between a teacher, myself, and a student, Pramiti, a form three Class A female student of Nepali heritage who was sixteen at the time, in which both participants begin with epistemological dialogue and eventually come to ontological understanding of the limits of our relations with others. I mark this episode's start with an instance of epistemological dialogue that was predicated on an ongoing dialogical relationship based on trust. Before and after this episode, over the course of three years, Pramiti, like many other students, messaged me with academic, emotional, social, and physical, epistemological, and ontological concerns. Students would message me at all hours of the day and night: to ask questions about homework, to elicit my perspectives on life, to share a photo they had taken of a sunset, to get a comment on a video they made of a newly mastered skateboarding trick, or simply to chat about nothing in particular. Through these messages, students extended and built upon our existing relationships at school, and sometimes created provocations for dialogue.

In our chats, Pramiti revealed to me the suffering she experienced that led her to commit herself to academics as a way to transform her life, shared with me the concerns she had about her peers, admitted instances in which she thought she made mistakes or had serious misconceptions, and expressed her appreciation for me and my support. Through our dialogic relationship, we opened ourselves to each other's tribulations and showed the value we had for ourselves, each other, and those beyond us. For Pramiti, as was also the case with other students, concern for others expressed itself through dialogic action around the generative theme of education. In Chapter 5, I discussed how commitment to my pedagogy, by students and me, was subject to interrogation. This concern is part of this episode, in which Pramiti initiated a four and a half hour dialogue via online messaging at 4:41 pm on 18 June 2014 around some of these questions and what answers could mean for her, her EM peers, for Chinese students at the school. This dialogue revealed to Pramiti her own stereotyping of others and brought me to deeper realizations about the limits of my CP, and where it could go next.

School exams had finished, and the end of the year included a flurry of activities for Pramiti. In mid-March, I prepared her and several other students to conduct presentations for Dr. M's course. Pramiti critiqued the dominant banking education practice at her school (see Extract 5.2) and displaying an understanding of her own learning needs, and the needs of her classmates, Pramiti implored the student-teachers in the audience to help students gain English academic vocabulary and writing skills through some of the methods we used within my classes. However, her most urgent piece of advice was to "maintain continuity with students" in order to know and address learning issues over time.

After this presentation, she did not slow down. In late March she and the rest of Class A attended a day camp run by students at an international college focused on progressive pedagogies. Through simulations, games, discussion, and lectures, the Class A students furthered understanding of various forms of social conflicts and ways to reach resolutions. Lagan had arranged for this activity for Class A after he met a teacher at the international college and learned of the student-led day camps. Pramiti, along with many other students, spoke, on Facebook and to me in person, of the experience as transformative in that they were able to see conflicts, and their roles in creating, maintaining, or solving them, through new perspectives. Then at a Gurkha history workshop I led off campus, she was interviewed by a local television station regarding her experiences as an EM youth. Applying her learning from the workshop, she delivered a speech at an annual Gurkha remembrance event headed by Lagan. Connecting not just to what she had recently learned about Gurkha history, but also to what she was learning through our study of the novel "1984" in our English class, she wanted to spread the message that knowledge of history is important for individuals and societies, and "every generation has its own struggle, or fight for freedom." She identified the intergenerational struggle for freedom faced by the young Nepalese generation had shifted to a fight "for education, or inclusion in the society." She reminded the audience, "Let's not forget what the Gurkha did for us, as we keep fighting for our freedom."

Following this rush of activities, Pramiti put into action her knowledge about conflict, the importance of knowledge of one's history for self-actualization, and the need for continuity and youth leadership into action. In late April, she and a dozen other Class A members of Nepali heritage brought a group of about twenty younger Nepalese students from the form two classes taught by myself and Tad to conduct activities similar to those they experienced at the day camp. To finish off her year, she appeared briefly on an international interview program that had taken an interest on EM education in Hong Kong after images of primary level textbooks containing ethnic stereotypes went viral.

Against a milieu of on-going action to educate herself, her peers, the Nepalese community with which she identified, and local and international media audiences, I received a question from Pramiti via Facebook instant messenger. I have broken up the episode into three extracts, beginning with Extract 6.7. Because this is part of a longer conversation that took place over four and a half hours, I've removed some bits that I will summarize. These bits involve me giving longer responses to Pramiti. I will take up three extracts one at a time. Each number on the left of the extracts represents an individual message that was sent.

Extract 6.7 "I have a question"

1	Pramiti:	Mr. C
2		I have a question
3	Mr. C:	of course you do
4	Pramiti:	We believe that we want the teachers to teach us with different pedagogy. But doesnt that mean we want something different than local Chinese students?
5	Mr. C:	it depends
6		do you also want it for the Chinese students?
7	Pramiti:	Even if we demand that we want that kind of education for all the students in Hong Kong but will the government be able to do that? We have our limitation.
8	Mr. C:	Do you want a totally different pedagogy, or do you want teachers to just have more diverse methods?
9		I other words, do want them to have more tools?
10		And do you want them to connect more to your lives, your cultures, while you also learn about HK, China, and the world?
11		Do you want them to build up your English language more carefully so you can read, write, and discuss in every subject?
12	Pramiti:	Yes I wish they would use basic technology tools or services such as movies, songs, and even fb!
13		I also hope that they not only prepare us for the exam but for the coming future. Things that is happening around us or around the globe and build up our problem-solving skills

{Mr. C (researcher) and Pramiti, messaging communication, June 18, 2014}

Extract 6.7 begins with Pramiti addressing me directly and posing a problem that sets a frame for our interaction, which will expand and get elaborated in the extract. She writes, "We believe that we want the teachers to teach us with different pedagogy. But doesnt that mean we want something different than local Chinese students?" (message 4). In this message, she sets up a conflict around ethnic groups and pedagogy, assuming that a "we," comprised of non-Chinese students, and possibly some of her teachers, desires different teaching and learning practices from "local Chinese students" (message 4). I avoid a direct answer, asking her instead to consider if she wants a similar pedagogy for the Chinese students at her school (message 6).

Pramiti takes my point into consideration, and hypothetically expands the scope of the conflict to include "all the students in Hong Kong" and the local government, but sees that a collective body, "we," has a "limitation" about what could be practically changed even if demands are made (message 7). My response is a lecture, in the form of questions, that invites her to consider how radical a change she seeks, offering "a totally different pedagogy" on one pole, and "more tools" on the other (messages 8 and 9). Furthermore, I suggest that connecting learning to interact with self, locality, nation, and world is important, as well as a prioritizing building English across the curriculum (messages 10 and 11). The extract concludes with Pramiti responding affirmatively, and elaborating further on pedagogical changes she desires. She adds the use of technology and popular cultures, and the specific use of Facebook (fb), the social media platform through which the dialogue was being experienced, and a preparation that builds up problem-solving skills and transcends exams to one's future and social and global changes (messages 12 and 13).

In Extract 6.7, Pramiti started an epistemological dialogue that was instrumentally oriented but was also informed by ontological concerns. Her question posed a dilemma in so far as her belief about pedagogy might cause a dilemma around what it means to be an EM student, making epistemology challenge ontology (message 4). In other words, if her belief about education makes her different from "Chinese" students, does that mean that her belief is isolating, and therefore, not liberating? She created a self-imposed pedagogical task and chose dialogue with me as a tool to meet her goal of understanding. She posed the question and I replied through discourse that suggested she may take my response or reject it, or perhaps was a veiled authoritative command to accept my response. Like Tara in the "Letters Dialogue," she shared ontological concerns about the educational needs and the well-being of her peers. While Tara pinpointed the emotional, social, and relational needs of youth, Pramiti looked at more practical issues of pedagogical practices on the part of teachers. Yet, the issue of who counted in Pramiti's "We," or with whom she felt solidarity, was still unclear to me. Equally important was what was motivating her desire for change. Was it that she could perform better on the Hong Kong Diploma of Secondary Education (HKDSE) and conform to existing structures that marginalized those around her, or was she motivated by a desire to transform oppressive limits around her?

I furthered our interaction through a series of eight messages stating my views on educational reform. In what I now consider an overly simplistic view of curriculum policy and practice, I explained that the government had also supported the changes she called for in its revised curriculum, but that teachers and schools either lacked understanding, resources, or caring, or simply believed that the current textbook and recitation practices were the best way to achieve high marks on public exams. I stated that some schools did understand the changes that should be made, but that the lack of implementation for her and her peers was "because you guys are working class, you [do not] have the resources." I finished with a provocation for action, pressing her to "stand up [for] all students who want a different education," and claim that a "multicultural education" in which "we…learn about different histories, literature, experiences, and perspectives" is "crucial." With this provocation, we pick up the dialogue with Extract 6.8, which takes an ontological turn as Pramiti examines her beliefs and experiences in the world.

Extract 6.8 "They wont understand our view"

14	Mr. C:	Away are you thinking about this?
15		*Why?
16		Many teachers at our school, maybe most, think I am not giving you a good education and not preparing you for the HKDSE. They are not interested in how I teach.
17	Pramiti:	Hmmm. we want different way of teaching from the teachers but this view makes us isolate from the local community.
18	Mr. C:	what view? wanting a different education? yes !
19	Pramiti:	yes !
20	Mr. C:	Explain. how does the desire, or need isolate you? And who do you mean by "local community"?
21	Pramiti:	Because our thinking and the Chinese students thinking are different. They wont understand our view and neither will we understand theirs. Soo if we dont agree on the same thing that led us to being divided into a separate group.
22	Mr. C:	Are you talking about the Chinese students in our school?
23	Pramiti:	yes.
24		Not only in our school, I assume even at other school, we'll have the same situation.
25	Mr. C:	Well, I think you are right and wrong.
26		There are definitely students who will still want to learn in a textbook exam oriented way, and for some, that might be the best way to learn. But tho might be because they have never learned in a different way.
27		that*
28	Pramiti:	yes yes
29		I wish we had the rights to choose between the two ways of teaching.
30		learning*

{Mr. C (researcher) and Pramiti, messaging communication, June 18, 2014}

After offering Pramiti my views, I inquire about the rationale for her initial question (messages 14 and 15) and engage her in epistemological dialogue by seeking out her misconceptions so I can expose them to her, while I divulge to her my positioning against teachers at ISS who "are not interested in how I teach (message 16)." Pramiti aligns herself with me and problematizes the stance for a different education stating that it, not lack of Chinese language proficiency, causes isolation "from the local community" (message 17). Pramiti explains "our thinking and the Chinese students thinking are different" (message 21). She sees this as an immutable fact, a reality not subject to transformation, that she "assumes" transpires beyond the immediate context of ISS. I challenge her misconception about divergent thinking based on ethnicity (message 25), causing her to change her position and assert her wish to have greater choice and rights in education (messages 27 and 28).

In an exchange of seventeen messages that follow the interaction in Extract 6.8 the epistemological dialogue about what education is desired by whom continued, as I provided Pramiti with examples of my experiences working with ethnic Chinese students of various socioeconomic backgrounds in Hong Kong. I reference that many ethnic Chinese students, especially those who attend international schools, might already learn through the pedagogical practices she thought would be incompatible with "Chinese" thinking. I also told her the story of when I went to a job interview at a band two school and saw a display in the school's main office which was decorated with students' comments from a viewing of the Bollywood movie, "3 Idiots," which had been a cornerstone of our form one curriculum in Class A. These messages were supposed to further expose Pramiti to what I saw as a misconception in her thinking. At this point, we arrive at Extract 6.9.

Extract 6.9 "I was being stereotype -.-"

31	**Pramiti**:	hmmmm. okay! I was being stereotype -.-
32	**Mr. C**:	Yes
33		but I do think there is much isolation in our school
34		I think if other students watched 3 Idiot and Taare Zameen Par, then we could all talk about what kind of teaching and learning we want. Do you know 3 Idiots was so popular with Chinese people in HK? Many people saw it
35	**Pramiti**:	yes sire I know!
36	**Mr. C**:	we need to communicate with Chinese students and find out what they want and need.
37	**Pramiti**:	My chinese friends love that movie!

{Mr. C (researcher) and Pramiti, messaging communication, June 18, 2014}

Extract 6.9 concludes this episode with a realization by Pramiti and further alignment by the two of us. She shows she is considering my previous messages and signals her arrival at a Eureka moment through her use of "okay!" understanding that she was stereotyping others and emphasizes her realization with an emoticon she explained to me expressed shock at herself (message 31). Then reasserts her belief that students at her school are isolated (message 33). I offer that sharing of two Bollywood movies that were part of our study of education could be bridging texts that would put ethnically diverse Chinese and non-Chinese students into dialogue with each other, and try to give credence to my suggestion by explaining "3 Idiots" had appealed to Chinese audiences (message 34). In my last message of the episode, I give us a call to action, to communicate with Chinese students at ISS to learn more about them, and receive Pramiti's positive reaction to my previous message (messages 36 and 37).

Through this dialogue, we both taught, learned, and changed. Pramiti became aware that she was stereotyping Chinese students, while I became more conscious of the authoritative discourses that can constrain myself and my students to a particular view of reality that legitimizes my practices. In the episode, Pramiti referred to a limitation impeding changing reality, the inability to reach understanding of perspectives between herself and Chinese students (message 21). What I see now is that she perhaps, adopting the discourses available to her, echoed my sentiment, shared with me by my collaborators, including my ethnic Chinese Panel Head Jane, that some teachers at our school, were not interested in my pedagogy or able to understand it. By failing to model or to consider with her how I could reach understanding with Chinese teachers, I failed to model how she could reach understanding with Chinese students beyond using the Bollywood texts I suggested (message 34) and suggesting more communication (message 36).

As a result, I used the dialogue to enact a collusion with her around pedagogy, but maybe positioned her against teachers. Though I had prompted Pramiti to reconsider her stereotype, positioning her against teachers by not entering into further dialogue, could mean that pedagogical violence was committed by me. Pramiti initiated the episode with an authorial confidence and provoked me into epistemological dialogue to define the problem of what different ethnic groups at the school wanted in education. Her question led to questions from me, and my questions led to more questions from her. As the hero of the dialogue she staged, I did not bring a new reality into our dialogic space. Instead my responses, which in my initial analysis looked like ontological dialogue in the form of a lecture, constituted the imposition of an intellectual framework that defined my own practices and choice of texts as what should be valid for her to consider (messages 8–11 and 34). What looked as a series of questions was an authoritative, monological, discourse disguised as questions. Rather than move both of us to new possibilities through genuine questions that required us to jointly imagine new texts and practices, I reinforced my practices as the only valid reality without having either one of us ponder if there were texts or pedagogical practices outside of what we experienced in my class that would be desirable for her and her peers. Because as a teacher, I have a deep sense of love and commitment to Pramiti, I should have respected our trust more by asking questions to which I did not know the answer or by questioning the validity of my responses.

It is in the moment of writing these words my eyes are opened to the possibility for humanizing other teachers and furthering dialogical questions between myself and students. What I understood as a fixed reality in the moment of the Messaging Dialogue I now understand, thanks to the work of Pramiti in bringing me into dialogue, as my own limit requiring further reflection and action in order to arrive at more change. This does not mean that there was necessarily more that I could have done at ISS to communicate to teachers my willingness to share and learn. Perhaps they did not want to engage in dialogue. Instead, it means that it is imperative to seek out spaces in which dialogue with teachers from more diverse backgrounds is possible, and if that space does not exist, then I should work to create it. Pramiti likewise came to an understanding of how she dehumanized others through biased thinking, and in the following weeks started speaking with Chinese students at our school to figure out what they wanted changed in the school, furthering her capacity for transformative resistance that went beyond herself and her ethnic allegiances. Thus, we both came to an understanding of the limits in which we relate to others. We both saw unchangeable realities that we later reimagined as a critical situation on which to reflect so we could carry out new action.

Students moving into transformative resistance

These episodes shared in this chapter speak to the empowerment that curriculum and dialogic relationships helped to generate. Students had voices in my classes, in online spaces, and in academic and community spaces to which access was opened by myself and collaborators. There were instances, as illustrated by the Levitation Dialogue, in which students became empowered to take on new creative and artistic challenges. Furthermore, students could express concerns, even with topics that were of grave consequence to them that may have not been allowed in other classroom spaces. On top of becoming empowered through voice and expression, students were empowered academically. Dialogic pedagogical spaces were set up around explicit instructional goals, including the use of vocabulary, speaking conventions, listening skills, and use of sentence patterns. As students met these pedagogical goals, the skills they needed to perform well on the HKDSE strengthened. Before my termination by ISS, I scheduled students who had remained in my class for form four to take a mock English HKDSE speaking exam administered through a local university, and Pramiti, Tara, Naija, and Jagan, all scored top-end marks.

Out of students' dialogue with themselves, transformative resistance emerged. Students had gained a social critique and were motivated to act for social justice. In this chapter, we saw how Tara resisted the culture of silence in her classroom and spoke up out of a sense of wanting to stop hatred. For Pramiti, her reflections on education led her to continued action speaking on behalf of education and her classmates. In the weeks and months after the Pyramid of Hate Dialogue and the Messaging Dialogue, before my departure from ISS and after, nearly all of the students in Class A continued with social action, either as participants or as organizers. I continued to work with a group of ten students from ISS in a research project, and as was our habit, they presented to university classrooms and participated in an international symposium on minority education in Asia. Some Class A students continued to speak out in the English, Nepali, and Chinese language media to advocate for the needs of youth in their communities, speaking with renewed understandings of the themes that had been integral in our curriculum and dialogue. More importantly, they organized activities at their school and off-campus to engage other EM youth in dialogue about what kind of education they wanted and how they could go about identifying and addressing conflicts in their lives.

Tara, who was previously reticent from presenting her letters to her peers, finally gave a talk to her peers and continued her attacks on the culture of silence. Through participation in a research program led by myself and Dr. M after I left ISS, she gave a talk titled "A Patriarchal/Sexist Discourse in the Nepalese Community" at a local university, and then decided to give the same presentation to her Nepali peers at ISS, which she did by soliciting Tad's assistance. The more sophisticated social critique and social action I had hoped for in 2012 were materializing.

Nevertheless, not all students were equally empowered. In the form three Class A, I did not manage to form the trusting relationship necessary as a foundation for dialogue with the boys who had joined the class in the third year. Without access to the previous curriculum, experiences, and networks, and relationship with me as the teacher shared by Class A, it is not surprising that this subset of students did not seemed staked in the social critique and action exhibited by others in the class. Within their marginalized participation in my class, even after having witnessed dialogue and participated in it, they did not generate empowered actions observed by me. So what does this chapter tell us about how dialogue was carried out and how it could be widened to include and empower more voices?

Establishing continuity with students, as both Tara and Pramiti identified, can be essential to building and maintaining empowering dialogic relationships. The episodes of dialogue in this chapter, and the actions that followed them, were facilitated by a continuity in the teacher-student relationships between myself and those students in Class A with whom I could build trusting relationships over the course of three years. Our classrooms were dialogic, though not always for everyone or at all times, yet a space was created in which dialogue, both epistemological and ontological, was always a possibility. This created a continuity in terms of dialogical relations that were present and ready to be activated. Maintaining a teaching continuity also allowed some students to undergo longer-term transformation, changing how they came to know the world and how they were in it. For example, in Levitation, Letters, and Pyramid of Hate Dialogues, Tara visibly moved from a playful ontological dialogue, free of social critique, to a dialogue acknowledging a culture of silence and self-defeating resistance, to dialogic action in which she broke through silence, respectively. As a form one student, she needed a world in which to practice (the pedagogical spaces opened by myself and others), so that life would not just be pages of a book revealing themselves to her one day at time. By the end of this research, she had taken greater hold of her life, even as problems persisted, and found ways to author dialogues in which others could engage.

Beyond the continuity provided by my presence and my CP approach, and students' involvement, the continuous presence of Lagan, Jane, Pragun, Tad, and Dr. M all figured in a wider community of dialogic relationships that was networked into the curriculum. They added voices and other resources to dialogue that increased the empowering limits of my pedagogy, including content, experiences, locations, and leadership. Besides speakers like our artist and Holocaust survivor, these collaborators brought to my students interlocutors capable of revealing their struggles and sharing their epistemological and ontological orientations, while imparting on students their critiques society and endeavors to change the world. Through their personal social capital, my collaborators provided locations, audiences, and additional participants outside the classroom into which dialogue could extend, including social networking sites, community centers, schools, social service organizations, and university classrooms.

Regardless of the continuity, resources, and spaces that facilitated dialogue, for empowerment to emerge, students and I had to open ourselves, and each other, to risk, discomfort, and being unsettled in the process of learning together and growing intellectually (Moriarty, Danaher, and Danaher 2008, p. 432). For Tara, discomfort came in a difficult process of investigating and writing about her pain then making it public, and later came in negotiating an uncertain situation with her classmates in order to speak out against hate. For Pramiti, discomfort first came in managing a cognitive and emotional dissonance between her desire for a liberating education and the isolation it seemed to be producing, and later the discomfort came in accepting that she was looking at others with stereotypes, even as she was searching for freedom within education for herself and for those she considered her peers. For me, it meant stepping into activities with apprehension and no knowledge of the outcome, and also opening myself to and feeling a visceral response to the sharing of students' struggles. Similarly, by being present during dialogue, students needed to be open to any discomfort that transpired in the course of unfiltered sharing by others as the class moved from relating to curricular content in epistemological dialogue to relating to each other in ontological dialogue. Furthermore, their names, actions, and utterances could at any moment become subject to dialogic examination, even if they had chosen to step back, as was the case in the Pyramid of Hate Dialogue. For students to invest in the discomfort of dialogue, and thus become empowered, they had to trust I was invested along with them.

Building trust involved reciprocal listening, an act that involved both hearing and talking. Through hearing, critical educators "increasingly prepare themselves to be heard by learners" and by talking "with learners, democratic teachers teach the learners to listen to them as well" (Freire 2004, p. 102). Listening to students helped to "develop and negotiate" interest in my dialogical provocations, making interest in the dialogue grounded in students' lives (Matusov and Miyazaki 2014, p. 10). Listening allowed for the noise, the multimodal utterances that we may disregard and misidentify as inconsequential, of the everyday concerns of students to enter the classroom space. This noise was audible on social media posts by students, which assisted in generating the Letters Dialogue, being aware of prejudiced attitudes and acts of discrimination they faced or perpetuated, making the Pyramid of Hate Dialogue possible, or making myself available when students wanted to talk face-to-face or online, as was the case with the Messaging Dialogue.

Listening to noise came in the midst of reading class work and doing data collection. For example, Tara shared musings on boredom in her writing for assignments and during an interview led me to interpreting them as "the absence of possibility for creative engagement with the world" (Pérez-Milans and Soto 2014, p. 226) and then to engaging her and her classmates in the Levitation Dialogue. Listening persisted after dialogue, as I was able to see that love and other generative themes, both in the Letters Dialogue and the Pyramid of Hate Dialogue, needed more reflection, action, and investigation in our curriculum, even though I had covered it in form two. Ultimately, listening to students allowed me to see "possibilities hidden within them" (Matusov and Miyazaki 2014, p. 33), and examples in this chapter illustrate students' latent potentials for being creative in the world, for acting as revolutionary leaders, and for intertwining concerns of the well-being of their peers with more immediate concerns of individual academic advancement. Moreover, my potential for change and greater understanding, of students and the limitations of my practice, through reflection and through dialogue with data, was also evident in this chapter and underscores the importance of listening. Without listening, there would have been no trust, and without trust, there would have been no dialogue, thus limiting the possibility for transformative empowerment.

Summary

Within my CP, dialogue in varied forms was useful and necessary—dialogue as an instrument of curriculum, dialogue as way to build and question knowledge, epistemological dialogue on concepts separate from our own experiences, and dialogue that brought us closer to each other's humanity. All forms were necessary for empowerment because "epistemological and ontological transformations are codependent on one another" (Kajner 2013, p. 14). Students, and I, could not dialogue about what we knew and how we knew it without first addressing how to be with each other, and we could not address how to be with each other without looking at generative themes that built our knowledge and vocabulary of the world around us. When I could build relationships that respected and expanded students' epistemological and ontological concerns, hope and humility pervaded our relationships. Through me they felt that the world could change, and through them, I felt that they could be the ones to create the change. They could accept when they were mistaken, or that their beliefs could be scrutinized, and I could accept no pedagogy could be a savior and that I was not a hero, unless it meant being the hero of the dialogue they authored for me to join.

7 Toward critical hope

> Where do we go, where do we go now? Where do we go? Sweet Child, where do we go now?
>
> – Guns N' Roses, "Sweet Child O' Mine"

Stories have power. They stir up emotions, motivate, and help us make sense of each other, the world, and ourselves. They ask questions and teach. They are written and re-written, and model the potential we all have to be, or to change. As bell hooks (2010, p. 56) put it, "Story, especially personal story, is one of the most powerful ways to educate." In my three years at Industrial Secondary School (ISS), I invested in the power of stories, both personal and fictional.

One prominent fictional story in my English classes was the Bollywood hit movie "3 Idiots" (Hirani 2009). In the movie's resolution, the protagonist, Rancho, is presented with a special pen by Dr. Viru, better known as "Virus," one he had been saving for an extraordinary student. Before this moment, the relationship between Virus and Rancho had been strained. Rancho openly challenged Virus' textbook-bound pedagogy and philosophy of education as a race, making himself a nuisance to Virus. But after Rancho exhibits ingenuity in a life-saving climax, Virus has a change of heart and presents Rancho with the pen. In the story's denouement, we see Rancho ten years later, at the school he founded, where creativity and playfulness abound. For my students, my collaborators, and myself, this story allowed us to understand models of pedagogy, led students to analyze personal conflicts, and inspired some of us to believe that a different vision of schooling was possible.

But real life does not always have a happy ending or the resolution we feel we deserve. After my dismissal from ISS I referenced this moment in "3 Idiots" in a message I shared on Facebook as I considered what to do next:

Extract 7.1: "This is real life, not a movie"

> A school faces many constraints, and within those constraints, a critical/transformative pedagogy is increasingly difficult. My goal now has to be to create a space for like-minded educators, families, and students to build the

DOI: 10.4324/9780429465215-7

> learning community they deserve. This is real life, not a movie. Virus does not give the pen to Rancho. If we want a different kind of education, we have to build it.
>
> {Carlos (researcher), Facebook post, October 26, 2014}

Likening myself to Rancho, I referenced "3 Idiots" to share an imagined possibility, that a school built on a different vision of education is possible. After the events of October 2014, students, colleagues, and I faced a choice: Do we accept that a critical pedagogy (CP) meant to empower ethnic minority (EM) students in Hong Kong can only go so far, or do we choose to write a new story? To borrow the lyrics from a song popular among my students, "Where do we go now?"

Where do we go now?

In the wake of my and Lagan's dismissal from ISS, some of my students chose the latter, and put their voices and academic skills to use. The week after our dismissal, a group of over sixty of my former students, along with a group of their parents, staged a boycott of the school and called a press conference. Pramiti, whose concern for education was featured in Chapter 6, was tasked with writing a letter to the school as a student representative of the boycotting group. In the letter, she included a list of demands:

Extract 7.2: The boycott's demand

> We demand: 1. an education which addresses our academic, social and emotional needs 2. an education which respects our identity and views it as an essential aspect of our education 3. teachers who can offer effective and flexible pedagogies which maximize the opportunities for us to reach our potential. We are tired of being used simply as pawns to keep the school alive. We require a vision and the strategies the school will implement to achieve it. Without teachers who can develop suitable curriculum, how can we students move ahead and prepare ourselves for the HKDSE, university and the world beyond?
>
> {Pramiti, letter to school, October 26, 2014}

Pramiti urged for students' holistic needs to be met through capable teachers and appropriate curriculum and pedagogies, along with the vision and practical work to achieve these goals, and admonished the school's use of EM students to maintain its enrollments. Her demands were in line with the Education Bureau's (EDB) vision of a reform process granting students a space to participate in implementing change. Tara, whose revolutionary leadership was also visible in Chapter 6, took it upon herself to write to an educator and journalist who had penned a story about the troubles students in band three schools faced. Looking for any source of support, she explained to the journalist what students lost as result of the sudden dismissals:

Extract 7.3: "These skills were also helping to let us prepare for the HKDSE"

We have been studying African-American literature, movies, poems, watching documentaries, learning how to write with complex words, learning to think critically, etc. We have also done presentations about pedagogies at the University of Hong Kong and at Baptist University. We were having transformative and generative pedagogies in our class and it helped us to connect these things to our real lives...These skills were also helping to let us prepare for HKDSE. There were only few teachers who supported us to have this kind of pedagogies in our school. These teachers gave us so many opportunities outside the school to let us learn what was outside the world, how we could solve a conflict. These teachers were the only ones we could trust. They were the only ones who supported us academically, psychologically and emotionally as well as in building community.

{Tara, letter to journalist, October 28, 2014}

Tara's writing provides a useful summary, from a students' perspective, of the CP I developed over three years at ISS. She mentions the literature, films, activities, and academic skills that were central to our learning, and she recognizes that our learning was in part about building a community based on trust that would be supportive in how we dealt with conflicts in our lives. At the same time, she continues to use her voice to build social capital. Other students from Class A joined in speaking out in favor of a different vision quality education, particularly in the Nepali language media.

Sometimes in recalling my time at New Territories Secondary School (NTS) and ISS, and more specifically in reflecting on my departure from ISS, I wonder where I went wrong. Could I have spent more energy understanding the struggles of the adults working at the schools, attempting to form more humanizing relationships with fellow teachers and administrators? Did my approach to education and research give rise to a fanaticism that relied on "emotion and sectarianism" (Shudak and Avoseh 2015, p. 468) and unfairly polarized students like Pramiti and Tara against their school? Or were my actions as a teacher and researcher, as well as those of some of my colleagues, justified because they addressed the pressing needs for humanization we found among the students we served? If an empowering CP was possible, but was ultimately unsustainable at ISS, where do we go now? I ponder questions like these often, not always answering them the same way.

Considering the story told in the preceding chapters, we return to my original research question: *What limits and possibilities exist in Hong Kong for empowering Ethnic Minority students through the practice of critical pedagogy?*

The remainder of this final chapter will take on this question, identifying the present constraints that through reflection and action have potential for new possibilities. First, I will consider how this study has advanced CP theory and practice, and how CP should: (a) push theoretical "critical deconstruction" of Hong Kong society, the experiences of youth, and colonized classroom practices and (b) increase engagement in projects of practical "critical construction" that provide "examples of how teaching and learning can be done alternatively" (Lin 2012, p. 82).

Second, I consider structural changes that would promote critical practices in Hong Kong, including changes in pedagogy, policy, and curriculum to facilitate the no-loser principle, defining an approach to diversity in education, opening new educational spaces that welcome critical practices, and developing critical educators and leaders. Finally, I will end with a summons for CP based on solidarity with marginalized groups in Hong Kong, and a call to maintain and struggle for critical hope (Duncan-Andrade 2009).

Advancing critical pedagogy as theory and practice

While this book opens the door for further theorizing in line with recent work examining critical, networked practices that build "community cultural wealth" (Yosso 2005), the sociolinguistic dimensions of empowerment (Pütz, Fishman, and Neff-van 2006), and the nature, development, and measurement of critical consciousness (Watts, Diemer, and Voight 2011), at its heart this book is a theory about how to practice a CP with a specific context and set of conditions. It advances the field of CP and expands possibilities for its practice in Hong Kong, where CP has made few inroads (Lin 2012), through its situated account that took on critiques of CP and adapted previous teacher-researcher accounts (Camangian 2008; Duncan-Andrade and Morrell 2008; Morrell 2002). Chapter 2 acknowledged critiques of CP: ambiguous terms, (Thomson-Bunn 2014), a dearth of explicit teaching tools (Emdin 2001), and curriculum materials, especially within an English as second language teaching context (Crookes 2010), narratives of redemption that overemphasize teachers as heroes (Fischman and Haas 2009), and a need to transform society by moving from single teacher narratives to building wider social movements (Tarlau 2014). Chapters 1 and 2 clarified my understanding of key terms, and subsequent chapters provided specific examples of generative themes, vehicles for engagement, curricular materials, dialogue, and student action. Thus, the content, processes, and related outcomes of this pedagogy are rendered tangibly.

Through this study, a wealth of junior secondary curricular materials, applicable to English language and Personal, Social and Humanities Education were developed, and only a general overview is provided in this book. Therefore, effort needs to be taken to organize and share these materials, and the rationales that underpin them, with members of the CP field and with teachers in and out Hong Kong. This book also addresses the critique of redemptive narratives in accounts of CP. While my collaborators and students at ISS give me much credit in regard to the leadership I took, my account emphasizes a collaborative effort involving colleagues, students, and literature, to which students affixed their own texts and experiences. Through its exploration of dialogue, Chapter 6 tempered my role as a bearer of hope and transformational agency against the heroic and authorial roles embodied by students. Tara, who gained a heroic, authorial confidence in the course of three years, made this clear to me responding to a questionnaire asking if and how she changed as a result of being in my class; she reflected as a form four student that studying with me changed her perspectives on herself and her communities, but added a caveat:

Extract 7.4 "It's not only your classes that influenced me"

But it's not only in your classes that influenced me or changed my thinking about myself and [my] communities. The surroundings, the situations, the people that I've met so far and the people whom I've heard about influenced me to. It has influenced me make changes in myself by respecting my mother and her decisions, by giving first priority to the Lord and second to my family and friends, by listening to those teachers who cared about our future and believing in myself that I can do something great in my life. I can't explain how it has changed the way I think about myself and about the communities because I am still figuring it out.

{Tara, online questionnaire, April 30, 2015}

Tara granted me credit in influencing her, but added me to a long list of other influences including her mother, friends, her religious faith, other teachers, and the experiences in her environment. She pointed out that her participation in my CP did not render her subjectivity complete. Tara was not left "saved," but was still in an ongoing process of "figuring it out." This qualification, in addressing redemptive narratives, reminds us of the possibility to build collaborative pedagogies that connect to and build on the experiences and social and professional networks of teachers, students, and families, as was the case with Pramiti, who in Chapter 6 displayed identity investment in working toward greater equity, in connection with her expanding network coming from our pedagogical work. We should not rely on a teacher to be a superhero fighting the evils in students' lives, and we should also understand that at times, students will be the heroes we teachers need as we face our adversities.

A redemptive narrative is further subverted through my story of NTS, and through the stories of other Class A students at ISS. Though I spent over a year at NTS, my involvement did not lead to significant changes in students, teachers, or the school. My modest contributions there, recounted in Chapter 4, can be neither considered redemptive nor heroic, even if CP guided my actions there. For some students from ISS Class A, my three-year commitment to them (and their commitment to my pedagogy) did not alter a trajectory leading them away from school academics. Two students of Nepali heritage from Class A dropped out of school near the end of the 2014–2015 academic year, and even some of the higher achieving students decided in later months to leave ISS and school altogether to complete their studies independently online with Lagan's help. These stories pose to critical pedagogues the question of how whether they wish to pursue transformation within or outside existing institutions, and illustrate the tentative, non-redemptive form that empowerment can take. It is not necessarily permanent or stable, particularly when the conditions that created it become subject to pronounced discontinuity. At the same time, they point to greater possibilities for CP through spaces that enhance continuity and stable relationships with trusted adults.

Taking on the final critique of CP mentioned in Chapter 2, the need to move from single teacher narratives to wider social movements, transpired in tandem with collaborators, particularly Lagan and Pragun who plugged me into their network of leaders, activists, journalists, and educators working for the betterment of Nepalese and wider EM community in Hong Kong. Activating this network provided us with media outlets through which to challenge the dominant media discourse on EMs in Hong Kong, and for students to become part of reshaping that narrative. I was also able to marshal my standing at my university to bring academic voices and resources to our efforts. These networks expanded students' social capital; giving them access to adults they could trust, besides the few teachers at ISS they saw as supportive. Students also became part of reshaping academic discourse and of bringing ideas of CP from the world of academia back to their own communities. However, ISS was a hub for activity, and with Lagan, Jane, and I no longer there, moving students and connecting them to a wider movement was hampered. Therefore, physical community spaces and university centers focused on critical practices, research, community education, and activism could augment the capabilities of critical educators to expand their practices beyond their classrooms.

In addition to advancing CP by taking on its critiques, this book exemplifies how practices generated in one context can be applied to another. Camangian (2008) and Duncan-Andrade and Morrell (2008) wrote their accounts of CP based on work with urban youth from marginalized communities in California, United States, and used literature, popular culture, including hip hop music, as vehicles for engagement of generative themes, and as bridges to academic literacy and canonical texts. They led students in projects of autobiographical investigation and community-based research. This group of critical teacher-researchers based their pedagogies on and shared with secondary students sociocultural theories of power, race, gender, education, and post-colonialism that provided students with a vocabulary for naming oppression in their worlds, but still connected this critical work to the standards set by the public school systems that employed them.

My CP fused my previous experience with the approaches advocated by this group of teachers and adapted it for a new context. English language literature and popular culture were essential vehicles for engagement that led students into greater learning and met EDB standards. However, adaptations were made. While in some cases I shared students' popular culture interests (for example, I shared a love of rock music), I often had to become a student of their interests

(Bollywood films, anime, manga, Korean pop music, for example) to gain insights into the themes these cultural products presented. Furthermore, my CP needed a different focus on teaching English as a second language at the junior secondary, requiring me to spend much time on more foundational skills. Still, teaching of theoretical vocabulary was included as a way for students to name oppression. Students learned terms to deconstruct their experiences, but rather than employ theories of race and post-colonialism that felt more immediately relevant to my work in the United States, I used theories of education, love, social mobility, and humanization that I felt would more directly speak to the realities faced by my students in Hong Kong. It was also necessary to include theories and perspectives from diverse cultural traditions I had not previously used in my teaching, including Muslim, Hindu, and Buddhist perspectives on the themes we studied.

A major difference in my approach to CP in this study is that I neglected to use a participatory action research (Duncan-Andrade and Morrell 2008) with students. I had hoped to do this work with students, but because I was never at ISS full-time, I found it overwhelming to carry out. I have taught through participatory action research previously, and even assisted Dr. Duncan-Andrade's students on a couple occasions with their projects, so I knew how consuming it could be. But the possibility to carry out this work in Hong Kong remains, and after my dismissal from ISS, Dr. M and I carried out a seven-month project teaching community-based research skills to ten students from ISS.

My CP is just one starting point that needs to be continuously made and remade. The generative themes of students' lives, and the dehumanizing or liberatory experiences schools provide, change, so creating new possibilities for CP in Hong Kong necessitates further critical deconstruction of students' lives, the schools that serve them and wider social forces. In the course of developing pedagogy, I looked back at students' personal histories, national histories, stories of migration, and also family legacies, and I expanded my knowledge of Hong Kong history and its EMs, comprehending their struggles here and their contributions to the formation of the territory. Going forward, research should shed light on how students' patterns of migration and transnational trajectories of identification across social fields (Pérez-Milans and Soto 2016), within a context of late modernity, in which traditions break down and individuals gain further reflexivity regarding their social worlds (Giddens 1991), interact with various forms of oppression and trauma, legacies of colonialism, and contemporary transformations in Hong Kong.

In terms of an understanding of schooling, it is imperative to examine how knowledge, literacy, and social class interact across the range of schools in Hong Kong, so that we understand the links between social class in Hong Kong and school knowledge (Anyon 1980) and can then consider how to move both teachers and students to new epistemological and ontological orientations. Developing a wider critical theory of Hong Kong society and schooling will allow us to "reconstruct education and promote multiple literacies appropriate to the novel material conditions, transformations, and subjectivities emerging in the contemporary era" (Kellner 2005, p. 59). This requires "broad-ranging and robust reconstructive theories in order to grasp the changing social and psychological conditions of life in a globalized, high-tech, digitized, multicultural, and highly conflicted world with its intense challenges, problems, and potential" (p. 58).

Bringing together researchers from different critical traditions that orient themselves either to critical deconstruction or teaching practices furthering critical construction can enhance this work. This was the case in the course of this research, as partnering with Dr. M's critical-sociolinguistic approach helped me link classroom dynamics I would have otherwise ignored, to wider institutional and societal tensions and transformations. At the same time, because of our collaboration, Dr. M was able to more clearly see pedagogy as a site for transformational resistance (Pérez-Milans and Soto 2014). Through critical deconstruction, we will arrive at new forms of critical construction. New generative themes will emerge, and untapped vehicles for engagement will be tested.

Over the past few years, I observed how students made intellectual, social, and emotional investments, went in search of identity, sought escape from pain and despair, or pursued creative and collaborative outlets through transnational mass media that included video games such as League of Legends and Minecraft, the sport of cricket, contemporary urban dance, music, famous YouTubers, and Korean serial dramas. These cultural forms have potential to become sites of critical learning for teachers and students. However, educators will need to critically examine these media and pay attention to what they omit, silence, or reproduce. Transnational media, "driven by the logic of commodity and consumption," erase "traumatic memories of oppression, violence, and injustice in both metropolitan centers and developing countries" through the "soap operas, disaster stories, glamorous geography, and historical dramas" (Kaplan and Wang 2008, p. 11) that our youngsters (and we) consume. Bollywood movies like "3 Idiots" (Hirani 2009), "Udaan" (Motwane 2010), and "Taare Zameen Par" (Khan 2007) are not free of biases and myths, but by studying them carefully, they became engaging classroom tools that could lead to dialogue, and the same can be true of other popular culture.

Though CP constitutes a powerful collection of theoretical and practical tools, and lays a foundation through which praxis leads to new forms of criticality to address unique contexts, on their own, theory and practice do not necessarily change structural conditions. Therefore, systematic changes should be pursued that will amplify opportunities for student empowerment and allow for critical practices to further be adapter for the Hong Kong context and achieve more sustainability.

Changing the system

Four possibilities for empowerment should happen at a systematic level. These are: (1) changes in pedagogy, policy, and curriculum, (2) defining a policy for diversity in education, (3) opening spaces where critical practices can flourish, and (4) fostering critical educators and leadership. Each of them will be further examined, in turn, in the sections below.

A no-loser principle through pedagogy, policy, and curriculum

Chapter 1 reviewed the wave of educational reforms and a no-loser principle that followed the handover of Hong Kong to China, and asserted that the spirit of these reforms has largely been unrealized within the context of EM education in Hong Kong. Chapter 4 showed that educational reforms meant to promote generic skills, and specific values and attitudes through student-centered pedagogies did not have a foothold at NTS and ISS where monologic, monocultural, textbook-based pedagogies, which did not adequately promote academic literacy, were dominant. Kennedy (2012) has already argued for broad changes in pedagogy, policy, and curriculum to ensure the "no-loser" principle applies to EM students, advocating that "all communities must be valued and must have a role to play in the development of the social fabric" and that schools must ensure "all students are treated fairly and provided with relevant curriculum and learning and guaranteed outcomes that will help them contribute in a productive way" (p. 20).

Kennedy suggested that positive feedback, encouragement, and cooperative learning be regular parts of pedagogy for students working with EM students (and also teachers working with ethnic Chinese students), and that policies which allow flexible usage of medium of instruction could be beneficial to EM students and build up a "socially resilient society" that would "ensure ethnic minority students are able to contribute to their own future as well as that of Hong Kong" (p. 19). This study supports Kennedy's proposal a way of ensuring the "no-loser" principle and illustrates the positive effects of practices such as relevant curriculum, encouragement, cooperative learning, and valuing and involving students' communities. Many of these practices, though, are possible now within the framework of the most recent reforms, so we need to consider how to make sure they are implemented, and change school cultures so that new practices are embraced.

We should also consider promoting not just pedagogies, policies, and curriculum that allow students to *contribute* to Hong Kong, but to maximize their potential to positively transform themselves, their families, their communities, and our society. In other words, we do not need pedagogy, policy, and curriculum "merely [preparing] students to fit into society and to experience social class mobility within existing structures" (Banks and Banks 1995, p. 152) already marked by inequity, bias, and discrimination. We need unified pedagogy, policy, and curriculum enabling "students not only to acquire basic skills but to use those skills to become effective agents for social change" (p. 152) individually and collectively. Also, we need to define what "diversity" is and what it means to Hong Kong society and the education system.

Defining an approach to diversity in education in Hong Kong

Over the past decade, various versions of an approach have been recommended, but either the EDB or the Hong Kong government has adopted none. The more common suggestions are based on awareness to cultural difference. For example, ten years ago, Ku, Chan and Sandhu (2005, p. 101) recommended a school-level approach to diversity based on "cultural sensitivity," including practices such as "cultural sensitivity training for teaching staff, developing curriculum suitable for the needs of minorities, extracurricular activities promoting cultural diversity, and review of school administration and management to eliminate cultural bias." Similarly, the Hong Kong Equal Opportunities Commission (2011, p. 10) endorsed a sensitivity-based approach, calling for "inclusive and racially harmonious" learning environments, training of principals and teachers in "awareness and sensitivity," and promoting "respect for diversity, equal opportunity values and human rights education" as a core module in the Liberal Studies subject.

Other views have gone beyond awareness to recommend taking on issues of power more directly. For instance, in a government commissioned report, Kennedy, Phillion, and Hue (2007) went past "cultural sensitivity" and advised "the development of policy on multiculturalism or cultural diversity" with emphasis "placed on training teachers on multiculturalism and minority education issues, and the introduction of anti-racist and critical multicultural education (including prejudice reduction) in teacher preparation courses." More recently, Erni and Leung (2014, p. 11) argued the need to move from a "benevolent multiculturalism" limiting itself to notions of fixed cultural groups and promoting assimilation of these groups by a dominant society to achieve harmony, to a "critical multiculturalism" recognizing power imbalances, the dynamic nature of cultures and identities, and the necessity of a "process of struggle and resistance to ethno-cultural hegemony" in order to make ethnic differences visible.

NTS and ISS paid lip service to approaches highlighting racial harmony and diversity, and reinforced fixed, and often stereotypical views of culture that did not take issues of power and social status into account. ISS not only used this language within the school but also made it a center piece of promotional materials. Rejecting these approaches, I advocate for critical approaches to diversity that validate the complexity of identities, cultures, and communities and also include anti-racist and anti-bias curriculum within schools. Chapter 6 offered an example of a curricular lesson, The Pyramid of Hate Activity, which tackles bias, prejudice, discrimination, and violence. But I also believe that more traditional approaches to multiculturalism continue to offer possibilities for policy and practice. For example, Banks and Banks' (1995) influential approach to multiculturalism in education advocates a framework based on five dimensions, including integration of content from students experiences and cultures into transformative curriculum and teaching, knowledge construction, prejudice reduction, and an empowering school culture, that all support an "equity pedagogy" that helps to "create and perpetuate a just, humane, and democratic society" (p. 153).

Banks and Banks' framework for multicultural education informed my work at ISS and can inform teachers and administrators within schools to set a direction at the class level, or policy at the school level. What is more important though, is not for the government, EDB, or schools, to just choose from any of approaches to diversity cited in this section. The fact that all these suggestions exist means that students, families, educators, and policy makers, need to learn about them, understand what is implied by each approach and how they differ from monocultural and assimilationist perspectives, and then engage in dialogue to move forward with action.

Creating spaces in which empowering practices thrive

During this research, I met committed and passionate educators who lacked the institutional space to fully collaborate with like-minded colleagues. Shum, Gao, and Tsung (2012, p. 260) have proposed the Hong Kong government establish "South Asian schools, an appropriate and standard curriculum for South Asian students, and an ad hoc assessment system." Though schools set up under the banner of being "South Asian" could lead to further segregation, establishing a school that values diversity and takes a critical multicultural approach is a step that could be taken through the direct subsidy scheme for schools, and could bring critically minded educators together to work with fewer constraints. I support the idea of schools focused on equitable educational opportunities for students of South Asian backgrounds, but promoting a "standard curriculum" over flexible practices might be unnecessarily constraining. Furthermore, these institutions need to be created in the images of students; schools need to be built from the ground up that acknowledge the diversity of knowledge, interests, heritages, cultures, struggles, and social statuses of students and are capable of adapting to changing needs of students and families.

Of course, creating dramatic change in schools, or founding new schools within a system with deeply engrained practices and beliefs, is no easy task. In imagining new possibilities for low-achieving urban schools in the United States, Noguera (2003) acknowledged the external and internal constraints that hinder schools seeking improvement. Schools are externally constrained by a "broad array of demographic and socioeconomic factors, including the arrival of new immigrants…and neighborhood instability" (p. 18). These factors were present at NTS and ISS and exerted influence over the students and the schools, as Noguera argued. Noguera insists that these external constraints be addressed because when they are ignored, they exacerbate the internal constraints of schools, which include "high turnover among superintendents, principals, and teachers." High turnover compounds "the sense of instability present in some schools and results in inexperienced professionals being assigned the most difficult and complex educational jobs" (p. 18).

NTS and ISS faced these same internal constraints, as well as additional constraints noted by Noguera, such as demoralized or burnt-out personnel, and a cynicism about the possibility reforms to be effective when past reforms have failed and not undergone proper evaluation (2003, p. 19). Despite the difficulties caused by external and internal constraints, optimism is still in order. Noguera reminds us that schools already exist where students from marginalized backgrounds thrive, and do so by facing internal and external constraints head-on (p. 19). So we need to believe that what is already happening in some schools should be possible in others. During this research, I was fortunate to be introduced to teachers and the principal of Village Primary School, a school in outer Hong Kong with a long history, that took on admitting EM students for its survival but managed to build an environment in which students felt supported.

A close friend of Lagan's, Amin, has worked at Village Primary School for ten years, teaching Nepali language lessons, developing support program for students, and using the school as a hub for his activism on behalf of EM communities in Hong Kong, in addition to his work in the Nepali media community. Amin advised the school about how to make the diversity of its student population an asset for changing the culture of the school, and the school's principal responded by taking on many of his suggestions and joining him in speaking out for the needs of students in the media and at forums concerning EM education policy. It was not surprising then, that my colleagues and I saw our ISS students who were Village Primary School alumni maintain a close bond with the school once they moved onto secondary. It was also not surprising that these students on average had higher academic skills in English, Chinese, reading, math, and science, compared to students coming to ISS from other primary schools.

I remember the first time I was invited to the Village Primary School's graduation ceremony, held in the town center's formal performance theater. At the beginning of the ceremony, the students sang the school's song, and my eyes swelled with tears as I heard students belt out their notes with a strong sense of pride for their school. In this moment, I knew that better schools for EM students in Hong Kong were possible. But realistically, building more humanizing schools is only possible with the human capital to make it happen, individuals committed to struggling in solidarity with students and families for equity.

Developing critical educators and leaders

What will it take for teachers to reorient themselves toward criticality and alternative, more empowering, humanizing beliefs and practices, and engaging in dialogue as a teacher-student? To answer these questions, let me consider the case of Paula, an English teacher at NTS. Paula was raised a working-class Hong Kong family and attended a low-banded secondary school. As a teacher she wanted to work in a band three school to help students with similar backgrounds. I asked her if she had any training related to working with EM, "band three," or working-class students:

Extract 7.5: "I kind of forget about the theory"

CARLOS: Okay. When you had your teacher training, was any of the training on the practical side or any of the training on the theory side? Was it related to working specifically with non-Chinese students or was it related to working specifically with Band 3 students or more low-income students?

PAULA: Well, it's hard to say because when I received my—when I study in the university, most of the lecturer believe that theory is good enough and they kind of ah, like to talk about all sorts of theories especially the teach, the pedagogical theories to us. However, when just like four years ago, when I started teaching in another Band 3 school, I find that ah, it's sometimes it's hard to integrate a theory into the practical, into such a practical way. And then so I kind of forget about the theory. Because theory is another thing, you got to learn from—I would prefer to learn from the—from my teachers because they kind of shared their experience with you. And just for example, when you face a particular difficult or troublesome students, if they would like to share some of their experience with you, and then you can sort of learn more from it.

{Paula, interview, July 8, 2011}

Paula, who was a caring and well-liked teacher, recounted her training as theory without practice, and her first few years teaching as practice devoid of formal theory. Finding theory as "hard to integrate into the practical," she decided to "forget about the theory." If the theories her colleagues circulate exist to cope with existing conditions or to reinforce myths, rather than to transform current conditions, then Paula effectively cut herself from the possibility of a critical praxis, choosing instead to seek strategies for facing "difficult or troublesome students." As a result, the teaching I observed found Paula, despite her kind intentions, trying in vain to muscle the working-class ethnic Chinese students through textbook-based, examination-oriented English curriculum that left the vast majority of them failing. Paula could not imagine an alternative pedagogy workable within her perceived constraints. I wonder still how Paula could be a different teacher if she could learn with professors and teachers who let her encounter examples of how critical theory informed their critical practice.

When I first began working with students in the United States, I was not the same critical educator I am today. My critique of society and subjugating education was much less developed, and at best, I thought by pushing students and having high expectations, and finding strategies for "troublesome students," I could get them to conform to the existing system so they could be academically successful. The notion of transformative resistance that would allow students to collectively name and struggle against social oppression was still foreign to me. Chapters 1 and 2 included a retelling of the trajectory my evolution as a critical educator followed. The training I received from critical pedagogues in my graduate education program, which had a concentration on equity and social justice in education, the opportunity to develop my practice at the Bay Area Education Program, and my own upbringing and learning in diverse environments accumulated into a powerful source of capital for melding theory with practice. Of note were the opportunities I had to learn from critical pedagogues who shared their praxis, making clear the theoretical foundations of their work and the practices those theories engendered.

Allman (2010, p. 172) informs us that adopting a critical approach "involves a personal and professional decision to engage in a process of self-transformation," one in which "teachers must be willing to undergo the process of 'rebirth' and to understand why it is necessary." Therefore, teacher training and development programs in Hong Kong must join with teachers in breaking "ideological chains of their own formal education, of past training, and the inertia of habit of past teaching" (Peterson 2003, p. 306). In this process, teachers begin by obtaining a philosophy of education that gives them perspective beyond "educational method" (Allman 2010, p. 172). Acquisition of philosophy of education should be supplemented by the cultivation of the ethnographic sensibility required delving into the cultures and communities of students and for the identification of generative themes.

Moreover, we cannot expect that pre- and in-service teachers in Hong Kong will have the same capital I used to negotiate my process of self-transformation, so we have to understand their funds of knowledge and experiences, to mobilize them into facilitating their journeys of rebirth. As young students need an empowering CP based on generative themes, vehicles for engagement, and dialogue, we need a CP for teacher education, with its own themes and vehicles. Similar to how my students needed theoretical concepts that they could use to name their immediate realities, pre- and in-service teachers need the stories and models of how other educators used theories to understand students and reshape practice. Stories of the trajectories of identification of critical teachers that illuminate the texts and experiences that shifted their perspectives and practices and inner beliefs would be of value. Fortunately, steps have been taken in this direction by intrepid teacher educators in local universities (Chan and Lo 2016; Chang 2018; Lo 2019).

All the possibilities discussed in this chapter, inclusive of a CP of teacher education, rest on the development of school leadership promoting equity and social justice in education. This too is a possibility that has already been imagined for Hong Kong by Ming Chiu and Walker (2007, p. 732):

> Given the palpable inequities within Hong Kong schools, it is incumbent upon the principal and other school leaders to work tangibly to promote social justice. However, concrete actions by a single or small group of actors, regardless of their position or power, only becomes meaningful if these actions are based on a clear set of authentic, just values shared within the school community. We suggest that reducing inequality in schools requires leaders to clarify understandings of their own value stances and those within their communities and; and to focus change efforts simultaneously on structural and cultural mechanisms.

In this view, building socially just learning communities places a responsibility of reflection on those who lead schools, otherwise, attempts at reducing inequalities within a school "might remain superficial" (p. 733). If leaders do not reflect deeply, then inequities remain invisible to them, and when leaders are blind, they cannot steer others in struggling against oppressive conditions. Ming Chiu and Walker (p. 737) elaborate:

> Inequality must be "seen" before it can be countered. However, it is not just a matter of seeing inequality, but of more clearly understanding one's place in its maintenance. Given the structural and cultural inequality in place in Hong Kong schools, leaders tend to view the status quo as the norm, perhaps not even as inequities. Change cannot emerge unless such assumptions are openly faced and subsequently challenged by leaders themselves, as well as by and in their communities.

Once they have carried out serious reflection, leaders with vision can then move to address persistent inequities in Hong Kong schools such as unequal allocation of resources, status differences assigned to students via tracking mechanisms, teacher bias against students, and lack of transparency in decision-making (p. 732). Beyond the capacity for critical reflection, school leaders need the capacity to support teachers in transforming themselves into critically oriented educators, meaning leaders too need a rebirth that brings them a new philosophy of education. Through this rebirth, they should gain a vision that allows them to see not just oppression, but a vision that lets them see empowerment. Only then will a leader be able to hear students like Pramiti and Tara, who articulated a critique of school, and provided suggestions for improvement based on their experiences, reflections, and previous actions to transform themselves, their classes, and their communities.

If a school leader cannot recognize students who feel loved by their teachers, are engaged in learning, and are fighting for justice for their communities, then they will not know what it looks like when inequities are being addressed. It is worth now moving to the importance of solidarity and critical hope, as emerging from the various voices, experiences, and practices examined in my study.

Conclusion: solidarity and critical hope

I mentioned in Chapter 1 that the school struggles for working-class ethnic Chinese students often parallel the experiences of EM students. There is an alienation from schooling that cuts across ethnicity, even if the dominant form of coping with it is different. Tara told us in Chapter 6 how some EM students "play" in class to forget their conflicts. But when I observed classes at NTS, and I walked around the halls of ISS, I often saw ethnic Chinese students coping by sleeping. In a large class, sometimes half the students would be asleep, and in smaller classes, ten out of a dozen students might lay their heads on their desks and shut their eyes to the world. These conditions are widely recognized, and there is an accompanying media discourse bemoaning the "zombie-like existence" of ethnic Chinese students in so-called "band three" schools (Yeung 2014, para. 1). Take this bit from a commentary in an English language newspaper:

> A decade of a daily diet of filling-in-the-blanks English ensures that school-leavers exit the system dumb, to face a bewilderingly uncertain future. But, as bad as this is, worse is yet to come. According to Alex Woo, a reform-minded school supervisor for 23 years until his recent retirement, as many as 50 per cent of students at these "Band 3" schools – that is, schools that cater to academically poor students – may have psychological issues stemming from broken homes, academic failure, alienation, boredom or school stress. Some display suicidal tendencies. This is a chilling report card on public education.
>
> (Yeung 2014, para. 7–8).

Seeing the alienation of ethnic Chinese students who put their heads down in search of respite, escape, or protest signaled the greatest limitation of my CP: it never put my EM students, or me, into dialogue with ethnic Chinese students sitting in the rooms or standing in the lines next to them. My pedagogy was confined to considering the problems my EM students faced, and the alienation of students from each other based on dominant and minority ethnicities was not a problem we took on in earnest. In Chapter 6, Pramiti was emblematic of this lack of solidarity; she harbored stereotypes about ethnic Chinese students and did not see how her concerns for educational equity might align with the needs of students across ethnic boundaries.

I recognize this limitation and the possibility for a CP of greater solidarity. Past thinkers in the field recognized "any genuine pedagogical practice demands a commitment to social transformation in solidarity within subordinated and marginalized groups" (Duncan-Andrade and Morrell 2008, p. 23). If EM students are to fight for educational equity and freedom, then we should build together an inclusive movement that brings in Hong Kong and transnational youth of more diverse backgrounds, including Hong Kong Chinese youth, and those who are fighting against gender, ability, sexuality, class, or refugee-status-based injustice. I had a taste of this possibility in May 2014 when I was given an opportunity to spend three hours with a unique group of students. Working with a fellow educator at an international college with a liberal school vision, Lagan assisted in organizing a week long camp to investigate issues of diversity at the college. They brought together about thirty-five students from a wide spectrum of socioeconomic backgrounds, including students from international schools and local system band one schools, first-year university students from mainland China, and thirteen of my former EM students. Following this experience, I was energized to work on myself and reflect so I may reach a new rebirth that widens my philosophy of education and pedagogical practices in expanded solidarity with others.

So we need hope, and lots of it. We need a belief that the future should be, can be, and will be more just, and the commitment to struggle to make it happen.

But it cannot be any hope (Duncan-Andrade 2009). It must not be a "hokey hope" through which we advise youth, without taking account of the inequities and pain they face, that if they "just work hard, pay attention, and play by the rules" (p. 182), they can achieve dominant notions of success. Nor can it be a "mythical hope" that is "a profoundly ahistorical and depoliticized denial of suffering that is rooted in celebrating individual exceptions" (p. 184), the *look, he did it, and so can you can you* narrative of hope. Nor a "hope deferred" that imagines life will be better for youth in "either a collective utopia of a future reformed society or, more often, the individual student's future ascent to the middle class." This hope fails to help students "cultivate their 'control of destiny'" because it ignores an education in the tools for negotiating the here-and-now suffering they face daily. When students see that teachers are not interested in taking on, or are unable to, this struggle in solidarity with them, they may "come to perceive a significant gap between their most pressing needs and the education we offer them" (p. 185).

Instead, as teachers, we can invest in a "critical hope" that gives students: (1) a material justification for hope through the strength of our teaching and the resources and networks to which we connect students, (2) resilience and strength to pursue a painful road, and (3) a value for solidarity with and sacrifice for others, that we all bloom (Duncan-Andrade 2009). A critical hope may give us the audacity to confront our limits and seize possibility. It can reassure us that no matter what pain we will feel vicariously through our students—because when they hurt, so do we—and what frustrations the struggle for humanization brings, that we can get up and start again. Our critical hope "models for our students that the painful path is the hopeful path" (p. 191). It comforts us in the knowledge that when we commit to our students, they commit to and walk beside us. And it gives us faith that one day, our students overtake us, and they lead the way.

I maintain and struggle for this critical hope because I know it is possible. I have heard it in my students' voices and their songs, I have seen it in their art, and I have read it in their words. I maintain this hope because I recall Tara's words in Chapter 1, and they remind me of walking into a classroom and talking with students, human-to-human. I did not merely instruct students to take out their textbooks and turn to a page. There was humanity in those classes: sharing our feelings, sharing our struggles, and changing our worlds.

Appendix
Transcription conventions

Numeral   Indicates lines of speech as organized in transcription
Name: name of the speaker in the following utterance
[ ]   Brackets around text indicate changes to language made by researcher during transcription; used when verbatim transcription needed clarification for reading purposes
—   Indicates a pause in the speaker's utterance
()   between parentheses indicates researcher's descriptive commentary
…   Indicates speech trailing off

References

Allen, R. L., and Rossatto, C. A. (2009). Does Critical Pedagogy Work with Privileged Students? *Teacher Education Quarterly*, 36(1), 163–180.
Allman, P. (2010). *Critical Education against Global Capitalism: Karl Marx and Revolutionary Critical Education*. Rotterdam: Sense Publishers.
Anyon, J. (1980). Social Class and School Knowledge. *Curriculum Inquiry*, 11, 3–41.
Au, K. H. (1995). Multicultural Perspectives on Literacy Research. *Journal of Reading Behavior*, 27(1), 85–100.
Banks, J. A., and Banks, C. (1995). Equity Pedagogy: An Essential Component of Multicultural Education. *Theory into Practice*, 34, 152–158.
Bartolome, L. I. (2004). Critical Pedagogy and Teacher Education: Radicalizing Prospective Teachers. *Teacher Education Quarterly*, 97–122.
Bhowmik, M. K. (2017). Equitable and Quality Educational Opportunities for Hong Kong's Ethnic Minorities: The Challenges to Achieve SDG4. *Curriculum Perspectives*, 37(2), 191–196.
Bhowmik, M. K. (2019). Ethnic Minority Young People's Education in Hong Kong: Factors Influencing School Failure. In J. Gube & F. Gao (Eds.), *Education, Ethnicity and Equity in the Multilingual Asian Context* (pp. 179–195). Singapore: Springer Singapore.
Bhowmik, M. K., and Kennedy, K. J. (2013). Equitable Provision for Hong Kong's Ethnic Minority Students: Issues and Priorities. *Educational Research Journal*, 27(1/2), 27–49.
Blommaert, J., and C. Bulcaen. (2000). Critical Discourse Analysis. *Annual review of Anthropology*, 29(1), 447–466.
Bourgois, P. (2003). *In Search of Respect: Selling Crack in El Barrio* (Vol. 10). Cambridge: Cambridge University Press.
Boushey, G., and Moser, J. (2006). *The Daily 5*. Portland, ME: Stenhouse.
Breuing, M. (2011). Problematizing Critical Pedagogy. *The International Journal of Critical Pedagogy*, 3(3), 2–23. Chicago.
Brosio, R. (2006). Critical Theory for Schooling-Education and Society. In K. Cooper & R. White (Eds.), *The Practical Critical Educator*. Dordrecht: Springer.
Burbules, N. C. (2000). The Limits of Dialogue as a Critical Pedagogy. In P. Trifonas (Ed.), *Revolutionary Pedagogies: Cultural Politics, Education, and the Discourse of Theory* (pp. 251–273). New York: Routledge.
Burbules, N. C., and Berk, R. (1999). Critical Thinking and Critical Pedagogy: Relations, Differences, and Limits. In T. S. Popkewitz & L. Fender (Eds.), *Critical Theories in Education: Changing Terrains of Knowledge and Politics* (pp. 45–65). New York: Routledge.

Camangian, P. (2008). Untempered Tongues: Teaching Performance Poetry for Social Justice. English Teaching. *Practice and Critique*, 7(2), 35–55.

Camangian, P. (2010). Starting with Self: Teaching Autoethnography to Foster Critically Caring Literacies. *Research in the Teaching of English*, 45, 179–204.

Camangian, P. (2014). The Personal Certainly Is Political: Our Past Must Inform Our Purpose as Educators in the Present. In I. Nuñez, C. Laura, and R. Apers (Eds.), *Diving In: Bill Ayers and the Art of Teaching into the Contradiction – A Tribute to Bill Ayers' Life's Work*. New York: Teacher's College, Columbia University.

Camangian, P. R. (2013). Reading in their Own Interests: Teaching Five Levels of Analysis. International *Journal of Multicultural Education*, 15(2), 1–16.

Cammarota, J., and Romero, A. F. (2009). A Social Justice Epistemology and Pedagogy for Latina/o Students: Transforming Public Education with Participatory Action Research. *New Directions for Youth Development*, 123, 53–65.

Canaan, J. E., Amsler, S. S., Cowden, S., Motta, S., and Singh, G. (Eds.) (2010). *Why Critical Pedagogy and Popular Education Matter Today*. Birmingham: C-SAP. Retrieved from http://aston.ac.uk

Carmichael, S. (2009). Language Rights in Education: A Study of Hong Kong's Linguistic Minorities. Centre for Comparative and Public Law Faculty of Law, The University of Hong Kong Occasional Paper No. 19. Retrieved from https://www.law.hku.hk/ccpl/pub/Documents/

Census and Statistics Department. (2017). *2016 population By-Census, Thematic Report: Ethnic Minorities*. The Government of the Hong Kong Special Administrative Region. Retrieved from http://www.statistics.gov.hk/pub/B11201002016XXXXB0100.pdf

Chan, C., and Lo, M. (2016) Exploring Inclusive Pedagogical Practices in Hong Kong Primary EFL Classrooms. *International Journal of Inclusive Education*, 21(7), 714–729.

Chan, D., and Mok, K.-H. (2001). Educational Reforms and Coping Strategies under the Tidal Wave of Marketisation: A Comparative Study of Hong Kong and the Mainland. *Comparative Education*, 37(1), 21–41.

Chang, B. (2018). Issues of Educational Equity, Curriculum, and Pedagogy in Hong Kong. In K. J. Kennedy & J. C. K. Lee (Eds.), *Routledge International Handbook of Schools and Schooling in Asia* (pp. 110–122). London: Routledge.

Chief Executive. (2014). The 2014 Policy Address: Support the Needy, Let the Youth Flourish, Unleash Hong Kong's Potential. Retrieved from http://www.policyaddress.gov.hk

Chiu, J. (2012, December 7). Jordan, Home to a Battling Nepali Community. *South China Morning Post*. Retrieved from http://www.scmp.com

Chiu, M., and Walker, A. (2007). Leadership for Social Justice in Hong Kong Schools: Addressing Mechanisms of Inequality. *Journal of Educational Administration*, 45(6), 724–739.

Choi, P.-K. (2005). A Critical Evaluation of Education Reforms in Hong Kong: Counting Our Losses to Economic Globalisation. *International Studies in Sociology of Education*, 15(3), 237–256.

Chow, Y. (2013, December 26). Ghetto Treatment Blocks Advance of Hong Kong's Ethnic Minority Students. Retrieved from http://www.scmp.com

Cohen, L., Manion, L., and Morrison, K. R. B. (2007). *Research Methods in Education* (6th ed.). London: Routledge Falmer.

Connelly, J., Gube, J., and Thapa, C. (2013). Hong Kong's Ethnic and Linguistic Minority Immigrant Students: An Evaluation of Educational Support Measures. In E. L. Brown & A. Krasteva (Eds.), *Migrants and Refugees: Equitable Education for Displaced Populations* (pp. 191–214). Charlotte: Information Age Publishing.

Creswell, J. (2002). *Research Design: Qualitative, Quantitative, and Mixed Methods Approaches*. Thousand Oaks: Sage Publications.
Creswell, J. (2013). *Qualitative Inquiry and Research Design: Choosing Among Five Approaches*. Los Angeles: Sage Publications.
Crookes, G. (2010). The Practicality and Relevance of Second Language Critical Pedagogy. *Language Teaching*, 43(03), 333–348. Chicago.
Cummins, J. (1996). *Negotiating Identities: Education for Empowerment in a Diverse Society*. Ontario: California Assn for Bilingual.
Cummins, J. (2000). Language, Power, and Pedagogy: Bilingual Children in the Crossfire (Vol. 23). Clevedon: Multilingual Matters.
Cummins, J. (2009). Multilingualism and Equity: Beyond the Effectiveness Paradigm: Exploring Inspirational Pedagogy for Bilingual Students [PowerPoint Slides]. Retrieved from http://www.londonmet.ac.uk/
Curriculum Development Council. (2000). *Learning to Learn: The Way Forward in Curriculum Development*. Hong Kong: Printing Department.
Davies, C. A. (1999). *Reflexive Ethnography: A Guide to Researching Selves and Others*. New York: Routledge.
Day, J. P. (2002). *Moving Forward with Literature Circles: How to Plan, Manage, and Evaluate Literature Circles that Deepen Understanding and Foster a Love of Reading*. New York: Scholastic Professional Books.
Delpit, L. (1995). *Other People's Children: Cultural Conflict in the Classroom*. New York: New Press.
Dewalt, K. M. D., and Dewalk, B. R. (2002). *Participant Observation: A Guide for Fieldworkers*. Walnut Creek, CA: Alta Mira Press.
Duncan-Andrade, J. (2009). Note to Educators: Hope Required When Growing Roses in Concrete. *Harvard Education Review*, 79(2), 181–194.
Duncan-Andrade, J., and Morrell, E. (2008). *The Art of Critical Pedagogy: Possibilities for Moving from Theory to Practice in Urban Schools*. New York: Peter Lang Publishing, Inc.
Durakoglu, A. (2013). Paulo Freire's Perception of Dialogue Based Education. *International Journal on New Trends in Education and Their Implications*, 4, 102–107.
Education Bureau. (2002). English Language Education Key Learning Area Curriculum Guide (Primary 1- Secondary 3). Retrieved from http://edb.gov.hk
Education Bureau. (2010). Personal, Social and Humanities Education Key Learning Area - Life and Society Curriculum Guide (Secondary 1–3). Retrieved from http://edb.gov.hk
Education Commission. (2000, September). Reform Proposals for the Education System in Hong Kong. Hong Kong Special Administrative Region of the People's Republic of China, Retrieved from http://www.e-c.edu.hk/eng/reform/index_e.html
Ellsworth, E. (1989). Why Doesn't This Feel Empowering? Working Through the Repressive Myths of Critical Pedagogy. *Harvard Educational Review*, 59(3): 297–324.
Emdin, C. (2011). Moving Beyond the Boat Without a Paddle: Reality Pedagogy, Black Youth, and Urban Science Education. *The Journal of Negro Education*, 80, 284–295.
Equal Opportunities Commission. (2011). Report on the Working Group on Education for Ethnic Minorities. Retrieved from http://www.eoc.org.hk
Erni, J. N., and Leung, L. Y. M. (2014). *Understanding South Asian Minorities in Hong Kong*. Hong Kong: Hong Kong University Press.
Fairclough, N. (2001). *Language and Power*. Harlow: Pearson Education.
Fairclough, N. (2006). *Discourse and Social* Change. Cambridge: Polity Press.
Ferguson, A. A. (2001). *Bad Boys: Public Schools in the Making of Black Masculinity*. Ann Arbor: University of Michigan Press.

Fischman, G., and Hass, E. (2009). Critical Pedagogy and Hope in the Context of Neoliberal Globalization. In W. Ayers, T. Quinn, & D. Stovall (Eds.), *Handbook of Social Justice in Education* (pp. 565–575). New York: Rutledge.

Fischman, G., and Sales, S. (2010). Formação de professores e pedagogias críticas: é possível ir além das narrativas redentoras? *Revista Brasileira de Educação*, 15(43), 7–20. Retrieved from http://www.scielo.br

Freire, P. (1970). *Pedagogy of the Oppressed*. New York: Continuum.

Freire, P. (2004). *Pedagogy of the Oppressed: 30th Anniversary Edition*. New York: Continuum.

Freire, P. (2005). *Education for Critical Consciousness*. New York: Continuum.

Freire, P., and Macedo, D. (1987). *Literacy: Reading the Word and the World*. South Hadley, MA: Bergin & Garvey.

FRIDE. (2006). Empowerment. *Development Backgrounder*, 1. http://www.fride.org/descarga/bgr_empowerment_eng_may06.pdf

Gao, F. (2012). Teacher Identity, Teaching Vision, and Chinese Language Education for South Asian Students in Hong Kong. *Teachers and Teaching: Theory and Practice*, 18, 89–99.

Gardner, H. E. (2006). *Multiple Intelligences: New Horizons in Theory and Practice*. New York: Basic Books.

Gee, J. P. (1989). Literacy, Discourse, and Linguistics: Introduction. *Journal of Education*, 171(1), 5–17.

Geertz, C. (1973). *The Interpretation of Cultures*. New York: Basic Books.

Gibbons, P. (2009). *English Learners, Academic Literacy, and Thinking: Learning in the Challenge Zone*. Portsmouth, NH: Heinemann.

Giddens, A. (1991). *Modernity and Self-identity: Self and Society in the Late Modern Age*. Stanford, CA: Stanford University Press.

Giroux, H. A. (1985). Teachers as Transformative Intellectuals. *Social Education*, 49(5), 376–379.

Gonzalez, M. C. (2003). An Ethics for Postcolonial Ethnography. In R. P. Clair (Ed.), *Expressions of Ethnography: Novel Approaches to Qualitative Methods*. Albany, NY: State University of New York.

Gore, Jennifer M. (1993). *The Struggle for Pedagogies*. New York, NY: Routledge.

Greene, M. (1997). Teaching as Possibility: A Light in Dark Times. *Journal of Pedagogy, Pluralism and Practice*, 1(1), 1–10.

Gube, J., and Burkholder, C. (2019). Unresolved Tensions in Hong Kong's Racialized Discourse: Rethinking Differences in Educating about Ethnic Minorities. In J. Gube and F. Gao (Eds.), *Education, Ethnicity and Equity in the Multilingual Asian Context* (pp. 105–121). Singapore: Springer.

Gube, J., and Gao, F. (Eds.). (2019). *Education, Ethnicity and Equity in the Multilingual Asian Context*. Singapore: Springer.

Harris, R., Lefstein, A., Leung, C., and Rampton, B. (2011). *Urban Classroom Culture: Realities, Dilemmas, Responses*. London: Centre for Language, Discourse & Communication, King's College London.

Hinchey, P. H. (2004). *Becoming a Critical Educator: Defining a Classroom Identity, Designing a Critical Pedagogy*. New York: Peter Lang.

Hirani, R. (Director). (2009). *3 Idiots* [Motion Picture]. India: Vinod Chopra Productions.

hooks, bell. (2010). *Teaching Critical Thinking: Practical Wisdom*. New York, London: Routledge.

Hue, M. T., and Kennedy, K. J. (2014). The Challenge of Promoting Ethnic Minority Education and Cultural Diversity in Hong Kong Schools: From Policy to Practice. *Revista Española de Educación Comparada*, 23, 117–134.

Hussien, S. (2007). Critical Pedagogy, Islamisation of Knowledge and Muslim Education. *Intellectual Discourse*, 15(1), 85–104.

Hytten, K. (2004). Postcritical Ethnography: Research as a Pedagogical Encounter. In G. W. Noblit, J. E. G. Murillo & S. Y. Flores (Eds.), *Postcritical Ethnography in Education* (pp. 95–105). Cresskill, NJ: Hampton Press.

Jackson, L. (2014). Under Construction: The Development of Multicultural Curriculum in Hong Kong and Taiwan. *The Asia-Pacific Education Researcher*, 23(4), 885–893.

Kajner, T. (2013). Beyond the Binary. In L. Shultz & T. Kajner (Eds.), *Engaged Scholarship* (pp. 9–20). Rotterdam: Sense Publishers.

Kapai, P. (2015). *The Status of Ethnic Minorities in Hong Kong: 1997–2014*. Hong Kong: Faculty of Law, The University of Hong Kong.

Kaplan, E. A., and Wang, B. (2008). Introduction: From Traumatic Paralysis to the Force Field of Modernity. In E. Ann Kaplan & Ban Wan (Eds.), *Trauma and Cinema. Cross-Cultural Explorations* (pp. 1–17). Hong Kong: Hong Kong University Press.

Kellner, D. (2005). Toward a Critical Theory of Education. In I. Gur-Ze'ev (Ed.), *Critical Theory and Critical Pedagogy Today: Toward a New Critical language in Education* (pp. 51–64). University of Haifa: Faculty of Education.

Kennedy, K. J. (2012). The 'No Loser' Principle in Hong Kong's Education Reform: Does It Apply to Ethnic Minority Students? Retrieved from http://edb.gov.hk

Kennedy, K. J., Philion, J., and Hue, M. T. (2007). *Educational Provision for Ethnic Minority Students in Hong Kong: Meeting the Challenges of the Proposed Racial Discrimination Bill (HKIEd8001 PPR-2)*. The Hong Kong Institute of Education. Retrieved from http://www.eduhk.hk.

Khan, A. (Director). (2007). *Taare Zameen Par* [Motion Picture]. India: Aamir Khan Productions.

Kincheloe, J. (2003). *Teachers as Researchers: Qualitative Inquiry as a Path to Empowerment*. New York: Rutledge.

Kincheloe, J. (2008). *Critical Pedagogy* (2nd ed.). New York: Peter Lang.

Ku, H. B., Chan, K. W., and Sandhu, K. K. (2005). *A Research Report on the Education of South Asian Ethnic Minority Groups in Hong Kong*. Hong Kong: Centre for Social Policy Studies, Department of Applied Social Sciences, The Hong Kong Polytechnic University.

Law, K., and Lee, K-M. (2013). Socio-Political Embeddings of South Asian Ethnic Minorities' Economic Situations in Hong Kong. *Journal of Contemporary China*, 22, 984–1005.

Law, W. (2007). Schooling in Hong Kong. In G. Postiglione & J. Tan (Eds.), *Going to School in East Asia* (pp. 86–121). Westport, CT: Greenwood Publishing.

LeCompte, M. D., and Shensul, J. J. (1999). *Designing & Conducting Ethnographic Research*. Lanham: Alta Mira Press.

Lee, K. M., Wong, H., and Law, K. (2007). Social Polarisation and Poverty in the Global City. *China Report*, 43(1), 1–30.

Legislative Council. (2006). The Committee on Teacher's Work: Final Report. Retrieved from http://www.legco.gov.hk/

Legislative Council. (2018). Overall Study Hours and Student Well-Being in Hong Kong. Retrieved from http://www.legco.gov.hk/

Lin, A. M. Y. (2004). Introducing a Critical Pedagogical Curriculum: A Feminist, Reflexive Account. In B. Norton & K. Toohey (Eds.), *Critical Pedagogies and Language Learning* (pp. 271–290). Cambridge: Cambridge University Press.

Lin, A. M. Y. (2012). Critical Practice in English Language Education in Hong Kong: Challenges and Possibilities. In K. Sung & R. Pederson (Eds.), *Critical ELT Practices in Asia* (pp. 71–83). Rotterdam/Boston/Taipei: Sense Publishers.

Lin, A. M. Y., and Man, E. Y. F. (2011). Doing-Hip-Hop in the Transformation of Youth Identities: Social Class, Habitus, and Cultural Capital. In C. Higgins (Ed.), *Negotiating the Self in a Second Language: Identity Formation and Cross-Cultural Adaptation in a Globalizing World*. London: Equinox.

Lo, M. M. (2019) Youth Mentoring as Service-Learning in Teacher Education: Student-Teachers' Ethical Accounts of the Self. *Teaching and Teacher Education*, 80, 218–226.

Loper, K. (2004). Race and Equality: A Study of Ethnic Minorities in Hong Kong's Education System. Project Report and Analysis. Retrieved from http://hub.hku.hk/bitstream/10722/54929/2/31801446.pdf

Macrine, S. (2009). What Is Critical Pedagogy Good For? An Interview with Ira Shor. In *Critical Pedagogy in Uncertain Times* (pp. 119–136). New York: Palgrave Macmillan.

Madison, D. S. (2005). *Critical Ethnography: Method, Ethics, Performance*. Thousand Oaks: Sage Publications, Inc.

Madison, D.S. (2012). *Critical Ethnography: Method, Ethics, Performance*. (2nd ed.). Thousand Oaks: Sage Publications, Inc.

Martín Rojo, L. (2010). *Constructing Inequality in Multilingual Classrooms*. Berlin, Boston: De Gruyter Mouton.

Matusov, E., and Miyazaki, K. (2014). Dialogue on Dialogic Pedagogy. *Dialogic Pedagogy: An International Online Journal*, 2(S.1.0), October.

McArthur, J. (2010). Achieving Social Justice Within and Through Higher Education: The Challenge for Critical Pedagogy. *Teaching in Higher Education*, 15(5), 493–504. Chicago.

McLaren, P. (2007). *Life in Schools: An Introduction to Critical Pedagogy in the Foundations of Education* (5th ed.). Boston: Pearson Education, Inc.

McLaren, P. (1988). Culture or Canon? Critical Pedagogy and the Politics of Literacy. *Harvard Educational Review*, 58, 213–234.

Meyer, E. (2010). *Gender and Sexual Diversity in Schools*. New York: Springer.

Michailova, S., Piekkari, R., Plakoyiannaki, E., Ritvala, T., Mihailova, I., and Salmi, A. (2014). Breaking the Silence about Exiting Fieldwork: A Relational Approach and Its Implications for Theorizing. *Academy of Management Review*, 39(2), 138–161.

Ming Chiu, M., and Walker, A. (2007). Leadership for Social Justice in Hong Kong Schools. Journal of Educational Administration, 45(6), 724–739.

Moorhouse, B. L. (2014). Using Critical Pedagogies with Young EFL Learners in a Hong Kong Primary School. *International Journal of Bilingual and Multilingual Teachers of English*, 2(2), 250–265.

Moriarty, B., Danaher, P. A., and Danaher, G. (2008). Freire and Dialogical Pedagogy: A Means for Interrogating Opportunities and Challenges in Australian Postgraduate Supervision. *International Journal of Lifelong Education*, 27(4), 431–442.

Morrell, E. (2002). Toward a Critical Pedagogy of Popular Culture: Literacy Development among Urban Youth. *Journal of Adolescent & Adult Literacy*, 46(1), 72–77.

Morrell, E. (2004). *Becoming Critical Researchers: Literacy and Empowerment for Urban Youth*. New York: Peter Lang.

Morrell, E., and Duncan-Andrade, J. M. (2002). Promoting Academic Literacy with Urban Youth Through Engaging Hip-Hop Culture. *English Journal*, 91, 88–92.
Motwane, V. (Director). (2010). *Udaan* [Motion Picture]. India: UTV Spotboy.
Noguera, P. (2003). *City Schools and the American Dream: Reclaiming the Promise of Public Education*. New York: Teachers College.
Orwell, G. (2003). *1984, Level 4, Penguin Readers*. New York: Pearson ESL.
Pérez-Milans, M. 2013. *Urban Schools and English Language Education in Late Modern China: A Critical Sociolinguistic Ethnography*. New York/Abingdon: Routledge
Pérez-Milans, M. (2017). Bilingual Education in Hong Kong. In S. May, O. Garcia & A. Lin (Eds.), *Encyclopedia of Language and Education. Bilingual Education*. Dordrecht: Springer.
Pérez-Milans, M., and Soto, C. (2014). Everyday Practices, Everyday Pedagogies: A Dialogue on Critical Transformations in a Multilingual Hong Kong School. In J. Byrd Clark & F. Dervin (Eds.), *Reflexivity and Multimodality in Language Education: Rethinking Multilingualism and Interculturality in Accelerating, Complex and Transnational Spaces*. London/New York: Routledge.
Pérez-Milans, M., and Soto, C. (2016). Reflexive Language and Ethnic Minority Activism in Hong Kong: A Trajectory- Based Analysis. *AILA Review*, 29(1), 48–82.
Peterson, R. (2003). Teaching How to Read the World and Change It: Critical Pedagogy in the Intermediate Grades. In A. Darder, M. Baltodano & R. D. Torres (Eds.), *The Critical Pedagogy Reader* (pp. 305–323). London: Routledge Falmer.
Pole, C., and Morrison, M. (2003). *Ethnography for Education*. Berkshire: Open University Press.
Postiglione, G. A. (1996). The Decolonization of Hong Kong Education. In G. A. Postiglione & Chang (Eds.), *The Hong Kong Reader: Passage to Chinese Sovereignty*. New York: M.E. Sharpe.
Pütz, M., Fishman, J. A., and Neff-van Aertselaer, J. (Eds.). (2006). *'Along the Routes to Power': Explorations of Empowerment through Language* (Vol. 92). Berlin: Walter de Gruyter.
Quantz, R. (1992). *On Critical Ethnography with Some Postmodern Considerations. In The Handbook of Qualitative Research in Education*. Edited by Margaret D. LeCompte, Wendy L. Millroy and Judith Preissle. (pp. 447–505) San Diego: Academic Press, Incorporated.
Rampton, B. (2007). Neo-hymesian Linguistic Ethnography in the United Kingdom. *Journal of Sociolinguistics*, 11(5), 584–607.
Rashidi, N., and Safari, F. (2011). A Model for EFL Materials Development within the Framework of Critical Pedagogy (CP). *English Language Teaching*, 4(2), 250. Chicago.
Rauniyar, D. (Director). (2010). *Pooja*. Nepal: BBC World Service Trust.
Sarroub, L., and Quadros, S. (2015). Critical Pedagogy in Classroom Discourse. Faculty Publications: Department of Teaching, Learning and Teacher Education. Paper 156. Retrieved from http://digitalcommons.unl.edu/teachlearnfacpub/156
Sassen, S. (1996). Cities and Communities in the Global Economy. *American Behavioral Scientist*, 39(5), 629–639.
Sassen, S. (1998). *Globalization and Its Discontents*. New York: The New Press.
Shor, I., and Freire, P. (1987). *A Pedagogy for Liberation: Dialogues on Transforming Education*. Westport: Bergin and Garvey Publishers, Inc.
Shudak, N., and Avoseh, M. (2015). Freirean-Based Critical Pedagogy: The Challenges of Limit-Situations and Critical Transitivity. *Creative Education*, 6, 463–471.

Shum, M., Gao, F., and Ki, W. W. (2016). School Desegregation in Hong Kong: Non-Chinese Linguistic Minority Students' Challenges to Learning Chinese in Mainstream Schools. *Asia Pacific Journal of Education*, 36(4), 533–544. doi:10.1080/02188791.2015.1005048

Shum, M., Gao, F., and Tsung, L. (2012). Unlocking the Racialized and Gendered Educational Experiences of South Asian Females in Hong Kong: The Case Study of Pakistani Girls. *Asian Ethnicity*, 13(3), 251–262.

Sofer, A. (2007). Global City School Systems. In T. Brighouse & L. Fullick (Eds.), *Education in a Global City: Essays from London*. London: Institute of Education.

Solórzano, D., and Delgado Bernal, D. (2001). Examining Transformational Resistance through a Critical Race and LatCrit Theory Framework: Chicana and Chicano Students in an Urban Context. *Urban Education*, 36(3), 308–342.

Souto-Manning, M. (2010). *Freire, Teaching, and Learning: Culture Circles across Contexts*. New York: Peter Lang.

Tarlau, R. (2014). From a Language to a Theory of Resistance: Critical Pedagogy, the Limits of "Framing," and Social Change. *Educational Theory*, 64(4), 369–392.

Thapa, C. B., and Adamson, B. (2018). Ethnicity, Language-In-Education Policy and Linguistic Discrimination: Perspectives of Nepali Students in Hong Kong. *Journal of Multilingual and Multicultural Development*, 39(4), 329–340.

Thomas, J. (1993). *Doing Critical Ethnography* (Vol. 26). Newbury Park: Sage Publications.

Thomson-Bunn, H. (2014). Are They Empowered Yet?: Opening Up Definitions of Critical Pedagogy. *Composition Forum*, 29. Retrieved from http://compositionforum.com/issue/29/are-they-empowered.php

Valenzuela, Angela. (1999). *Subtractive Schooling: U.S.-Mexican Youth and the Politics of Caring*. Albany: State University of New York Press.

Viola, M. (2009). The Filipinization of Critical Pedagogy: Widening the Scope of Critical Educational Theory. *Journal for Critical Education Policy Studies*, 7(1), 1–28.

Watts, R. J., Diemer, M. A., and Voight, A. M. (2011). Critical Consciousness: Current Status and Future Directions. *New Directions for Child and Adolescent Development*, 134, 43–57.

Weiner, E. (2007). Chapter 3: Critical Pedagogy and the Crisis of Imagination. *Counterpoints*, 299, 57–77.

Willis, P. E. (1977). *Learning to Labour: How Working Class Kids Get Working Class Jobs*. Farnborough: Saxon House.

Wink, J. (2000). *Critical Pedagogy: Notes from the Real World* (2nd ed.). New York: Addison-Wesley Longman Inc.

Yang, K. W. (2009). Mathematics, Critical Literacy, and Youth Participatory Action Research. *New Directions for Youth Development*, 123, 99–118.

Yeung, P. (2014, August 27). Teach English for the Real World to Hong Kong's Struggling Students. *The South China Morning Post*. Retrieved from www.scmp.com

Yi, L. (2008) *Cultural Exclusion in China: State Education, Social Mobility and Cultural Difference*. London: Routledge.

Yosso, T. J. (2005). Whose Culture Has Capital? A Critical Race Theory Discussion of Community Cultural Wealth. *Race Ethnicity and Education*, 8(1), 69–91.

Yung, K. (1997). What Happens to the Attainment of Our Bottom 20% of Students at the End of Their Nine-Year Compulsory Education? *Educational Research Journal*, 12, 159–173.

Index

Note: **Bold** page numbers refer to tables and *italic* page numbers refer to figures.

academic goals of writing 109–10
accountability 9, 36, 52, 54
"active membership" 48
activism 43, 49, 115, 156
advocacy 10, 11, 49
alienation 2; classroom rules 58; conflicts 59–60; EM students 58; ethnic Chinese students 58; feelings of 58–60; inter-class competition 57; physical and school conditions 57–8
Allman, P. 158
application of critical pedagogy 21
aspirations 56; academics 62–3; music 63–4; teachers avenues for 74–5

Bakhtin theory of language 118–19
banding/streaming system 6–7
band three schools 11, 44, 114, 146, 156, 159–60
banking concept of education 19; Cantonese and English proficiency 72–3; class status 73–4; conformity 66; dynamics 66, 72; failure 66; four skills in English 70; knowledge about Hong Kong and China 72–3; language difficulties 71–2; materials use and pedagogy 68–9; student materials choice 70; teacher's proficiencies 72–3; teaching and learning 66–7; Territory System Assessment 70; textbooks as primary material for exam 69–70; two form one classes 69; unit plan **67**, 67–8; *see also* challenges
Banks, C. 154
Banks, J.A. 154
Berks, R. 29

Bollywood films: educational theme 97–8; "3 Idiots" 96–7, 102; "Taare Zameen Par" 97; "Udaan" 102; vocabulary 98–9
Breuing, M. 28
Burbules, N.C. 29

Camangian, P. 23–5, 30, 150
Campus TV 55–6
Cantonese 4, 5
Cantonese and English proficiency 72–3
challenges: Chinese teacher mindset 79; institutional and relational constraints with racism 76–7; knowledge about Hong Kong and China 78–9; language abilities and individual effort 74–6; student-teacher relationship 77–8; teachers training and development 76
Chan, K.W. 154
Chinese language education 14–15
Chinese medium of instruction (CMI) 4, 9, 71, 112
Chiu, M. 6
classroom cultures and communities 91
classroom interaction 116
class status 73–4
"co-intentional education" 19–20
collaborative relations of power 31
commitment and human liberation 36–7
"committed intellectuals" 29
communicative resources 116
community/communities of practice 23, 53, 112
constrained empowerment: dialogue 83–4; generative theme of aspirations 80–2, *81*; hard work 83; scavenger hunt 82–3, **83**; social mobility 80, 82;

Index

transformative resistance 83; voice and expression 80, 83
constraints of schools, external and internal 155–6
context 52
conventional ethnography 37, 40–2
coping mechanisms 103
critical consciousness 124–5
critical discourse analysis 36
critical educators and leaders 156–9
critical ethnography (CE) 3, 14; commitment and human liberation 36–7; conventional ethnography 37, 40–2; critical discourse analysis 36; criticality 36–7, 46–9; data analysis 35–6; data collection 35; emancipation 37; ethical commitments 52–4; linguistic ethnography 36; monological to dialogical action based 38, **39**, 40; personal relationships 52; qualitative approach 34–5; radical teacher 42–6; reflexivity 49–52; semi-structured interviews 35, **36**
critical hope 159, 161
critical pedagogy theory and practice: autobiographical investigation and community-based research 150; Camangian's lesson plan 67–8; collaborative pedagogies 149–50; communities 149; content, processes, and related outcomes 148; context and set of conditions 148; critical construction 152; critical deconstruction practices 151–2; criticality 152; English language literature and popular culture 150–1; epistemological and ontological orientations 151; participatory action research 151; redemptive narratives 148–9; transnational mass media 152
criticality 33, 36–7, 46–9, 86
critical multiculturalism 154, 155
critical teaching 17, 34
critiques of critical pedagogy: definitional precision and transparency 28; empowerment and social change 29–30; heroic teacher 28–9; lack of clarity 28; "redemptive narratives" 29
cultural sensitivity training 154
culture of silence: in classroom 126; food equity 120; ignorance and lethargy 115; interpersonal relationships 120; love 121–4; oppressive reality 124; reactionary and self-defeating resistance 124, 126; trust 120–4; *see also* hate dialogue
curricular poetry-based curricular unit 23–5, **24**
curricular reforms 57
curriculum 15, 22, 44–5, 49; academic literacy 91; dialogic relationships 143; English proficiencies diversity 88–9; formal curriculum 126; generative themes 86; interactions and classroom dynamics 89; limited range of content 89–90; multimodal 90–1; new knowledge and skills 90; pedagogical sequence 90; policy and practice 137–8; self-revelation (*see* self-revelation); simulations against injustice 95–6; teaching unit outline 93, **93**; three-year junior secondary 91, **92**, 93; *see also* Bollywood films
curriculum guides 8–9

definition of critical pedagogy 17
dehumanization 108–10, 112, 127, 130
demands of schooling 2
dialogical skills/dialogue skills 22
dialogue: conflict 134–7; continuity with students 135; educational reform 137–9; epistemological dialogue 118, 126, 132, 134, 137, 139, 140; interpersonal relationships 120–1; Levitation Dialogue 141; mono-topic dialogue 118–19; ontological dialogue 124–5, 135, 137; against oppressive/hegemonic conditions 115; progressive pedagogies 135; realization 139–40; relationship 134–41; rules and boundaries for 127; self-actualization 134, 137; and student actions 15; trust 115, 120–4, 134; understanding of limits 141; *see also* culture of silence; hate dialogue
"disadvantaged group" 3
discontinuity in life 123
disorientation 55
diversity in education 153–5
drug addiction and systematic oppression 24–5
Duncan-Andrade, J. 1, 22, 23, 50, 150, 151
dynamics 66, 72

education reform 146
emancipation 37, 54
Emo aesthetic 60

empowerment: collaborative relations of power 31; conformist resistance 32; curriculum 141; definition 31; dialogic relationships 141–3; limit situation concept 32; self-defeating resistance 31–2; and social change 29–30; social justice 141–2; systematic level 152; transformational resistance 31, 32; *see also* constrained empowerment
English language teaching 25, 26
English Language with English Language Arts 43
English medium of instruction (EMI) 4, 9, 56, 71, 73
epistemological dialogue 118, 126, 132, 134, 137, 139, 140
equity and social justice in education 158–9
"equity pedagogy" 154
Erni, J.N. 154
ethical commitments 35, 49, 52–4
ethnic Chinese students 26
ethnicity 2, 139, 159
ethnic minority (EM) students: academic success 5–6; banding/streaming system 6–7; Chinese language skills 5; class-based inequities 6; collaboration and commitment 10; colonial government and working class labours 3–4; curriculum guides 8–9; efficacy and competitiveness 7–8; English-medium-based private international school 4; enrolments in government schools 4; free education 8; Indonesian and Filipino origin 3; market-based reforms 9–10; meritocratic ideology 6; Pakistani and Nepalese descent 3; second language curriculum 5; self-actualization 55; teacher perceptions 7

"Five Levels of Analysis" framework 30
Four Cs ("Communication," "Cooperation," "Conflict," and "Community,") 91
four skills in English 70
Frankfurt School of Critical Theory 18
free education 8
Freire, P. 1, 13, 14, 18, 29, 32, 37, 115, 127

Gao, F. 155
General Certificate of Education (GCE) A/AS Levels 42

generative model of education 97
generative themes: of aspirations 80; boundaries and limits 55; curricular engagement with 40, 45; curriculum 86; definition 14; and dialogue 20, 23; of education 20, 30, 65–6, 125; and empowerment 80–3; of freedom 116; hard work 56; identification of 158; individual effort 63–4; of love 105–6, 125; pedagogical spaces 86; scavenger hunt 82–3, **83**
global centers of power 2
Gonzalez, M.C. 52, 53
Gurkha Brigade of security forces 3–4

hate dialogue: dehumanization 127, 130; epistemological and ontological dialogue 134; homophobia 128–30, 132, 133; prejudice discrimination/violence 128–30; rules and boundaries 127; violence against women 131
hip hop music: English skills and self-confidence 26; as vehicle of engagement 25
history theme 111
holistic needs 146
homophobia 128–30, 132, 133
Hong Kong Diploma in Secondary Education Examination (HKDSE) 8, 42, 137
Hong Kong Equal Opportunities Commission 5, 154
Hong Kong Special Administrative Region of the People's Republic of China 7
hooks, bell 1, 145
Hue, M.T. 10, 154
humanization of educational practices 1–2, 75–6, 147

identity 56, 60
improvization 134
income inequality 6
in-service teachers 26
institutional space 155–6
instrumentality 118, 119
intergenerational oppression 124–5
intergenerational poverty 125
International General Certificate of Secondary Education qualification (IGCSE) 42
International Section for EM students 42
interpersonal relationships 120

Kennedy, K.J. 10, 153, 154
Ku, H.B. 154

language difficulties 71–2
learn through interaction 76
Leung, L.Y.M. 154
Levitation Dialogue 116, 141, 144
liberatory pedagogy 13, 30, 116
limits and possibilities of critical pedagogy 15, 147–8, 160
limits and possibilities of empowerment 17, 30–2
limit situation concept 32
Lin, A.M.Y. 26, 27
linguistic ethnography 36
listening 94, 118, 143–4
literary analysis techniques 108–9
literature curriculum 44

Madison, D.S. 36
market-based reforms 9–10
materials use and pedagogy 68–9
medium of instruction (MOI) 4, 9
Messaging Dialogue 134–41
Ming Chiu, M. 158, 159
mono-topic dialogue 118–19
Morrell, E. 1, 22, 23, 150
multicultural education 43, 138
multiculturalism/cultural diversity 154
multimodal and multilingual interactions 60
multimodal curriculum 90–1

Native English Teacher scheme 26
Newly Arrived Students (NAS) 40, 42
"1984" 108–10, *109*
Noguera, P. 32, 155
no-loser principle 8, 10, 148, 153
non-Chinese speaking (NCS) 40, 71–2

"one country, two systems" mode of governance 7
online pedagogical space 86
ontological dialogue 125, 135, 137, 142
optimism 18, 155
Orwell, George 107, 108

pain 123, 124
pain and injustice 58–61
participatory action research 23, 151
participatory dynamics/dynamics of interaction 22
pedagogical spaces 86, 105, 117, 141
pedagogy of oppressor 29

personal relationships 52, 104, 120, 133
Personal, Social, and Humanities Education Curriculum Guide 9
Phillion, J. 154
poetry writing 23–5, **24**
"Pooja" 106–7, 120
possibilities and constraints 56
Postiglione, G.A. 6
praxis 19, 23, 115, 157
praxis-based dimension 45–6
pre-service teacher 27

Quadros, S. 28

radical teacher 42–6
reflexivity 49–52
reformed schools 9
revolutionary leaders 21

Sandhu, K.K. 154
Sarroub, L. 28
scavenger hunt 82–3, **83**
"Schindler's List" 108
schools types 6
self-defeating resistance 31–2
self-harm 60
self-reflexivity 49
self-revelation: about puberty 103–4; coping mechanisms 103; emotional and social conflicts 102; homework 101–2; inter-generational domestic violence 103; love 106–7; self-worth and visibility to world 105; "Udaan" 102–3
self-transformation 158
Shor, I. 1, 13, 16
Shum, M. 155
silence 115
social injustice 94–5
social mobility 56; English music 63–4; families' "old" thinking 61–2; gender and social class norms 62–3
Soto, Carlos: Bay Area Education Program 10; critical practices 11; education 12; family background 11; racial identity 12; transnational solidarity 12
special educational needs (SEN) 42
stories, personal and fictional 145–6
structural factors of critical pedagogy 22
students' perspective of critical pedagogy 146–7

"Taare Zameen Par" 64, 65, 91, 97, 152
teacher development program 26
teacher's proficiencies 72–3

teacher-student relationships *see* dialogue
teaching duties 48, **48**, 49
Territory System Assessment 70
theory of pedagogy for liberation: "banking concept" 19, 21; "co-intentional education" 19–20; critical consciousness 19; dialogue 20–1; generative themes 20; humanization 18, 19; oppression through praxis 19; revolutionary leaders 21; "transformative intellectuals" 20; transmission-based educational modes 18
"thick description" 35
Thomas, J. 35
Thomson-Bunn, H. 28
"3 Idiots" 64, 88, 93, 96–8, 102, 139, 140, 145, 146, 152
transcription conventions 163
"transformative intellectuals" 20
transformative resistance 25, 31; classroom cultures and communities 91; criticality 86; cultural silence 133; curriculum within critical pedagogy 85–6; definition 97; dialogical tensions 126; dialogic relationships 142–3; emotional and social changes 85; EM students presentation of International Section 99; listening 94, 143–4; notion of 157; online pedagogical space 86; as personal and social change 100; responses 86–7, 87; social injustice 94–5; social justice 141–2; *vs.* transmission pedagogy 100–1; trust 120–1, 142; *see also* Bollywood films; curriculum
transmission pedagogy 97–9; *see also* banking education
transnational mass media 152
trust 120–1
truthfulness 52–3
Tsung, L. 155
two form one classes 69

"Udaan" 64, 65, 84, 85, 102–3, 120, 152
unfinalizability 118, 125
unit plan **67**, 67–8

vehicles for engagement 22–5; academic skills 22, 23, 55, 57; Bollywood films 64–5 (*see also* Bollywood films); definition 14; expression of identities 80
verbalism 115
Village Primary School 156
voice and expression 80, 83

Walker, A. 6, 158, 159
Weiner, E. 17
western progressive liberal pedagogies 27

Yang, K. Wayne 50
Yung, K. 7

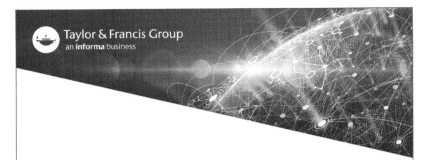